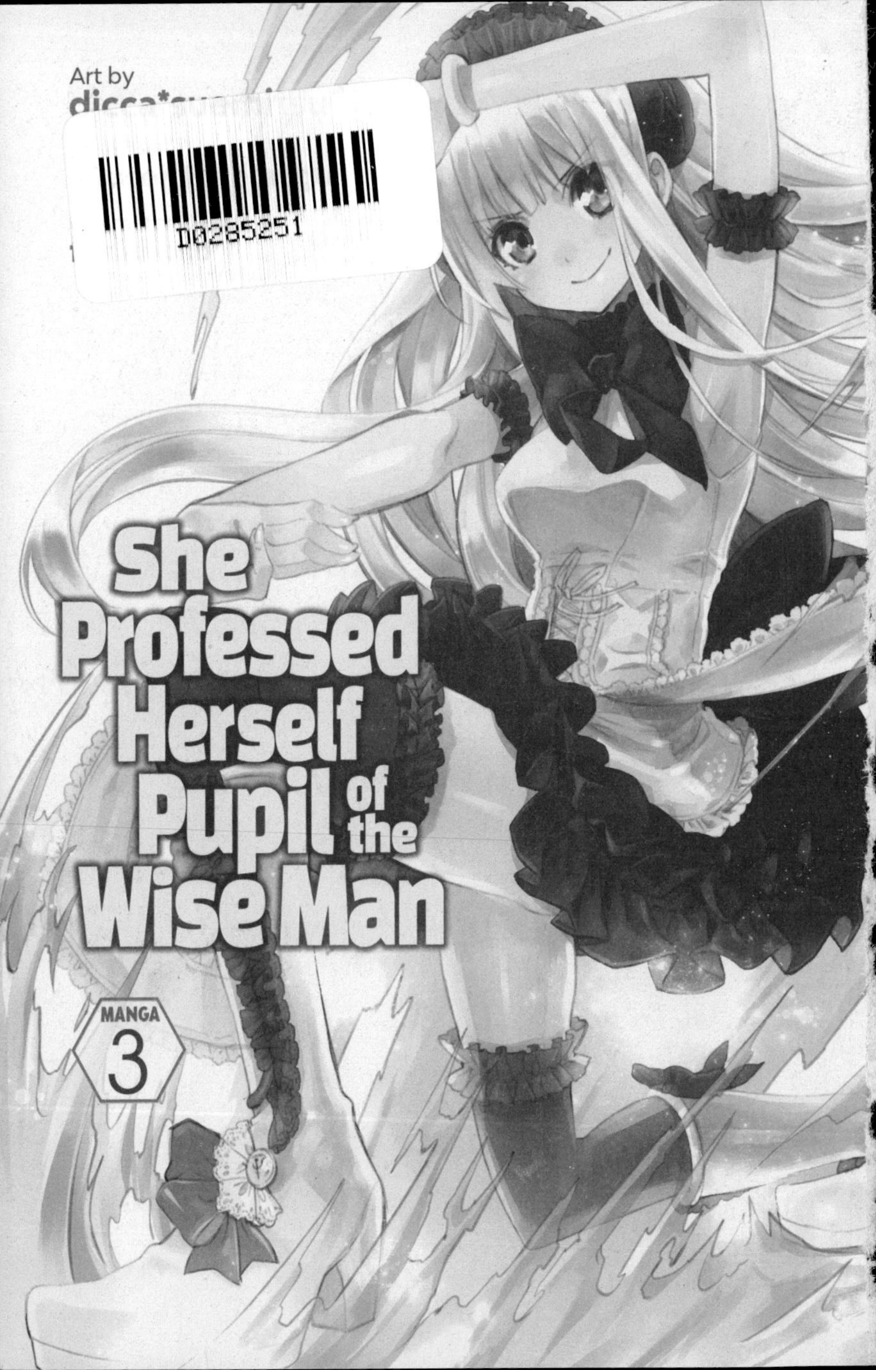
Art by
She Professed Herself Pupil of the Wise Man
MANGA
3

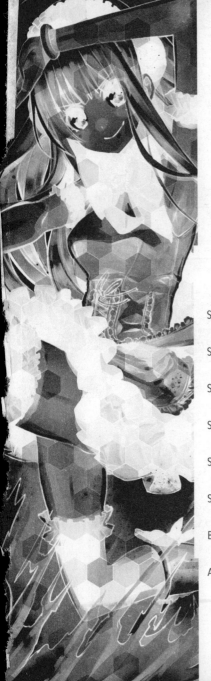

CONTENTS

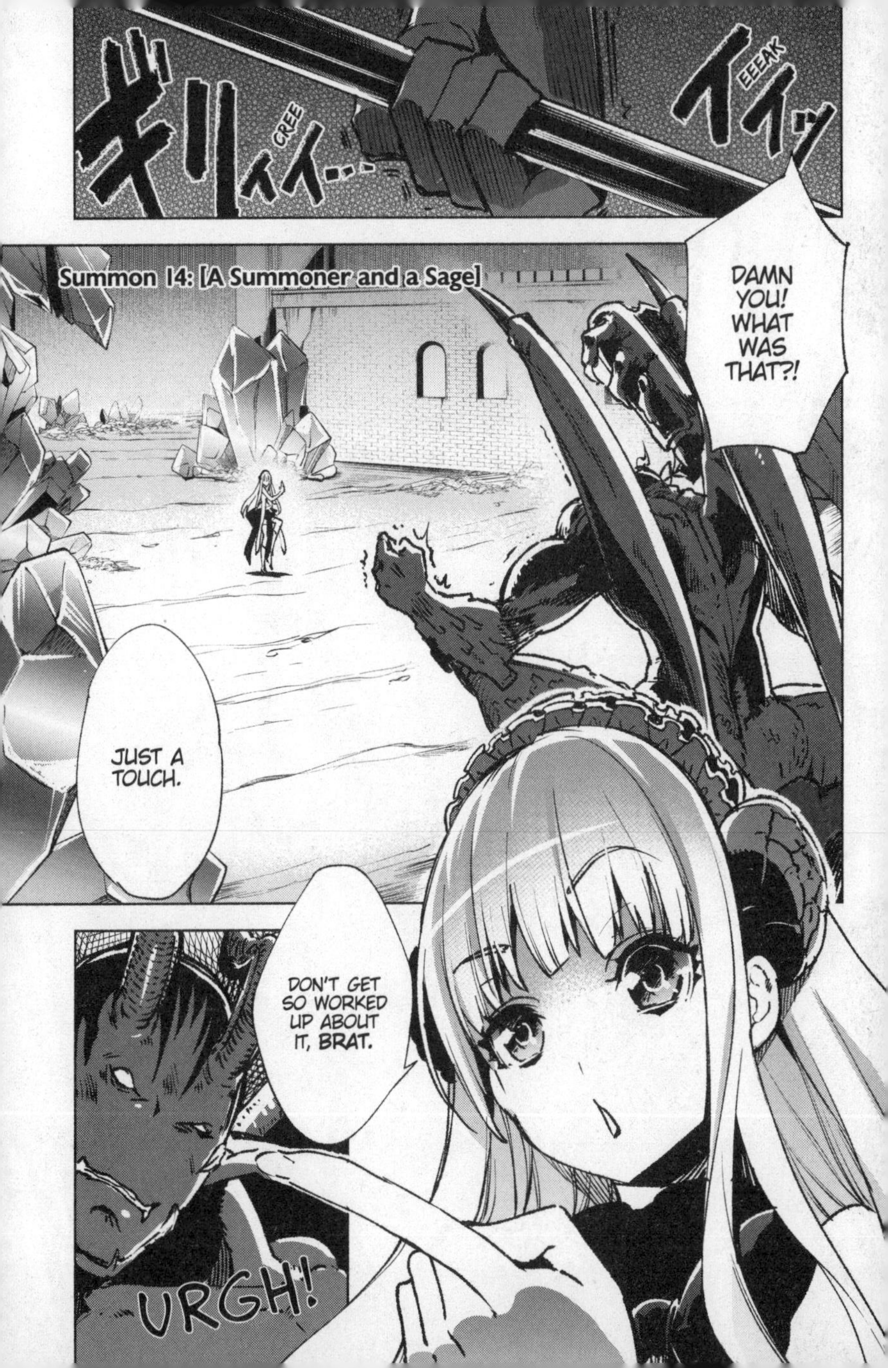

イィッ
EEEAK
ギリィイ…
GREE
DAMN YOU! WHAT WAS THAT?!
Summon 14: [A Summoner and a Sage]
JUST A TOUCH.
DON'T GET SO WORKED UP ABOUT IT, BRAT.
URGH!

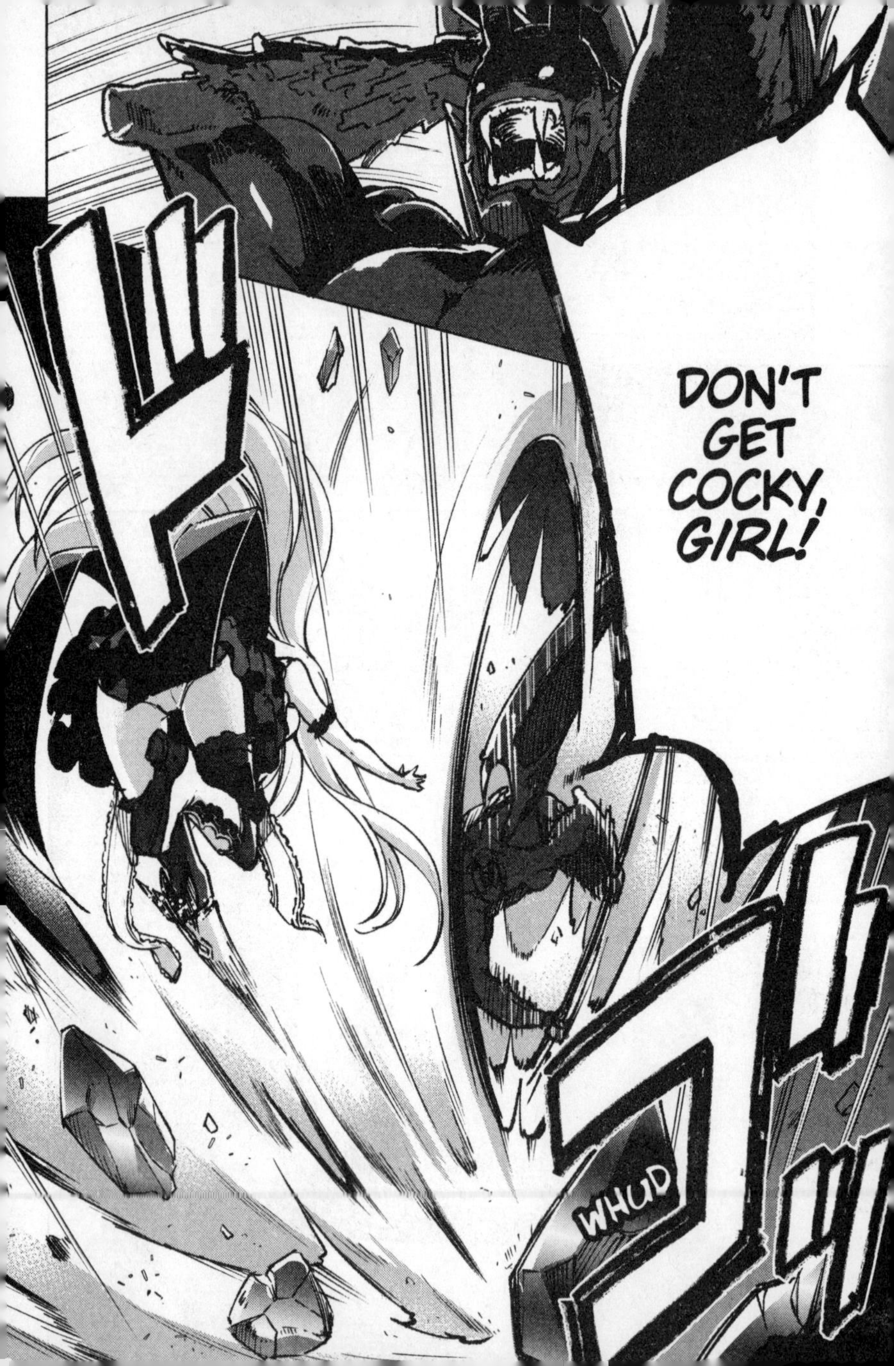
DON'T GET COCKY, GIRL!
WHUD

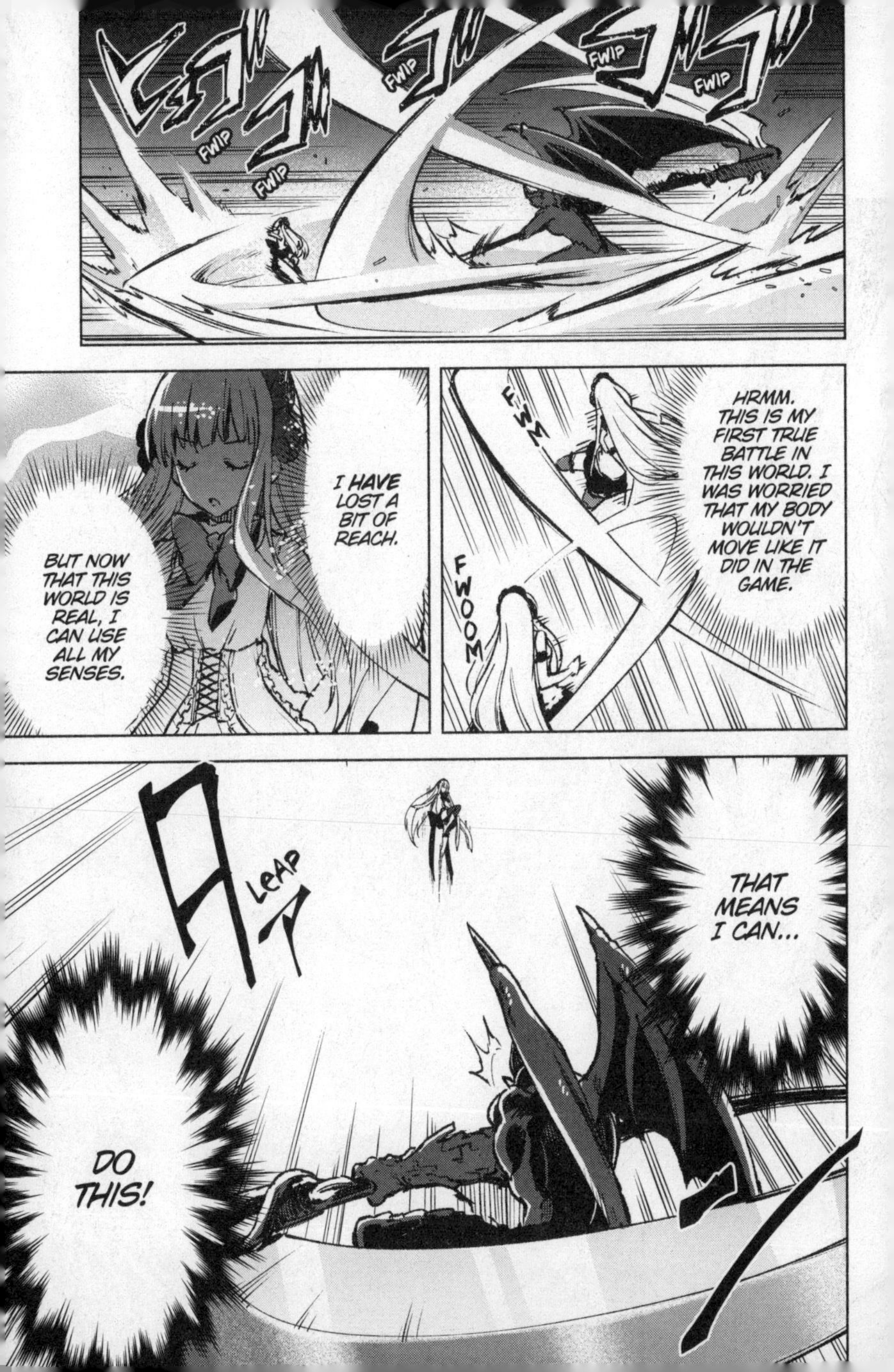
FWIP
FWIP
FWIP
FWIP
FWIP
HRMM. THIS IS MY FIRST TRUE BATTLE IN THIS WORLD. I WAS WORRIED THAT MY BODY WOULDN'T MOVE LIKE IT DID IN THE GAME.
FWM
FWOOM
I HAVE LOST A BIT OF REACH.
BUT NOW THAT THIS WORLD IS REAL, I CAN USE ALL MY SENSES.
THAT MEANS I CAN...
LEAP
DO THIS!

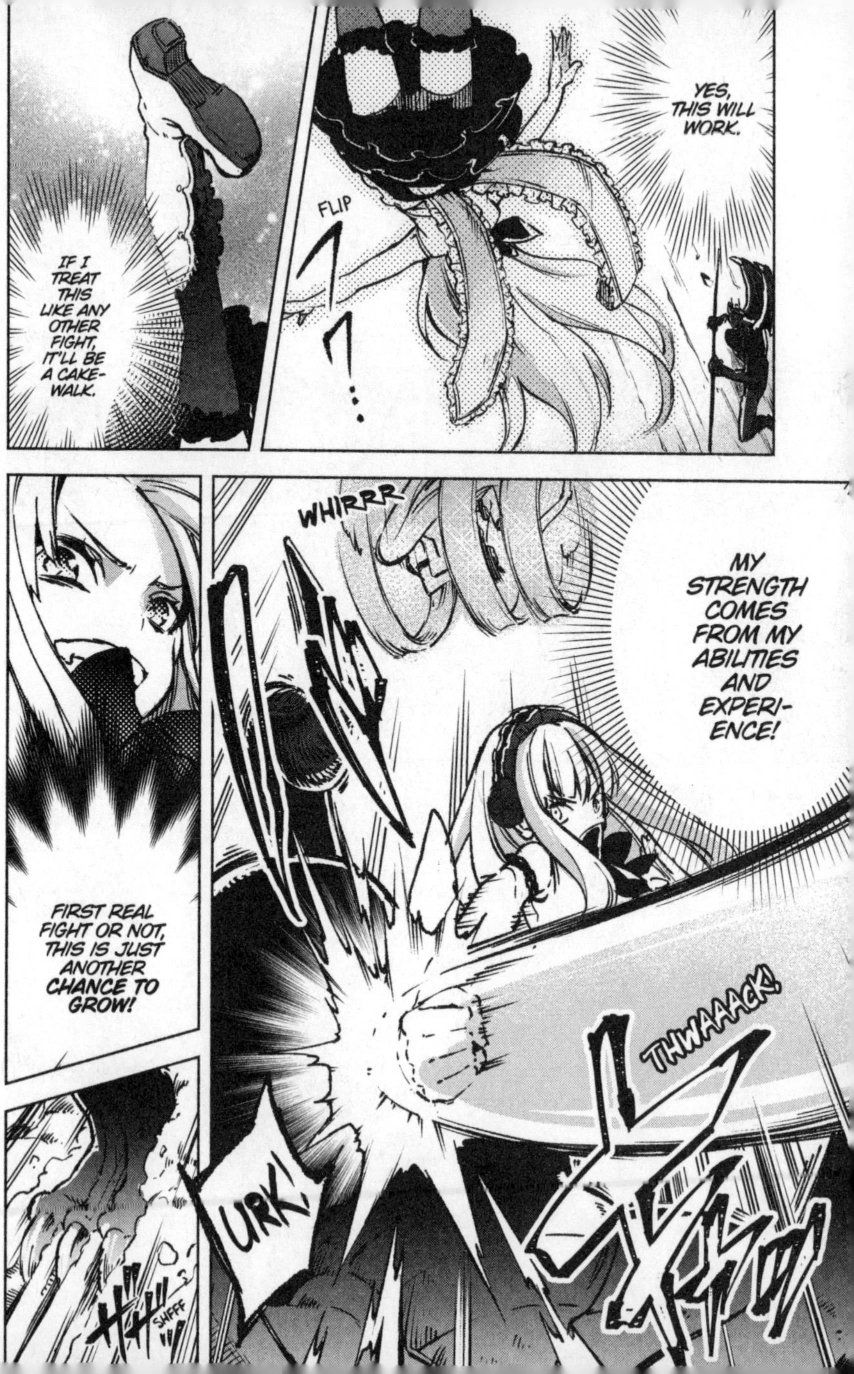
YES, THIS WILL WORK.
FLIP
IF I TREAT THIS LIKE ANY OTHER FIGHT, IT'LL BE A CAKE-WALK.
WHIRRR
MY STRENGTH COMES FROM MY ABILITIES AND EXPERI-ENCE!
THWAAACK!
URK!
FIRST REAL FIGHT OR NOT, THIS IS JUST ANOTHER CHANCE TO GROW!
SHFFF

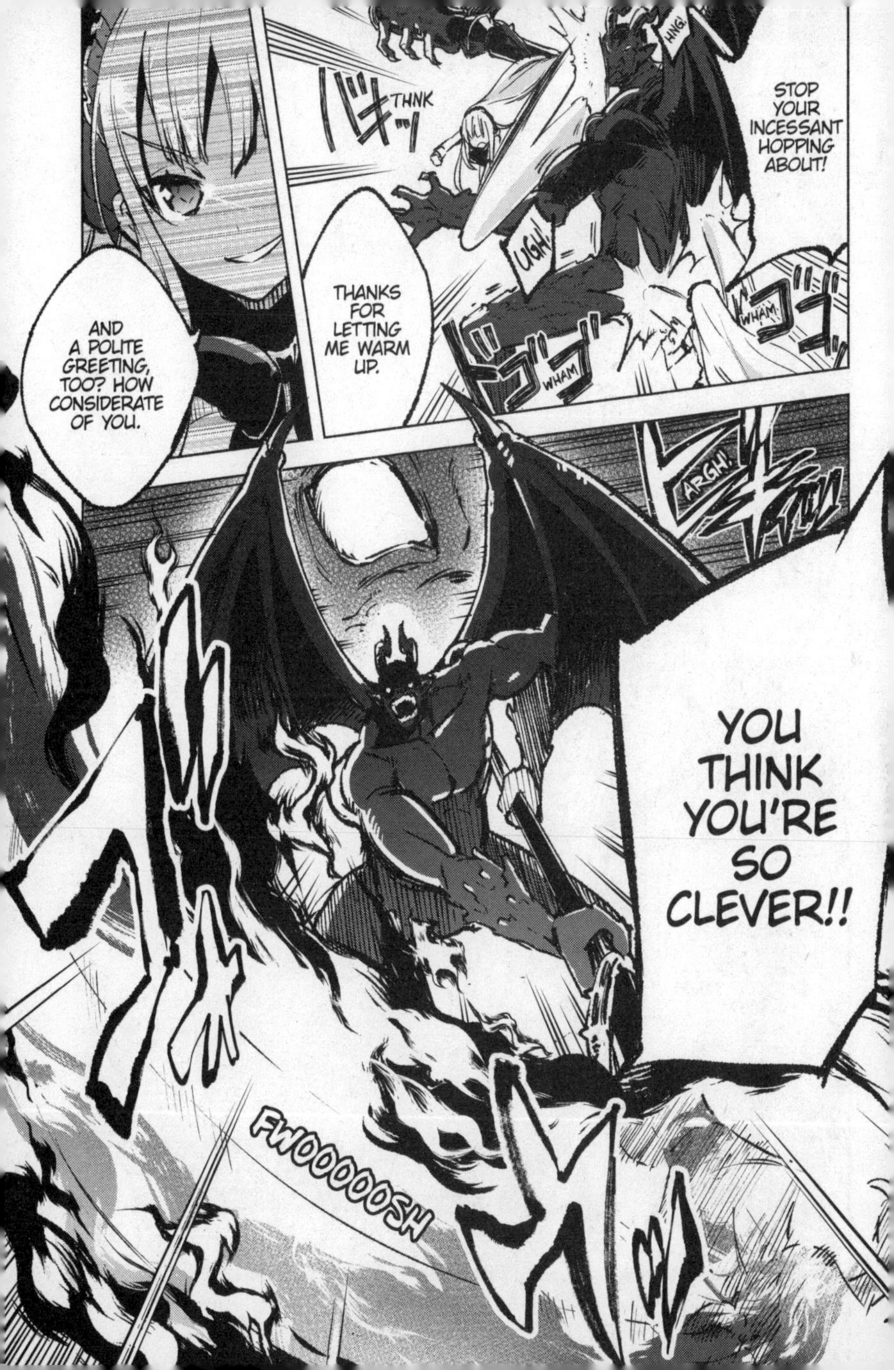
HNG!
STOP YOUR INCESSANT HOPPING ABOUT!
THNK
UGH
WHAM
WHAM
THANKS FOR LETTING ME WARM UP.
AND A POLITE GREETING, TOO? HOW CONSIDERATE OF YOU.
ARGH!
YOU THINK YOU'RE SO CLEVER!!
FWOOOOOOSH

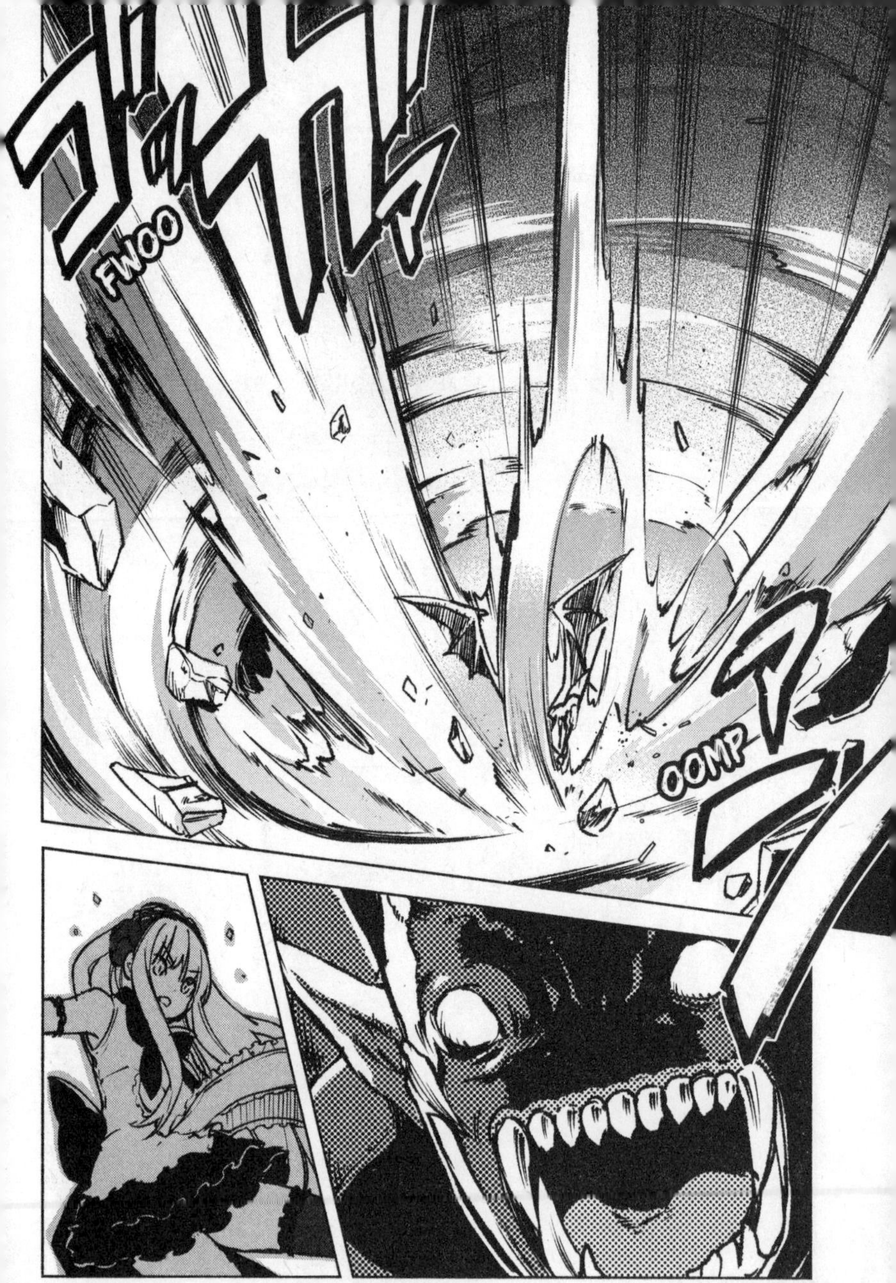
FWOO
OOMP

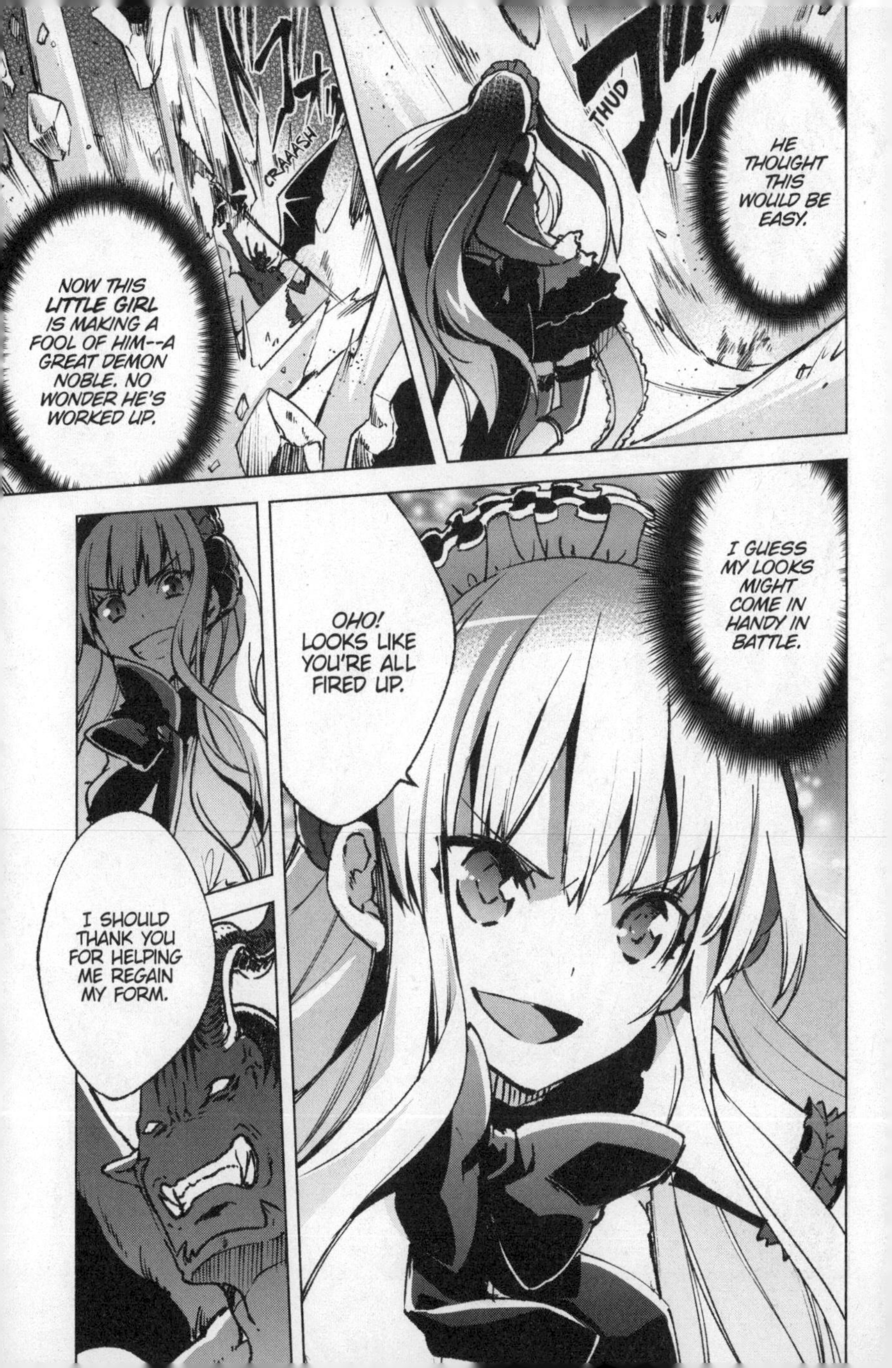
THUD
HE THOUGHT THIS WOULD BE EASY.
CRAAASH
NOW THIS LITTLE GIRL IS MAKING A FOOL OF HIM--A GREAT DEMON NOBLE. NO WONDER HE'S WORKED UP.
I GUESS MY LOOKS MIGHT COME IN HANDY IN BATTLE.
OHO! LOOKS LIKE YOU'RE ALL FIRED UP.
I SHOULD THANK YOU FOR HELPING ME REGAIN MY FORM.

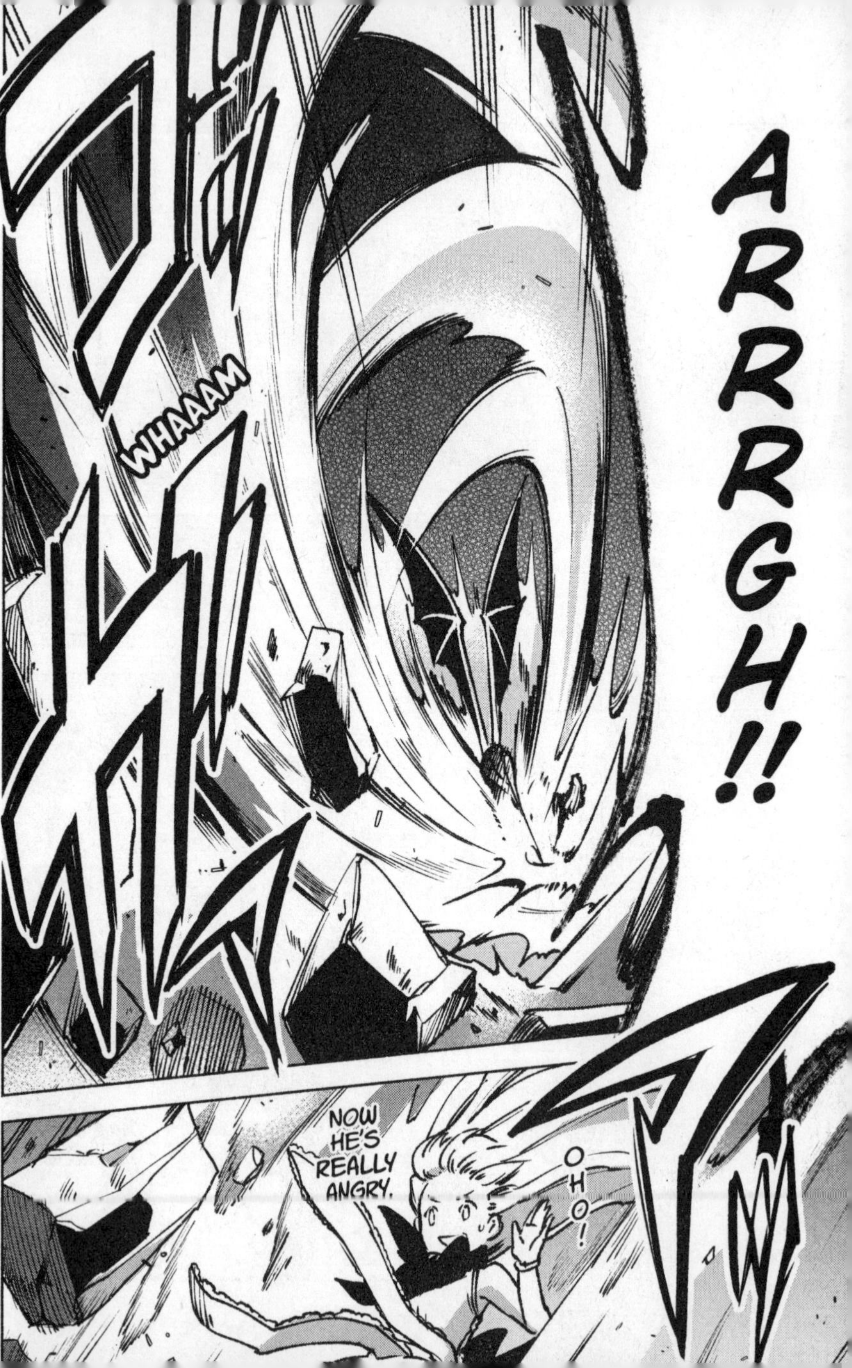
ARRRGH!!
WHAAAM
OHO!
NOW HE'S REALLY ANGRY.

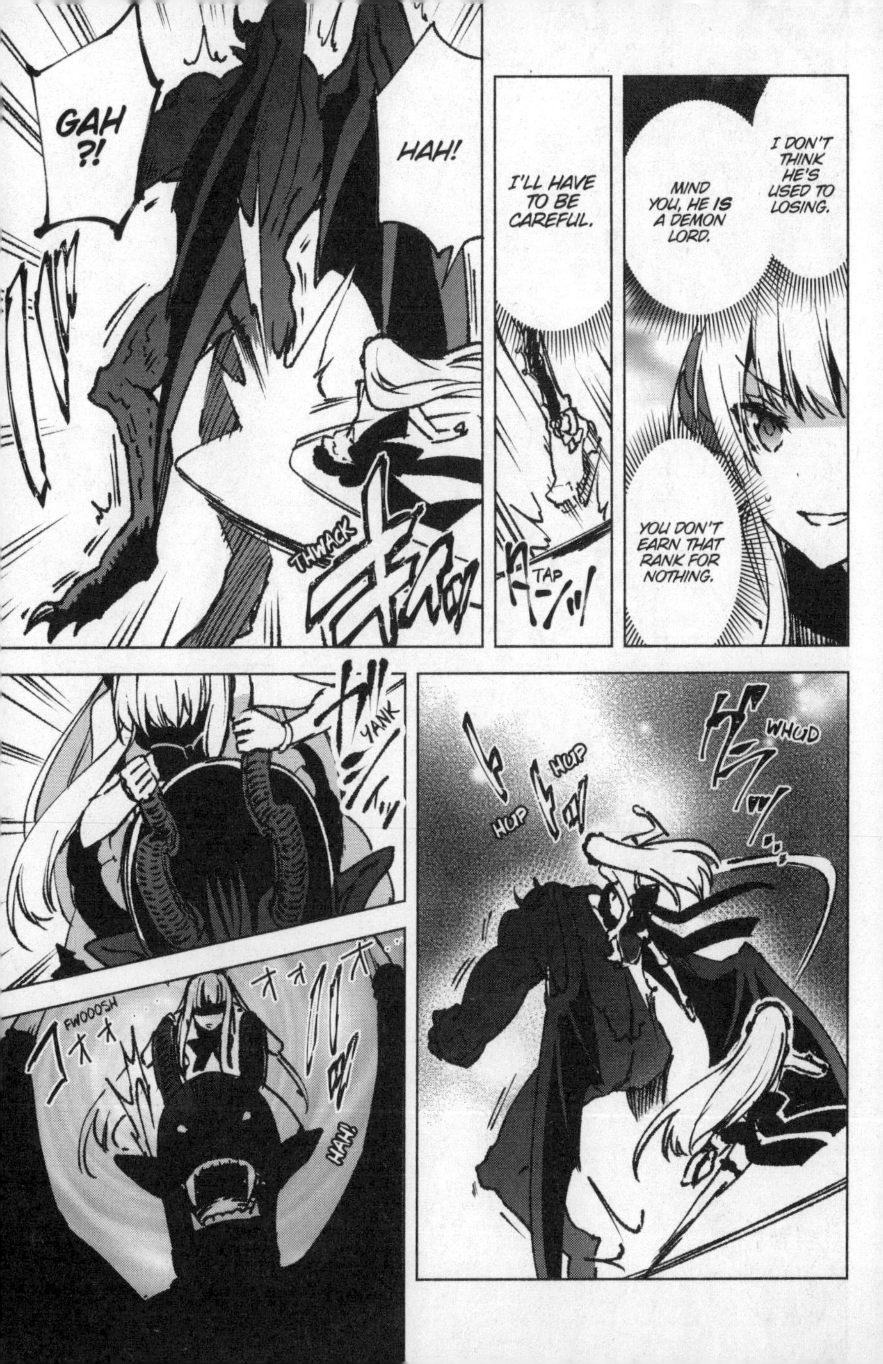
I DON'T THINK HE'S USED TO LOSING.
MIND YOU, HE IS A DEMON LORD.
YOU DON'T EARN THAT RANK FOR NOTHING.
I'LL HAVE TO BE CAREFUL.
TAP
HAH!
THWACK
GAH ?!
WHUD
HUP
HUP
YANK
FWOOOSH
HAH!

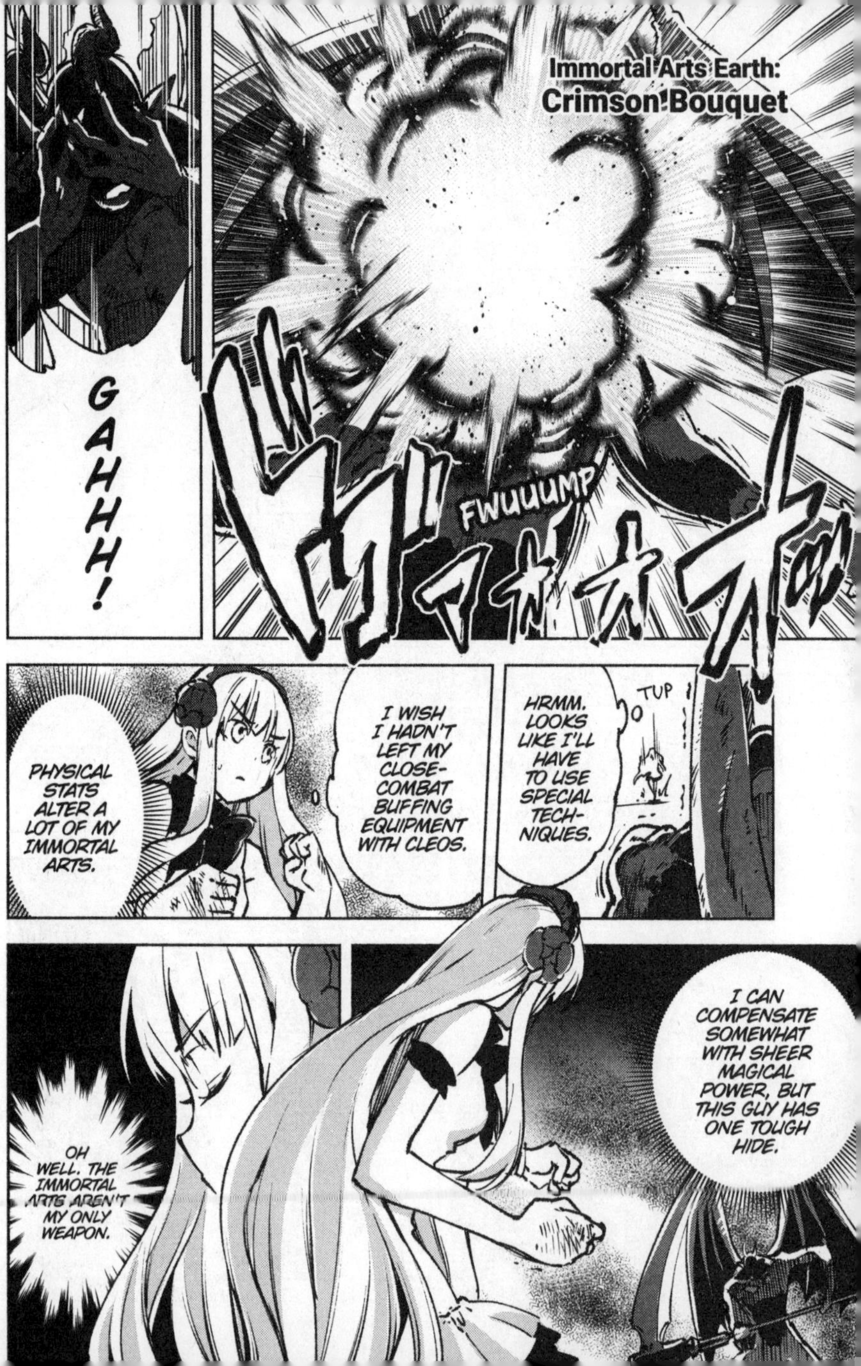
Immortal Arts Earth:
Crimson Bouquet
FWUUUMP
GAHHHH!
TUP
HRMM. LOOKS LIKE I'LL HAVE TO USE SPECIAL TECH-NIQUES.
I WISH I HADN'T LEFT MY CLOSE-COMBAT BUFFING EQUIPMENT WITH CLEOS.
PHYSICAL STATS ALTER A LOT OF MY IMMORTAL ARTS.
I CAN COMPENSATE SOMEWHAT WITH SHEER MAGICAL POWER, BUT THIS GUY HAS ONE TOUGH HIDE.
OH WELL. THE IMMORTAL ARTS AREN'T MY ONLY WEAPON.

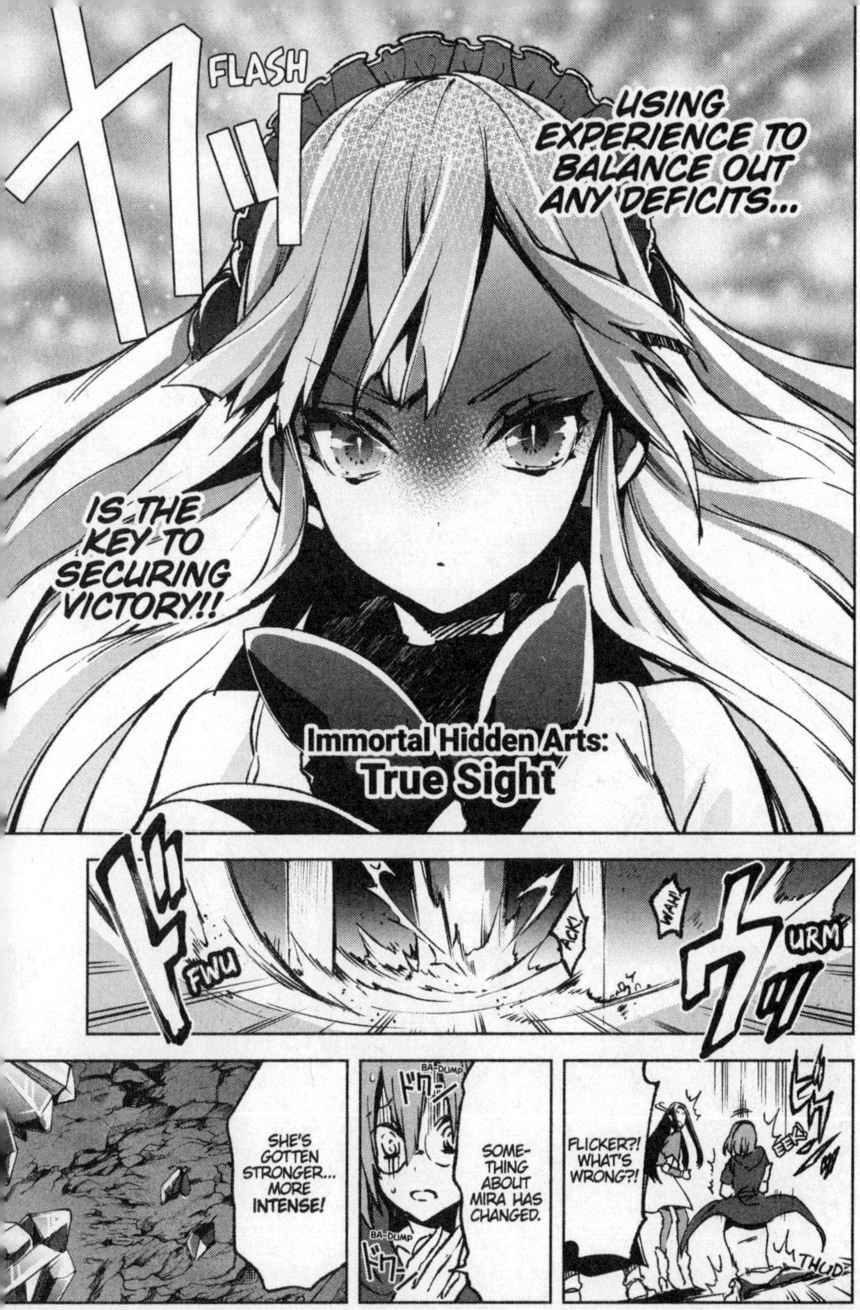
FLASH
USING EXPERIENCE TO BALANCE OUT ANY DEFICITS...
IS THE KEY TO SECURING VICTORY!!
Immortal Hidden Arts:
True Sight
URM
WAH!
ACK!
FWU
FLICKER?! WHAT'S WRONG?!
EEK
THUD
BA-DUMP
SOME-THING ABOUT MIRA HAS CHANGED.
BA-DUMP
SHE'S GOTTEN STRONGER... MORE INTENSE!

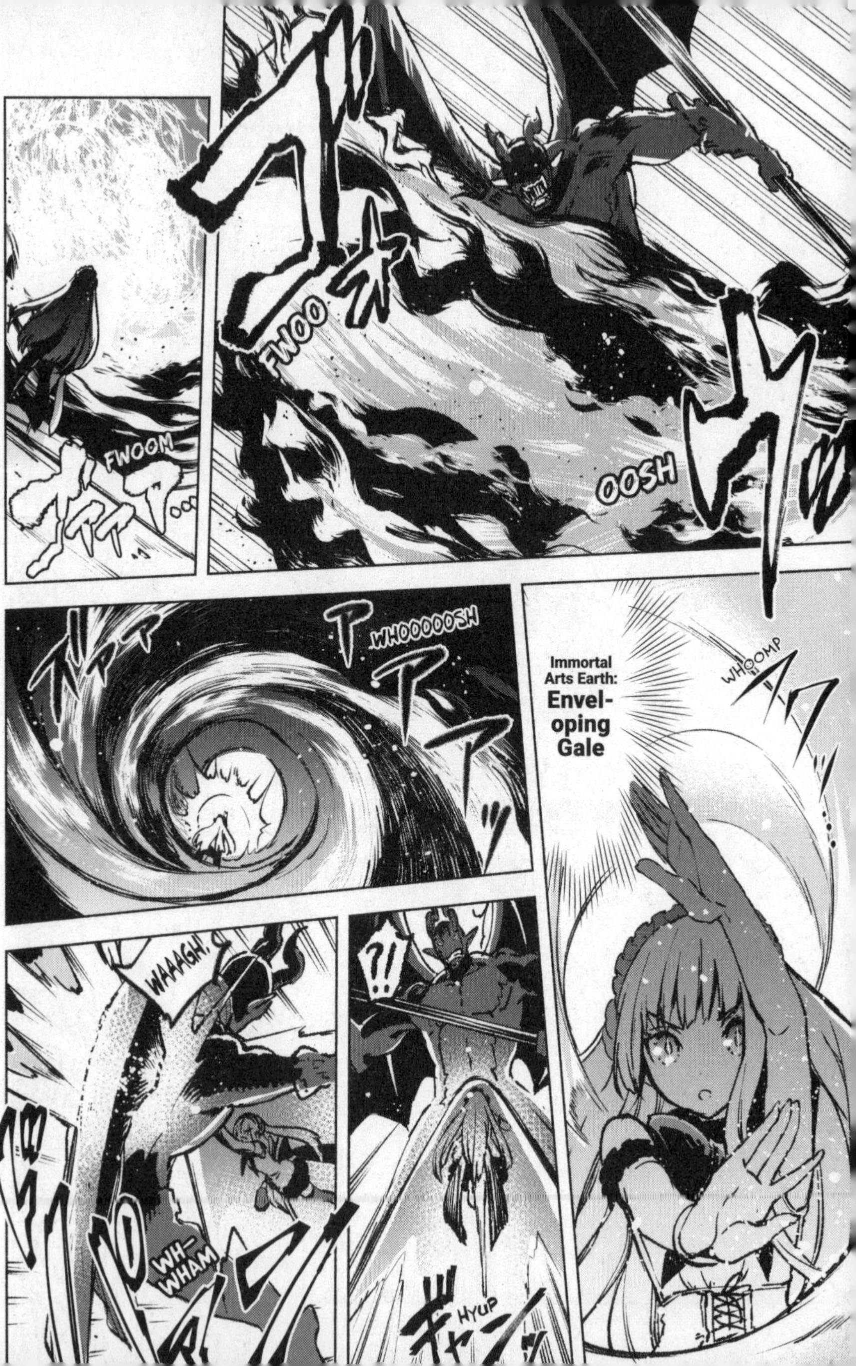

FWOO
OOSH
FWOOM
Immortal Arts Earth: Envel-oping Gale
WHOOMP
WHOOOOOSH
?!!
HYUP
WAAAGH
WH-WHAM

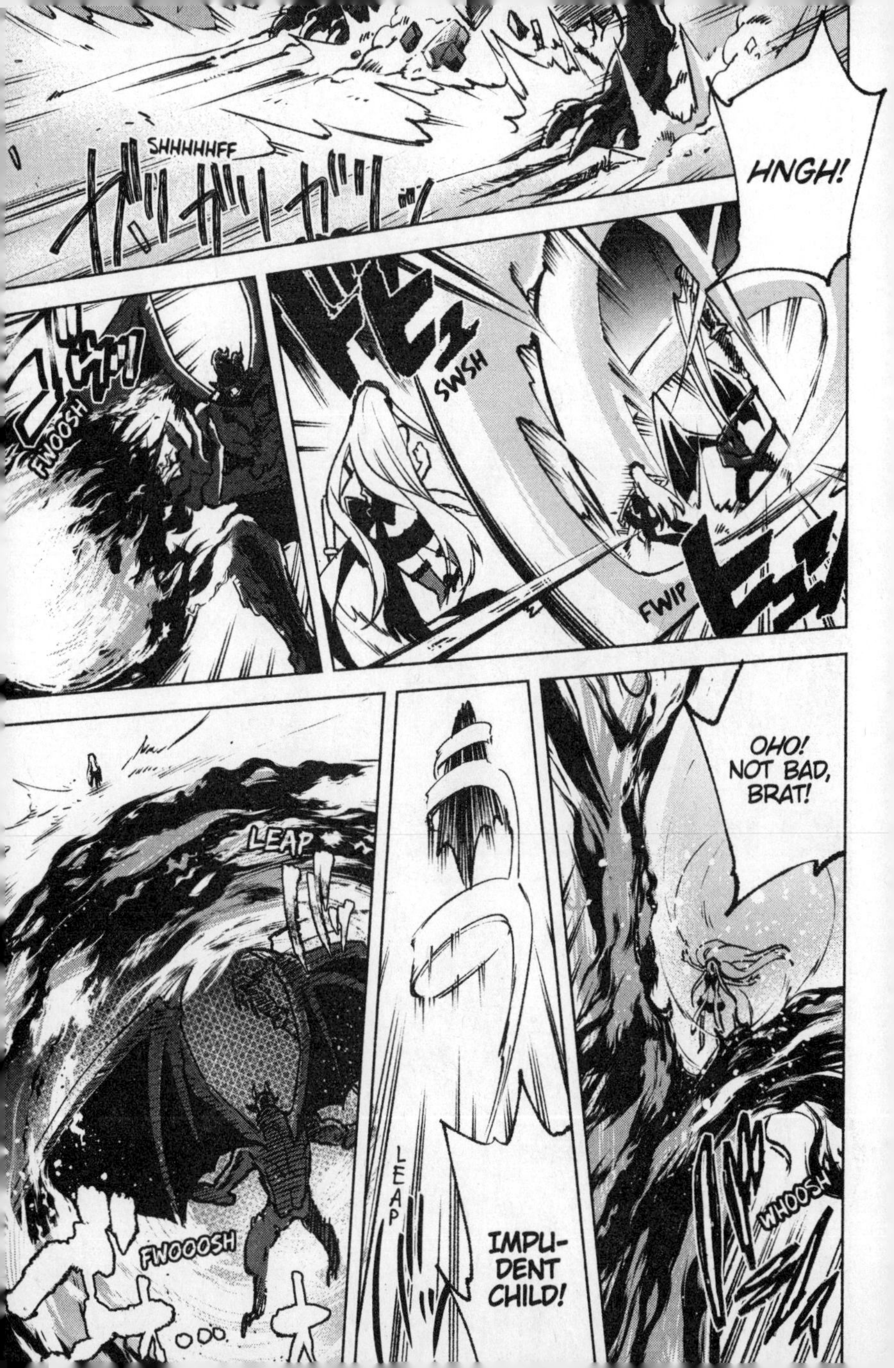
HNGH!
SHHHHHFF
FWIP
SWSH
FWOOSH
OHO! NOT BAD, BRAT!
WHOOSH
LEAP
IMPU-DENT CHILD!
LEAP
FWOOOSH
OOO.

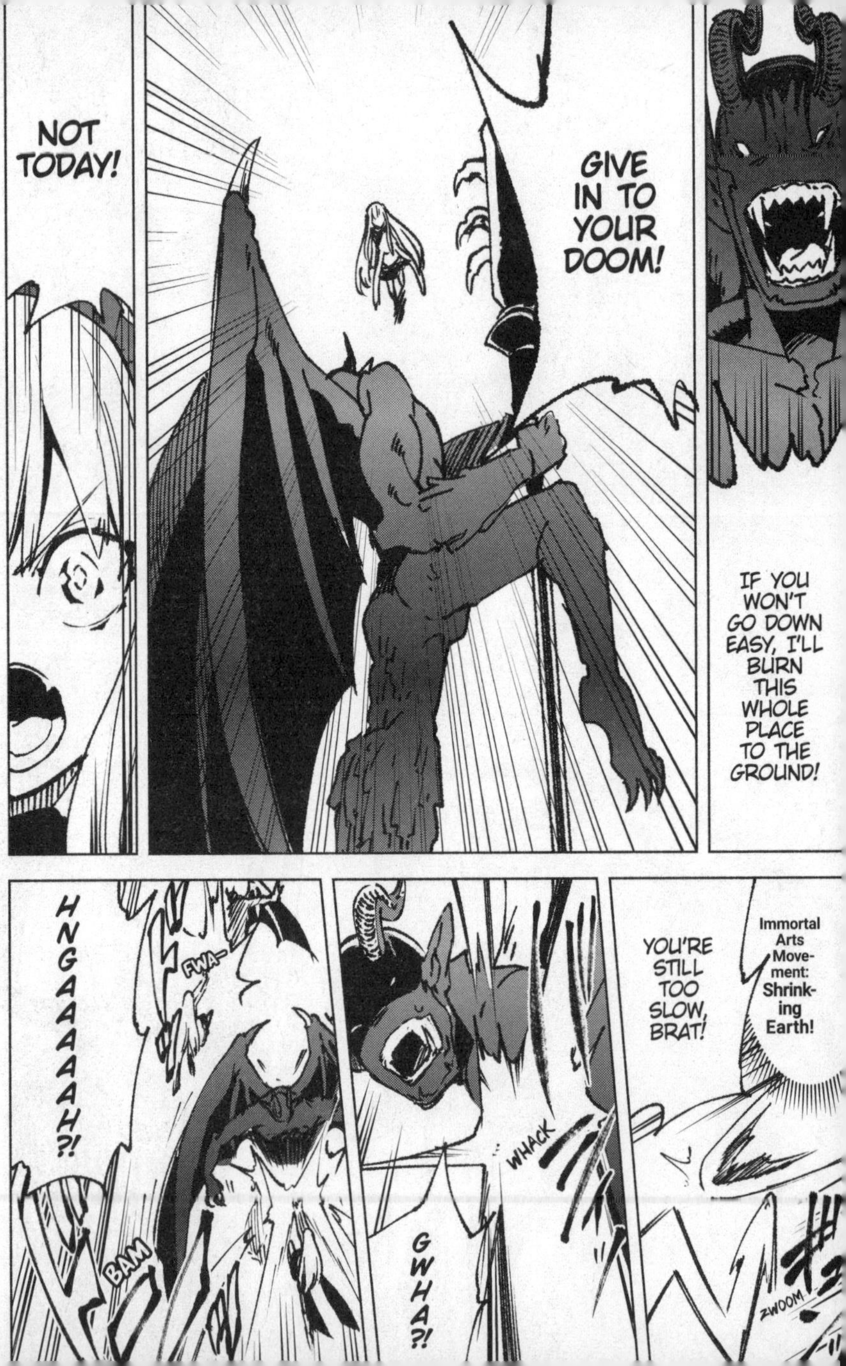
IF YOU WON'T GO DOWN EASY, I'LL BURN THIS WHOLE PLACE TO THE GROUND!
GIVE IN TO YOUR DOOM!
NOT TODAY!
Immortal Arts Movement: Shrinking Earth!
YOU'RE STILL TOO SLOW, BRAT!
ZWOOM
WHACK
GWHA?!
FWA-
HNGAAAAAAAH?!
BAM

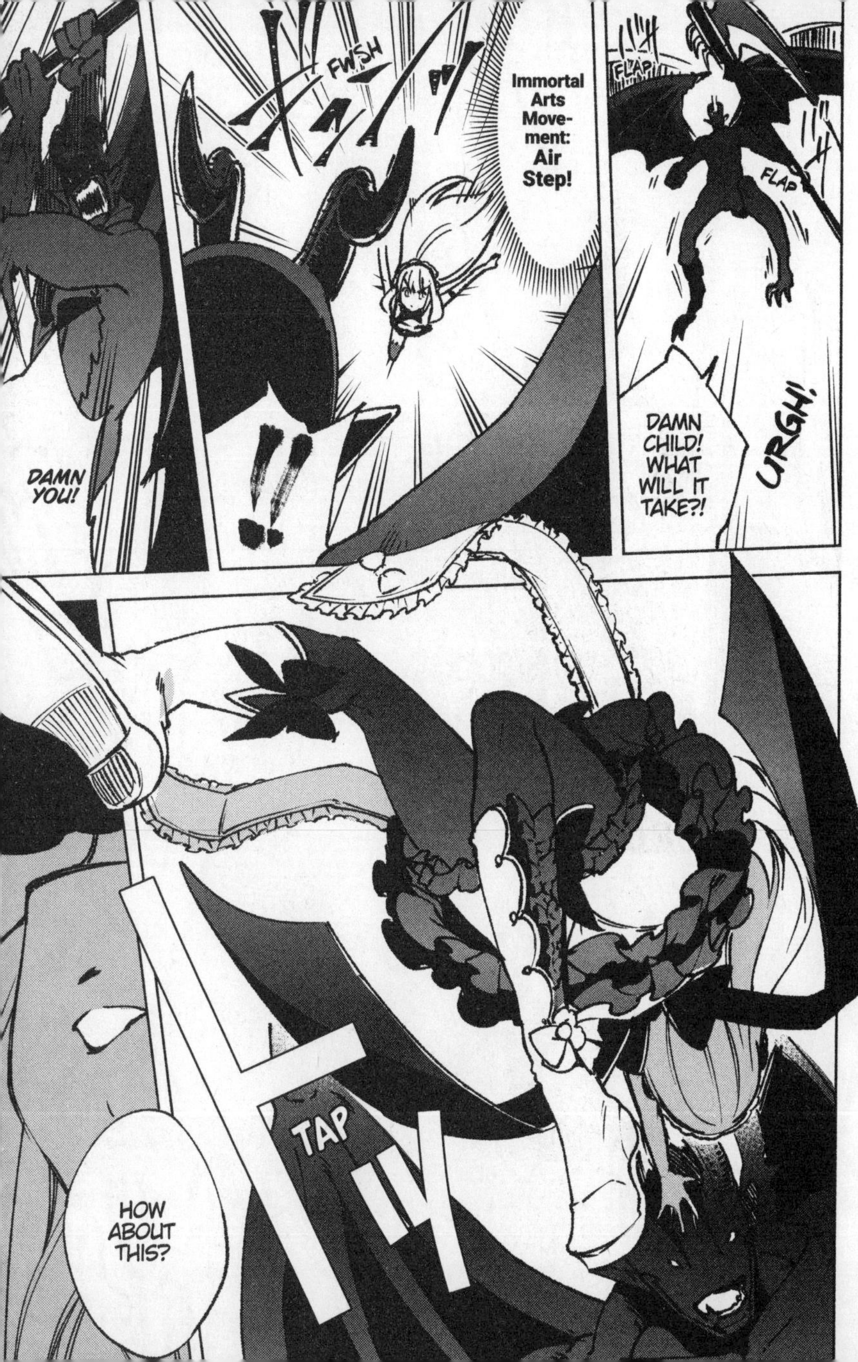
FLAP
FLAP
DAMN CHILD! WHAT WILL IT TAKE?!
URGH!
FWSH
Immortal Arts Movement: Air Step!
!!
DAMN YOU!
TAP
HOW ABOUT THIS?

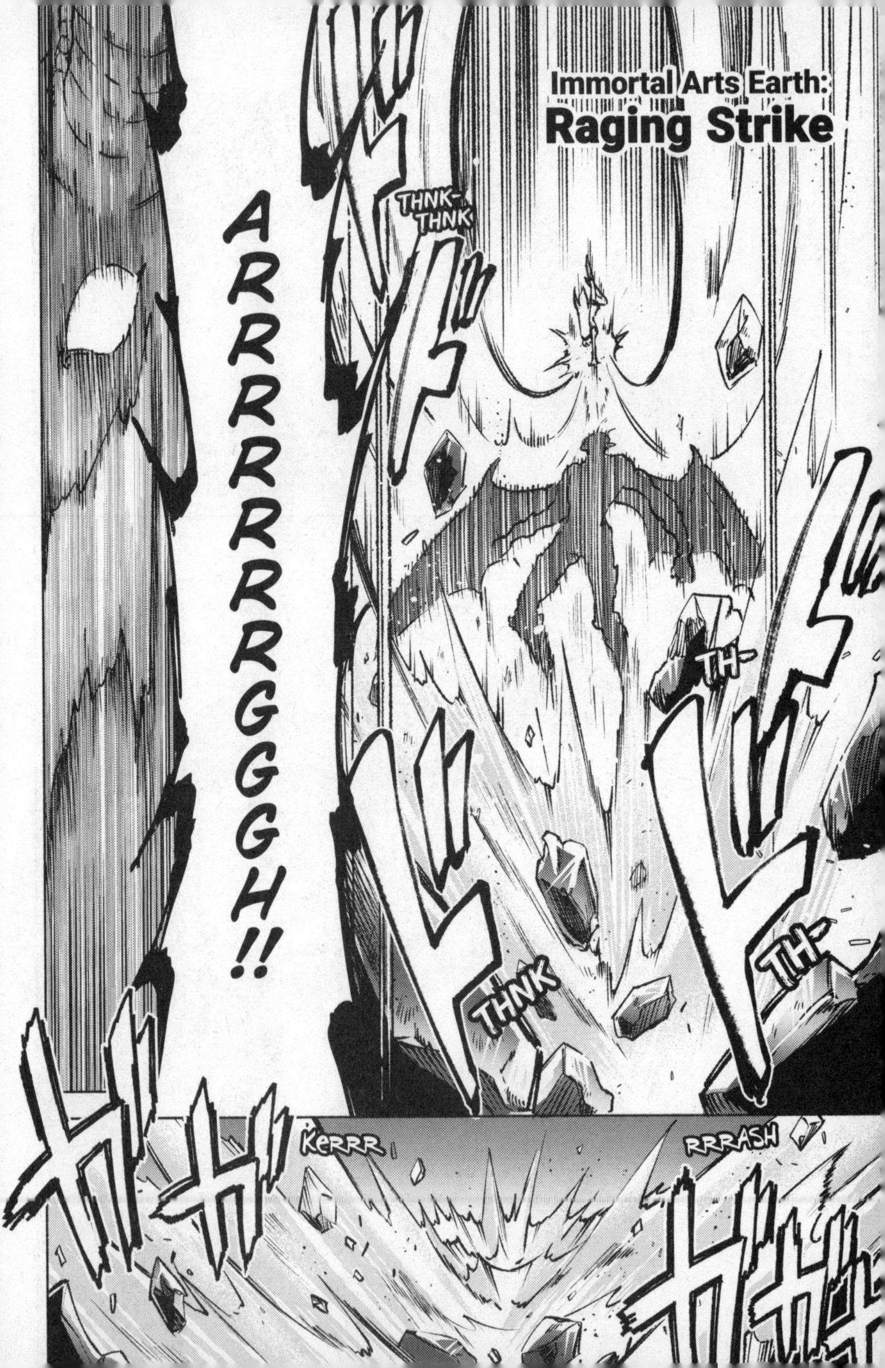
Immortal Arts Earth:
Raging Strike
THNK-THNK
ARRRRRRRGGGH!!
TH-
TH-
THNK
KERRR
RRRASH

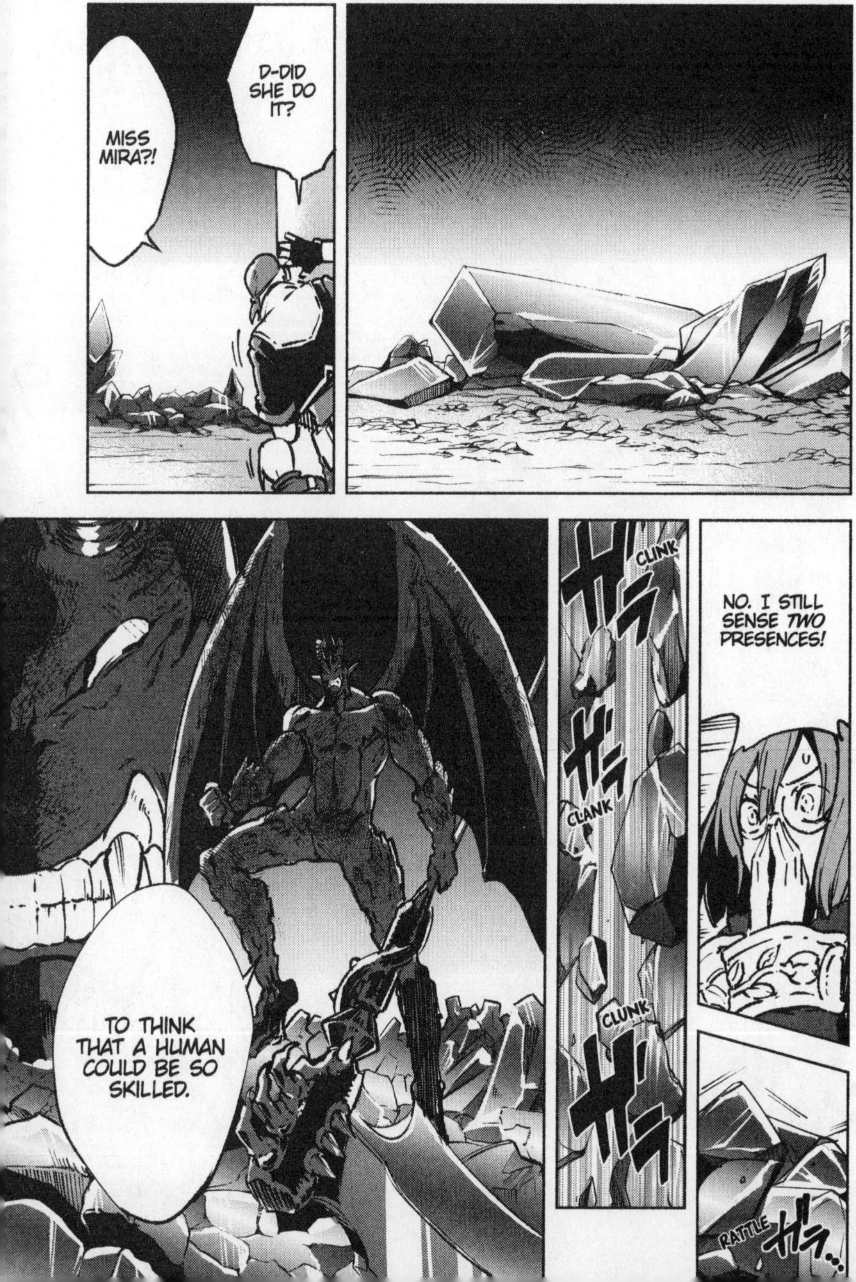
D-DID SHE DO IT?
MISS MIRA?!
NO. I STILL SENSE *TWO* PRESENCES!
RATTLE
CLINK
CLANK
CLUNK
TO THINK THAT A HUMAN COULD BE SO SKILLED.

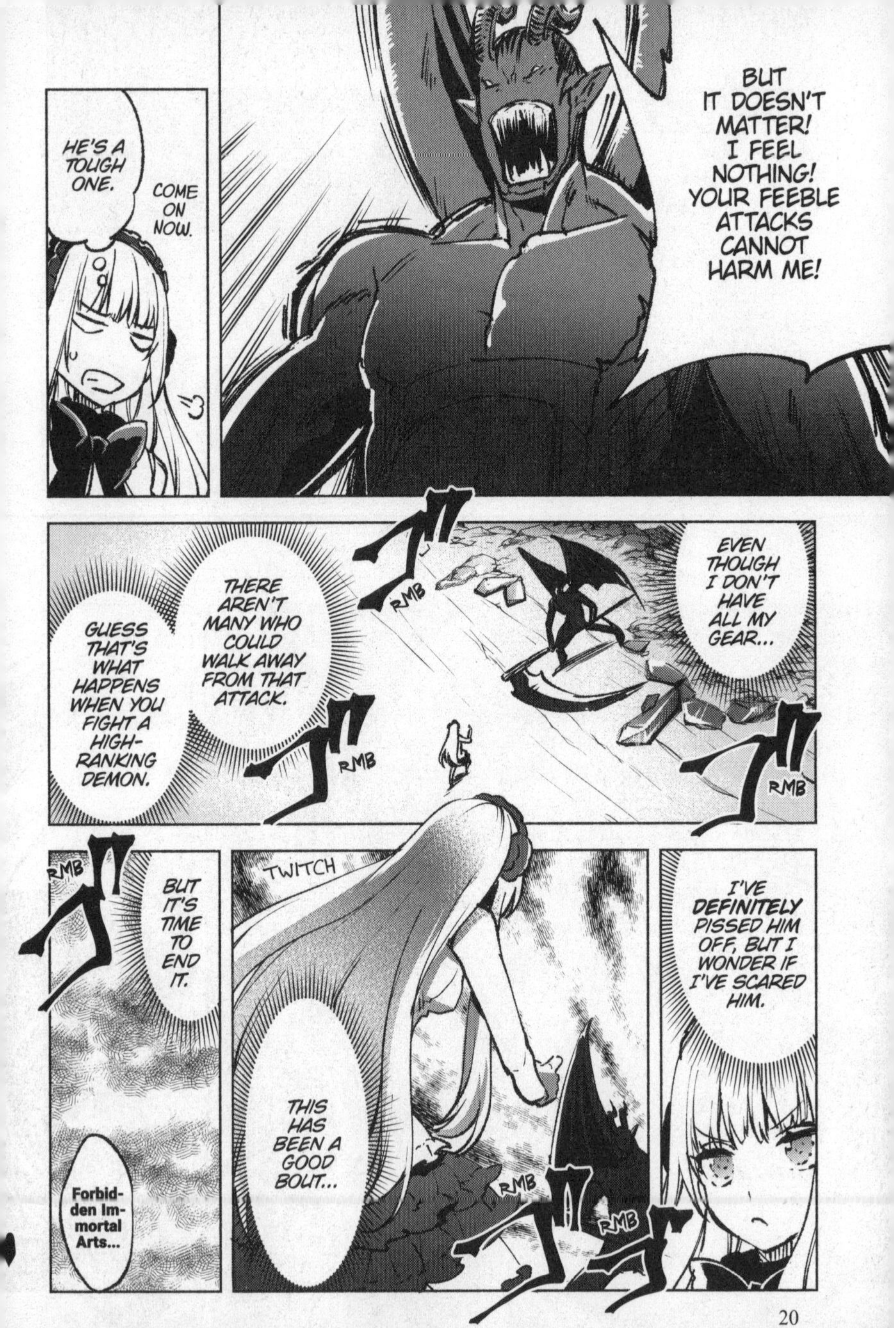
BUT IT DOESN'T MATTER! I FEEL NOTHING! YOUR FEEBLE ATTACKS CANNOT HARM ME!
HE'S A TOUGH ONE.
COME ON NOW.
EVEN THOUGH I DON'T HAVE ALL MY GEAR...
RMB
THERE AREN'T MANY WHO COULD WALK AWAY FROM THAT ATTACK.
GUESS THAT'S WHAT HAPPENS WHEN YOU FIGHT A HIGH-RANKING DEMON.
RMB
RMB
I'VE **DEFINITELY** PISSED HIM OFF, BUT I WONDER IF I'VE SCARED HIM.
TWITCH
THIS HAS BEEN A GOOD BOUT...
RMB
RMB
RMB
BUT IT'S TIME TO END IT.
Forbidden Immortal Arts...

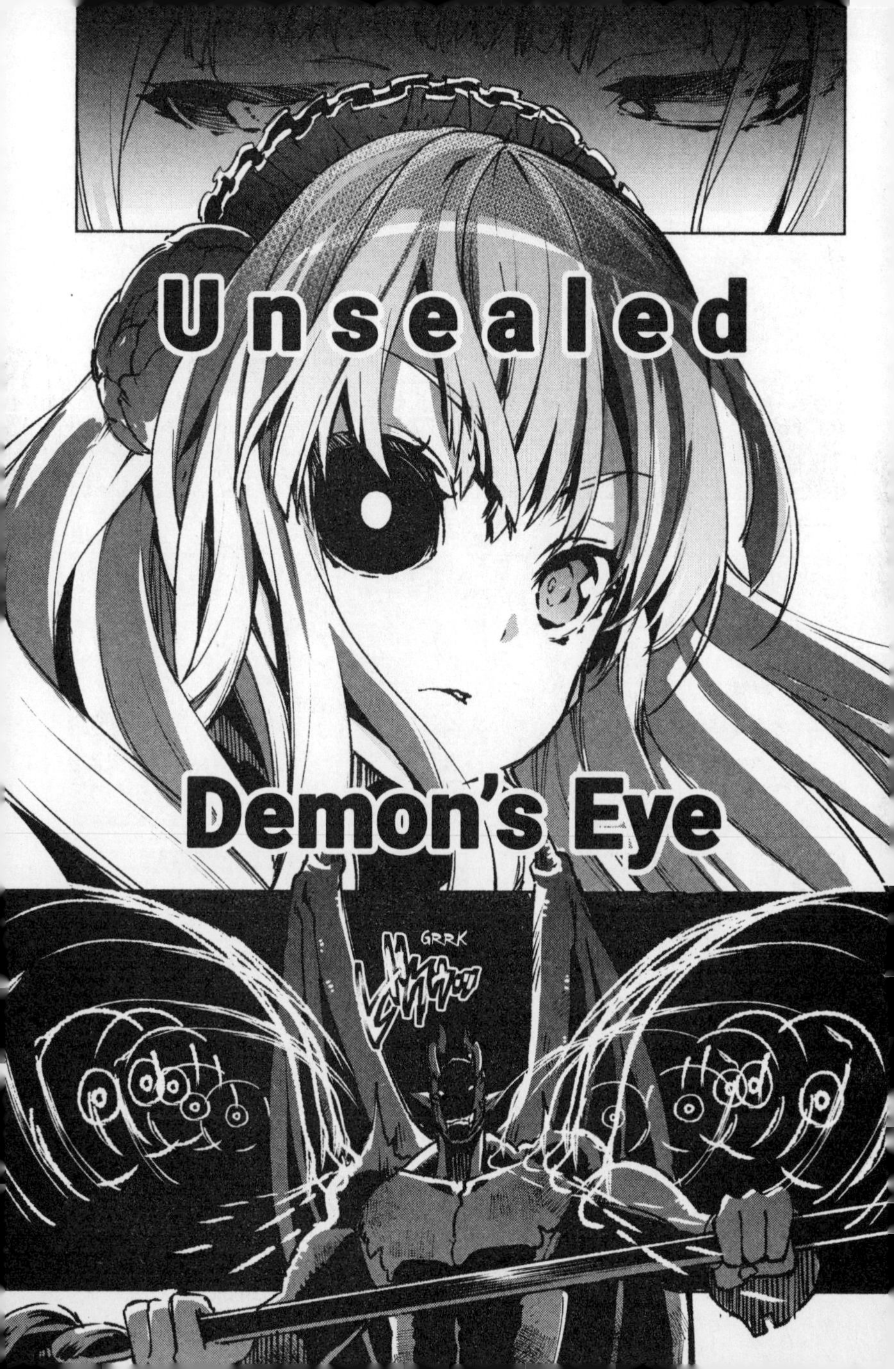
Unsealed
Demon's Eye
GRRK

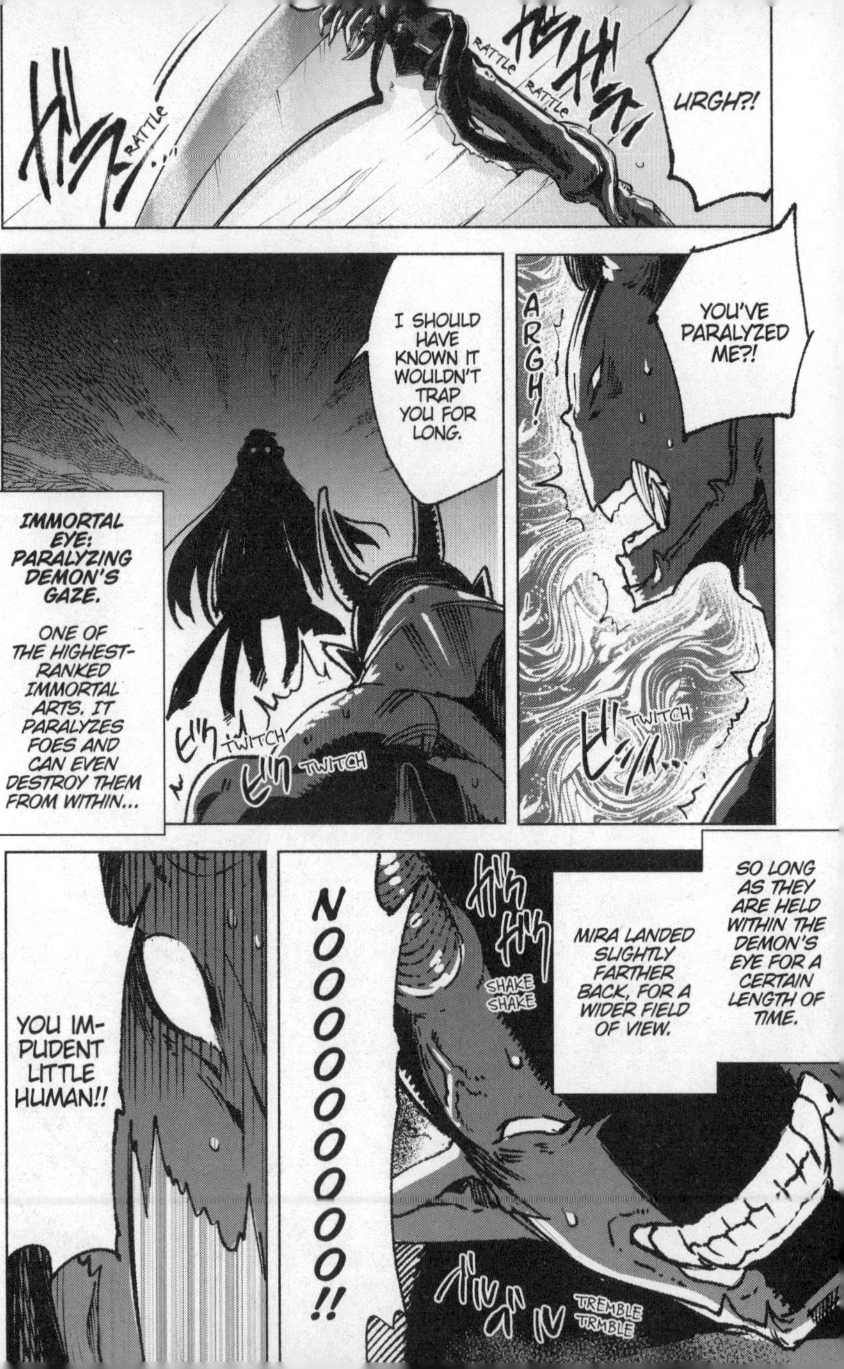
RATTLE RATTLE
URGH?!
RATTLE...
YOU'VE PARALYZED ME?!
ARGH!
TWITCH
I SHOULD HAVE KNOWN IT WOULDN'T TRAP YOU FOR LONG.
IMMORTAL EYE: PARALYZING DEMON'S GAZE.
ONE OF THE HIGHEST-RANKED IMMORTAL ARTS. IT PARALYZES FOES AND CAN EVEN DESTROY THEM FROM WITHIN...
TWITCH
TWITCH
SO LONG AS THEY ARE HELD WITHIN THE DEMON'S EYE FOR A CERTAIN LENGTH OF TIME.
MIRA LANDED SLIGHTLY FARTHER BACK, FOR A WIDER FIELD OF VIEW.
SHAKE SHAKE
NOOOOOOOOOOOO!!
TREMBLE TRMBLE
YOU IMPUDENT LITTLE HUMAN!!

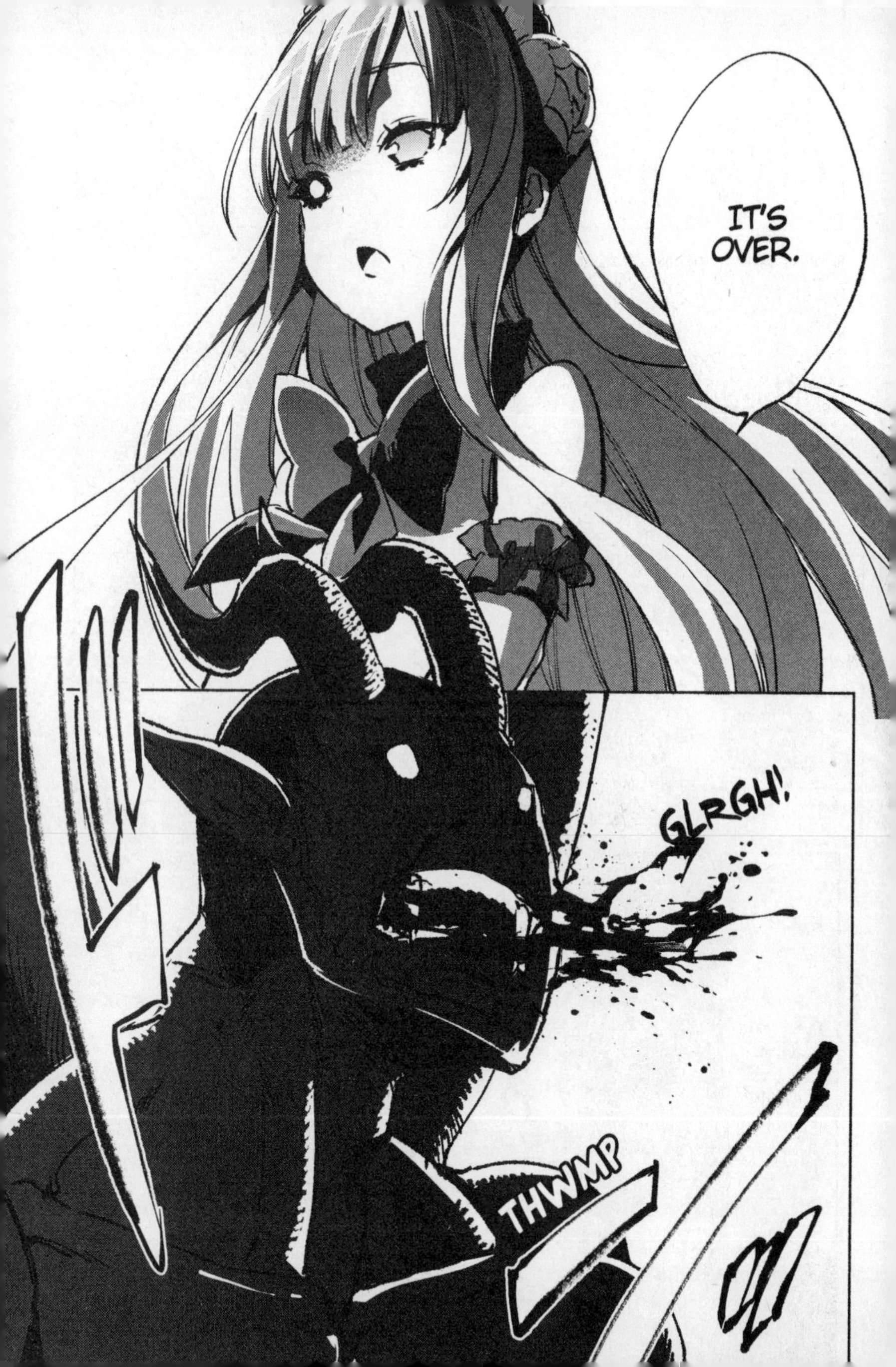
IT'S OVER.
GLRGH!
THWMP

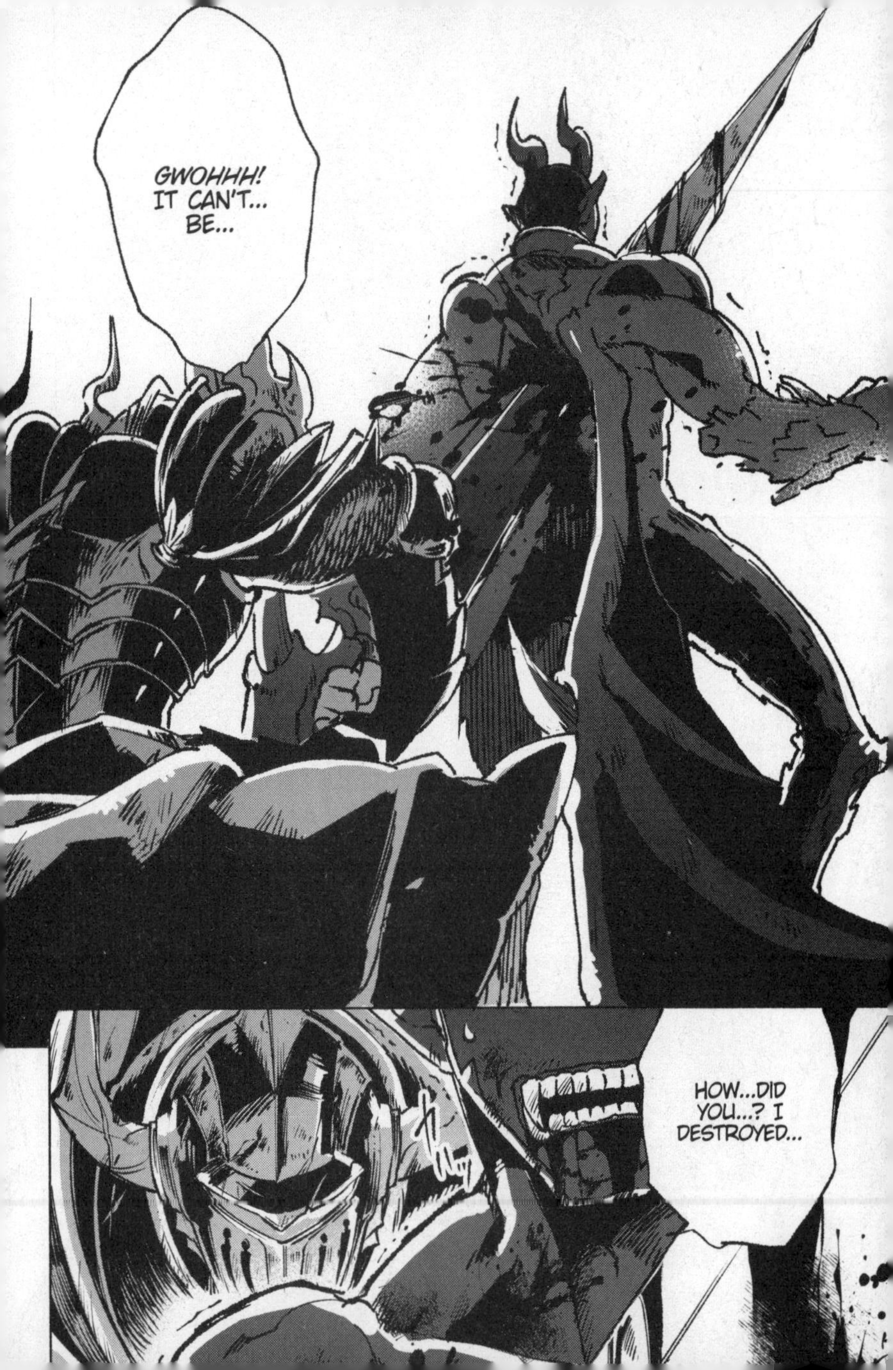
GWOHHH! IT CAN'T... BE...
HOW...DID YOU...? I DESTROYED...

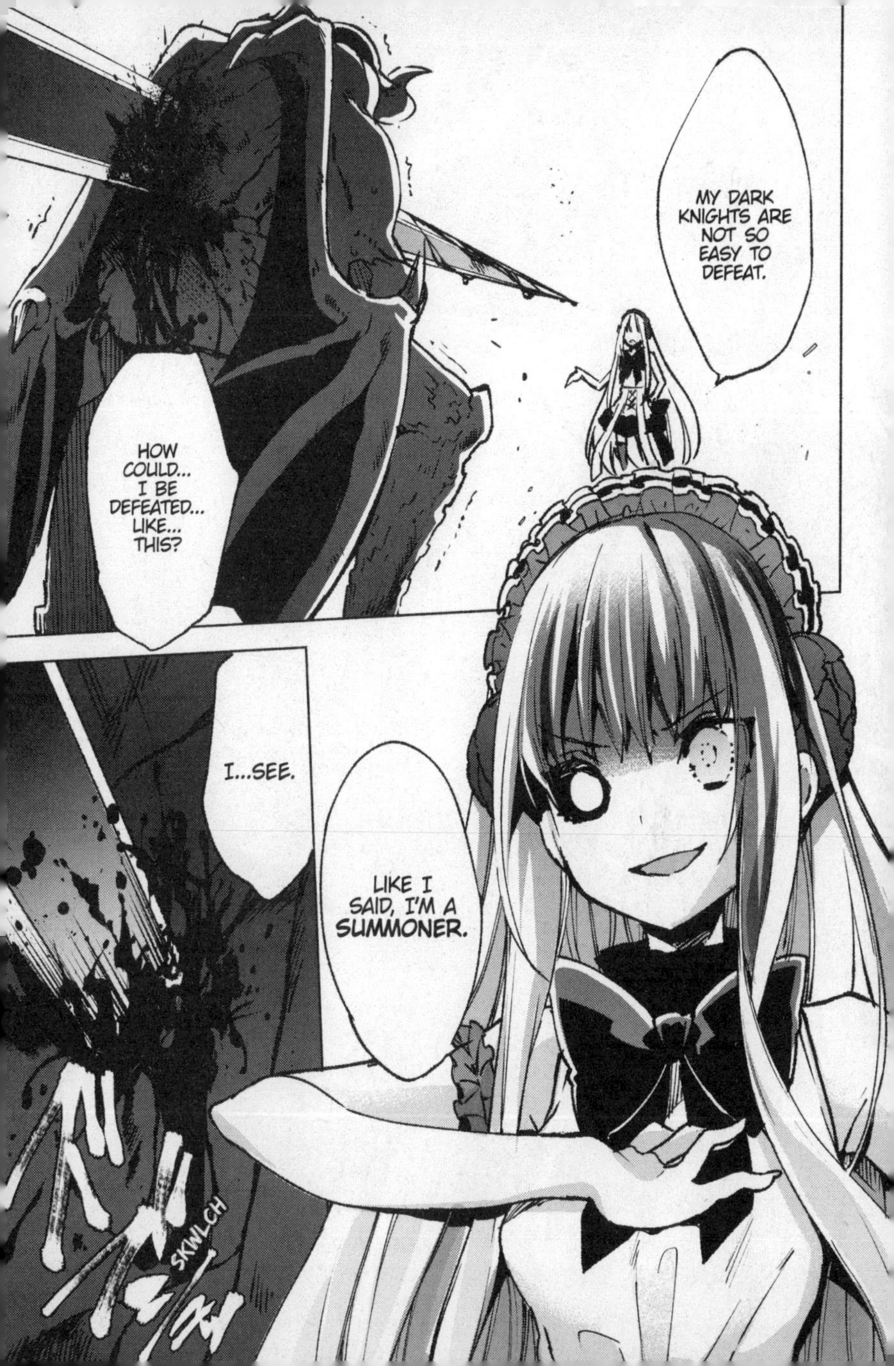
MY DARK KNIGHTS ARE NOT SO EASY TO DEFEAT.
HOW COULD... I BE DEFEATED... LIKE... THIS?
I...SEE.
LIKE I SAID, I'M A SUMMONER.
SKWLCH

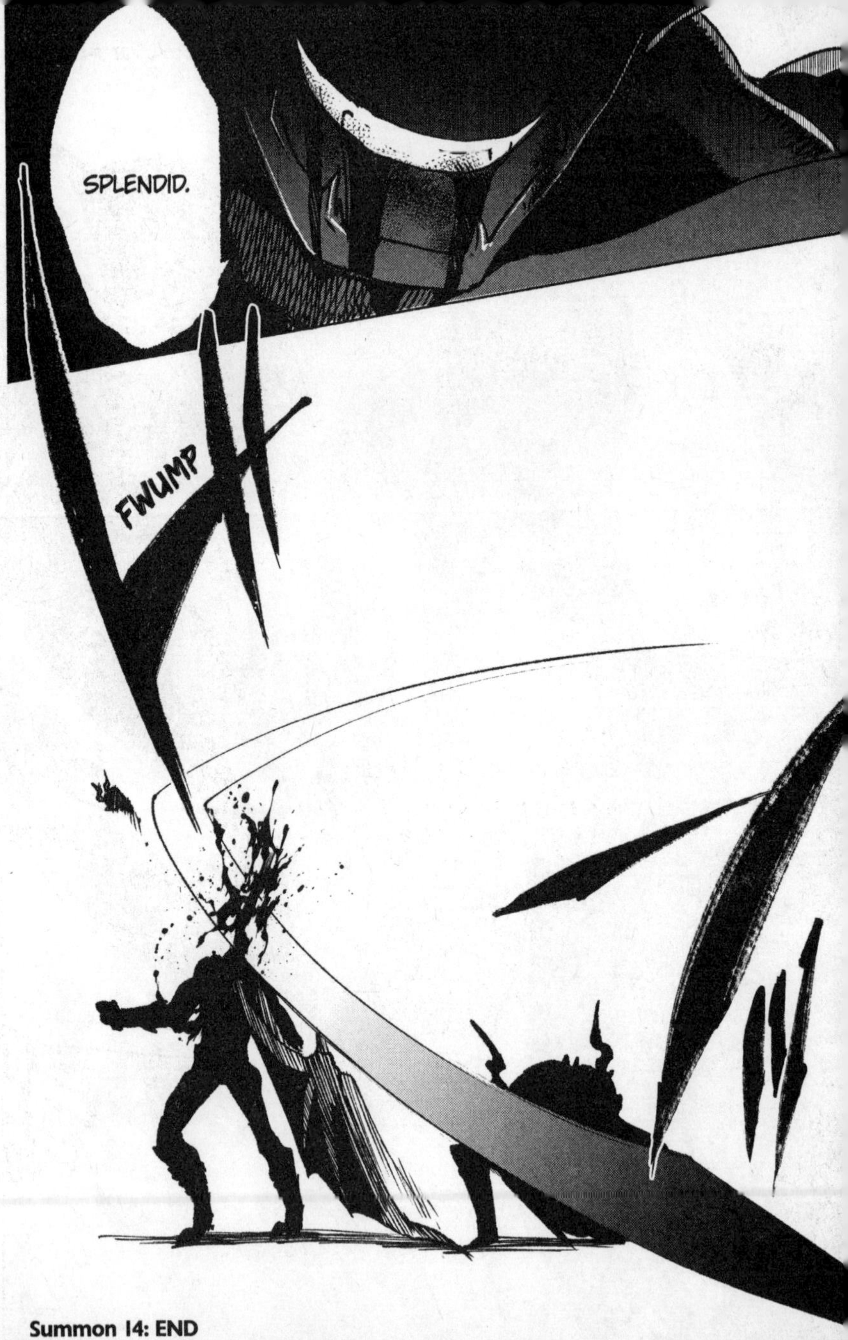
SPLENDID.
FWUMP

Summon 14: END

Summon 15: [One Thing After Another]

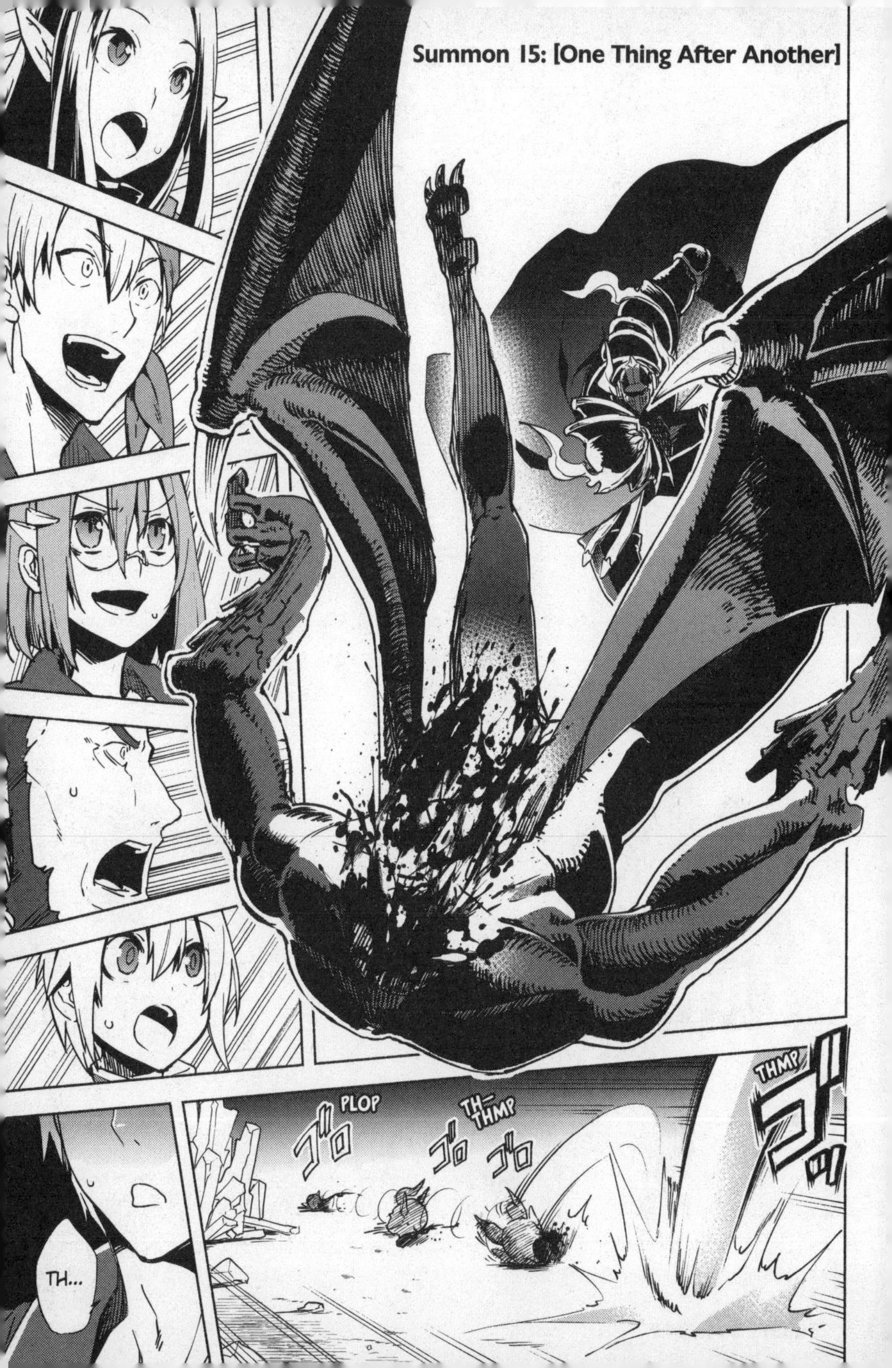
THMP
TH-THMP
PLOP
TH...

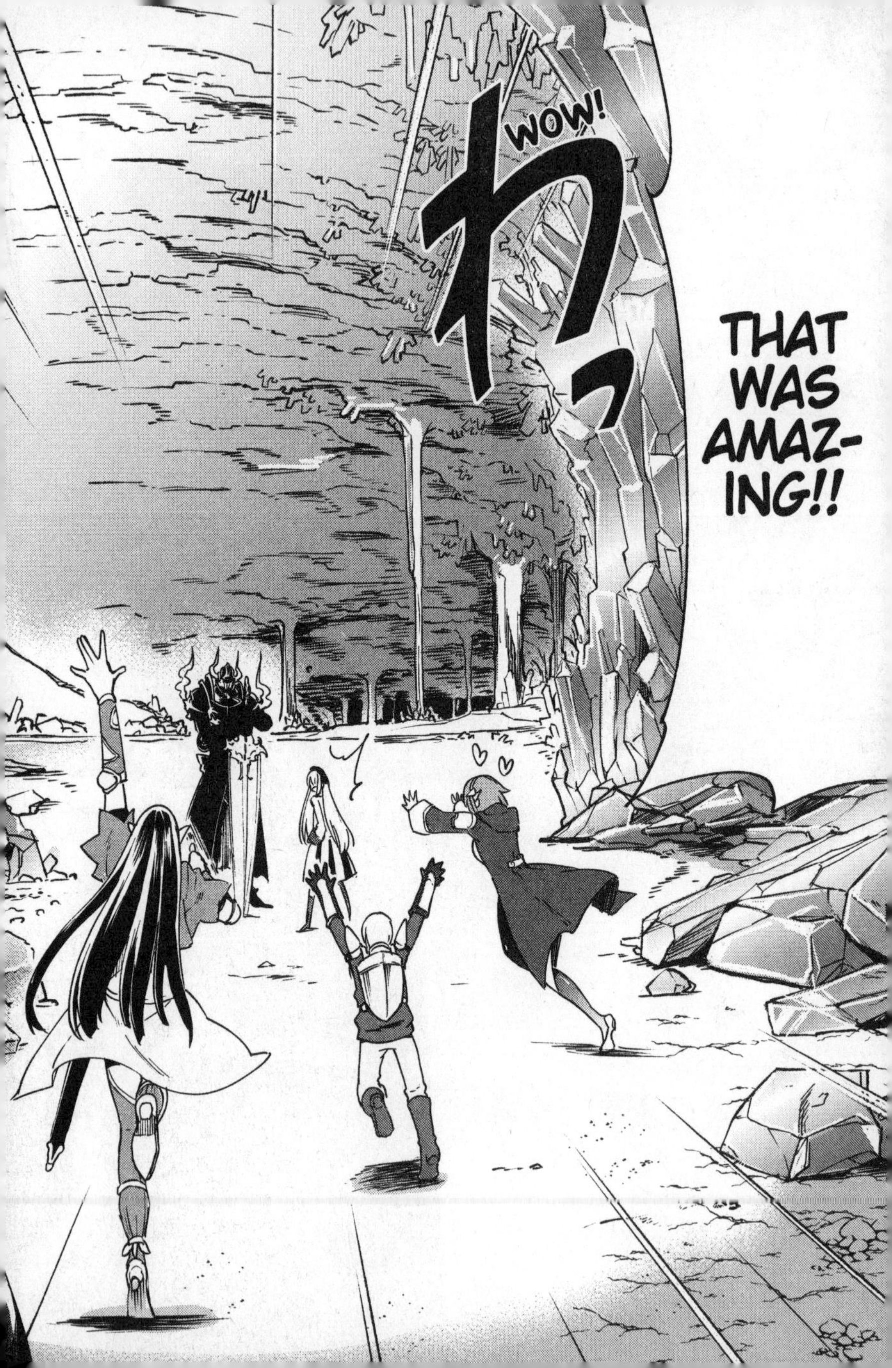
ワッ
WOW!
THAT WAS AMAZ-ING!!

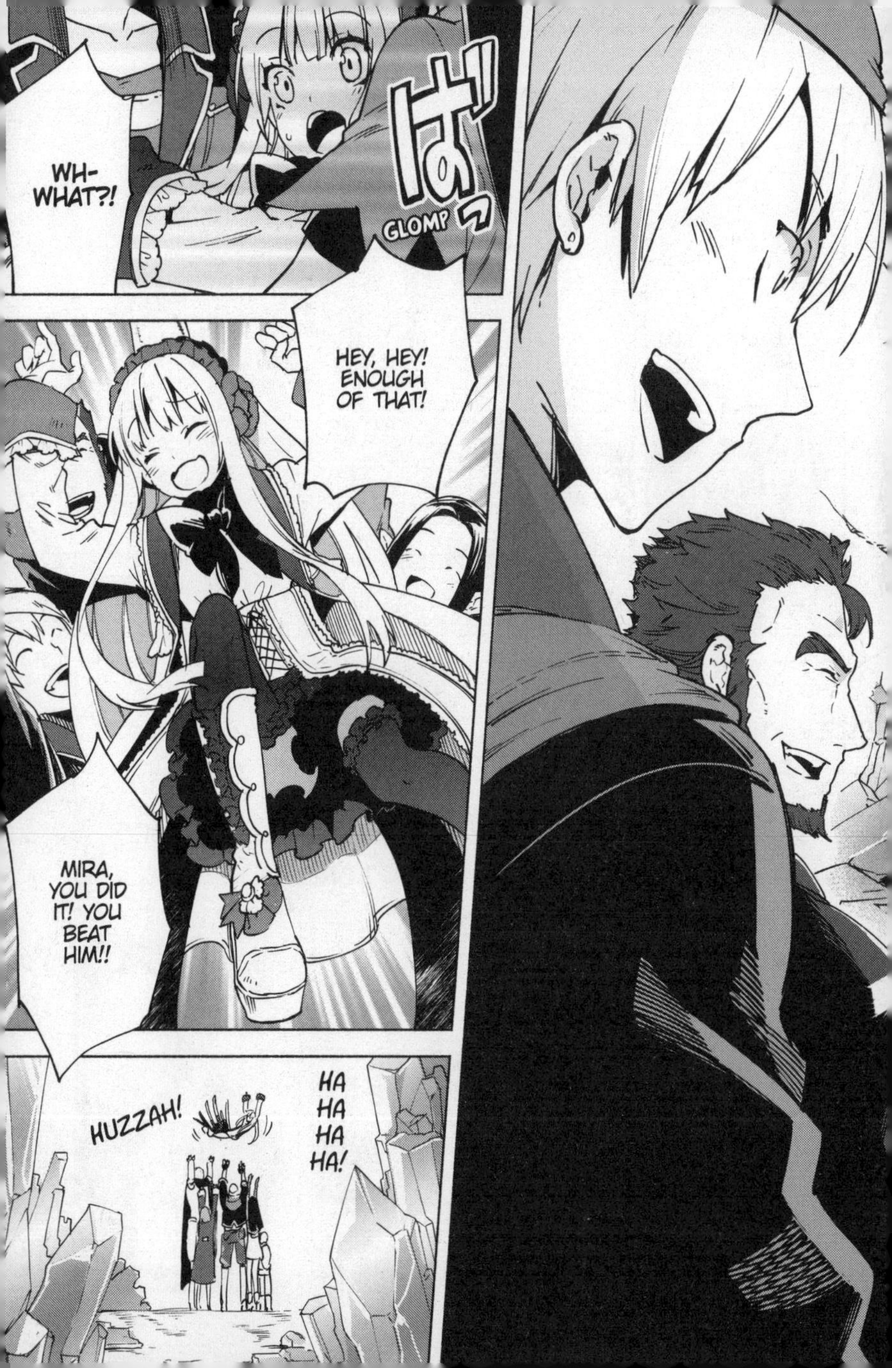
ばっ
GLOMP
WH-WHAT?!
HEY, HEY! ENOUGH OF THAT!
MIRA, YOU DID IT! YOU BEAT HIM!!
HA HA HA HA HA!
HUZZAH!

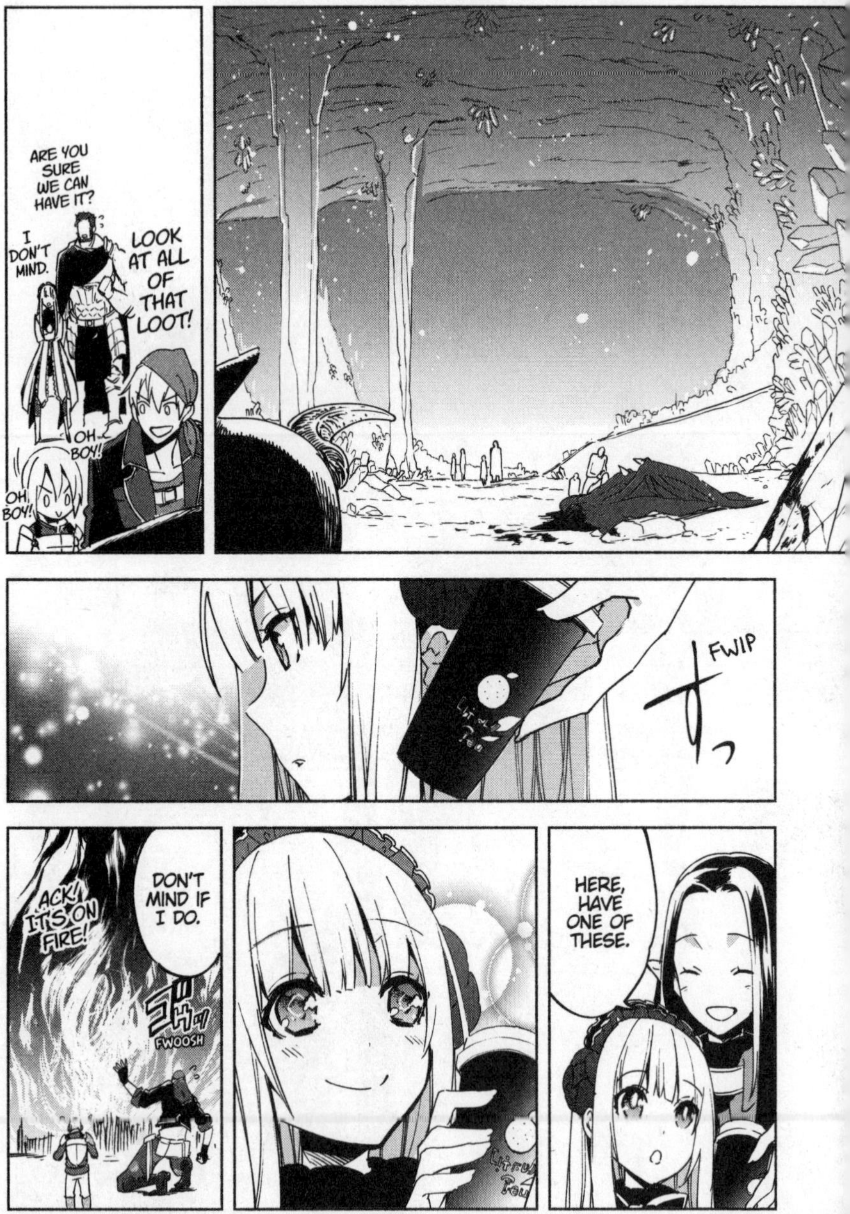
ARE YOU SURE WE CAN HAVE IT?
I DON'T MIND.
LOOK AT ALL OF THAT LOOT!
OH BOY!
OH BOY!
FWIP
HERE, HAVE ONE OF THESE.
DON'T MIND IF I DO.
ACK! IT'S ON FIRE!
FWOOSH

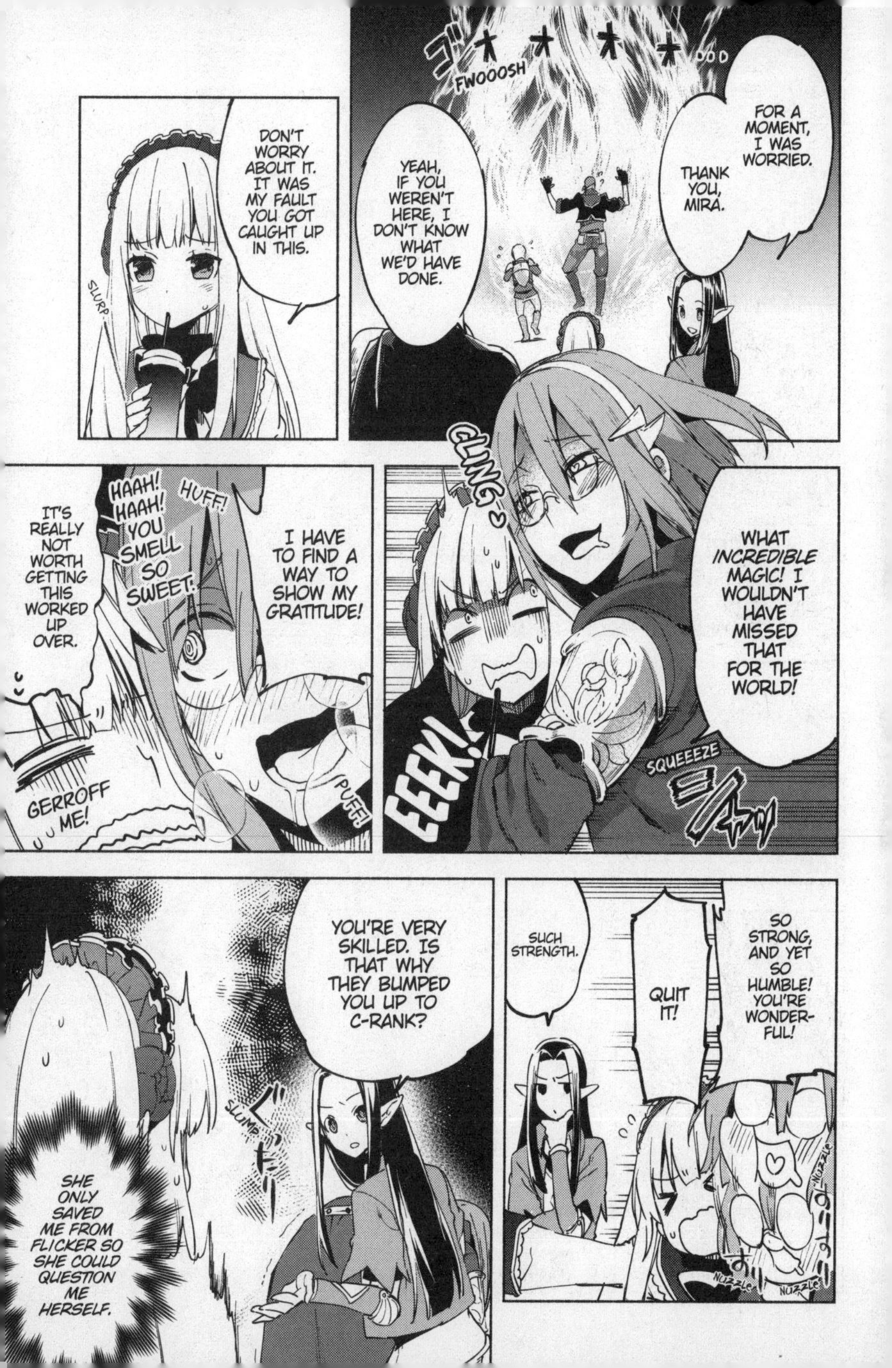
FWOOOSH
FOR A MOMENT, I WAS WORRIED.
THANK YOU, MIRA.
YEAH, IF YOU WEREN'T HERE, I DON'T KNOW WHAT WE'D HAVE DONE.
SLURP
DON'T WORRY ABOUT IT. IT WAS MY FAULT YOU GOT CAUGHT UP IN THIS.
CLING
WHAT INCREDIBLE MAGIC! I WOULDN'T HAVE MISSED THAT FOR THE WORLD!
SQUEEEZE
EEEK!
HUFF!
I HAVE TO FIND A WAY TO SHOW MY GRATITUDE!
HAAH! HAAH! YOU SMELL SO SWEET.
IT'S REALLY NOT WORTH GETTING THIS WORKED UP OVER.
PUFF!
GERROFF ME!
SO STRONG, AND YET SO HUMBLE! YOU'RE WONDERFUL!
QUIT IT!
SUCH STRENGTH.
NUZZLE
NUZZLE
NUZZLE
YOU'RE VERY SKILLED. IS THAT WHY THEY BUMPED YOU UP TO C-RANK?
SLUMP
SHE ONLY SAVED ME FROM FLICKER SO SHE COULD QUESTION ME HERSELF.

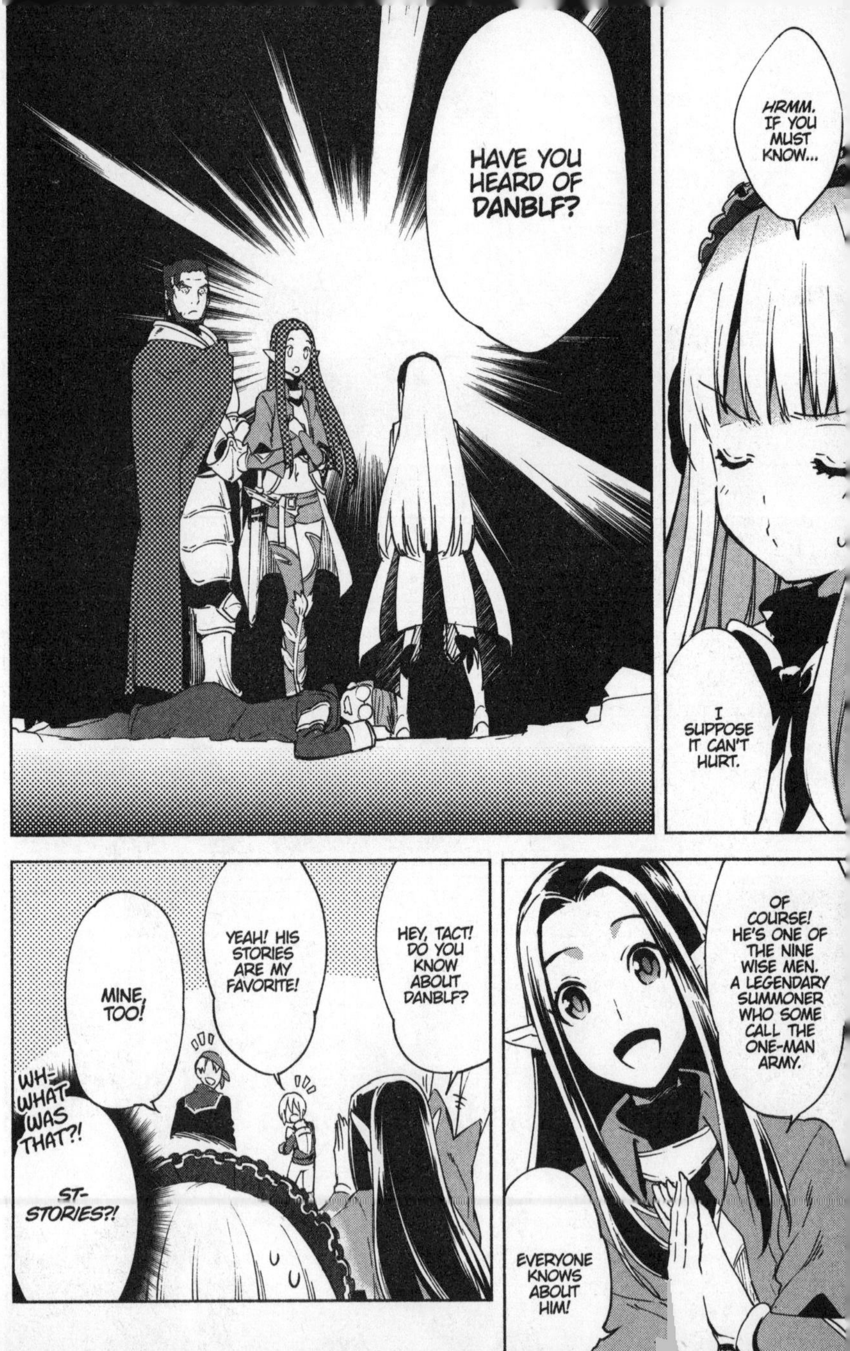
HRMM. IF YOU MUST KNOW...
I SUPPOSE IT CAN'T HURT.
HAVE YOU HEARD OF DANBLF?
OF COURSE! HE'S ONE OF THE NINE WISE MEN. A LEGENDARY SUMMONER WHO SOME CALL THE ONE-MAN ARMY.
EVERYONE KNOWS ABOUT HIM!
HEY, TACT! DO YOU KNOW ABOUT DANBLF?
YEAH! HIS STORIES ARE MY FAVORITE!
MINE, TOO!
WH- WHAT WAS THAT?!
ST- STORIES?!

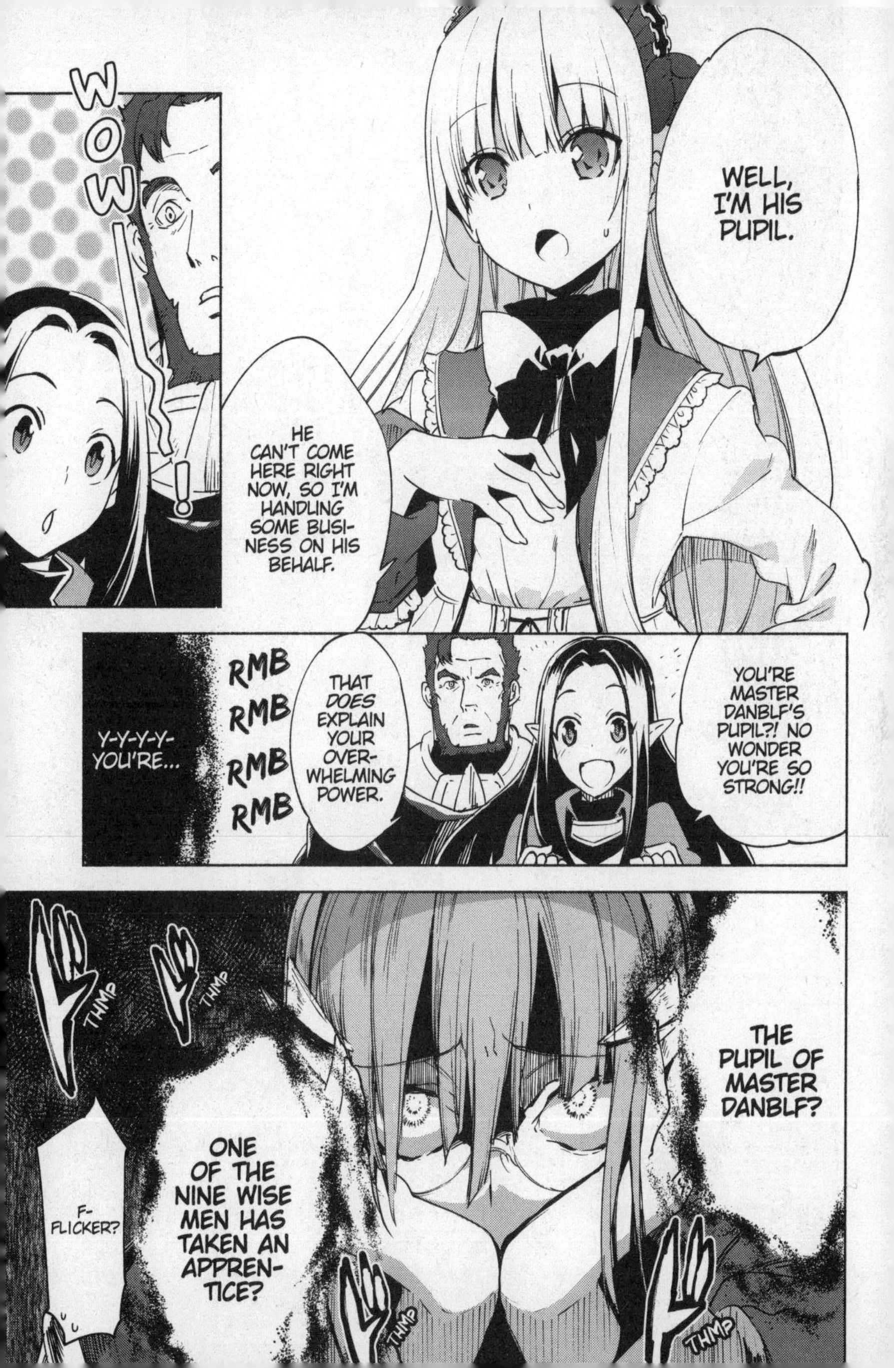
WELL, I'M HIS PUPIL.
HE CAN'T COME HERE RIGHT NOW, SO I'M HANDLING SOME BUSINESS ON HIS BEHALF.
WOW!
YOU'RE MASTER DANBLF'S PUPIL?! NO WONDER YOU'RE SO STRONG!!
THAT DOES EXPLAIN YOUR OVERWHELMING POWER.
RMB RMB RMB RMB
Y-Y-Y-Y-YOU'RE...
THE PUPIL OF MASTER DANBLF?
ONE OF THE NINE WISE MEN HAS TAKEN AN APPRENTICE?
F-FLICKER?
THMP THMP THMP THMP

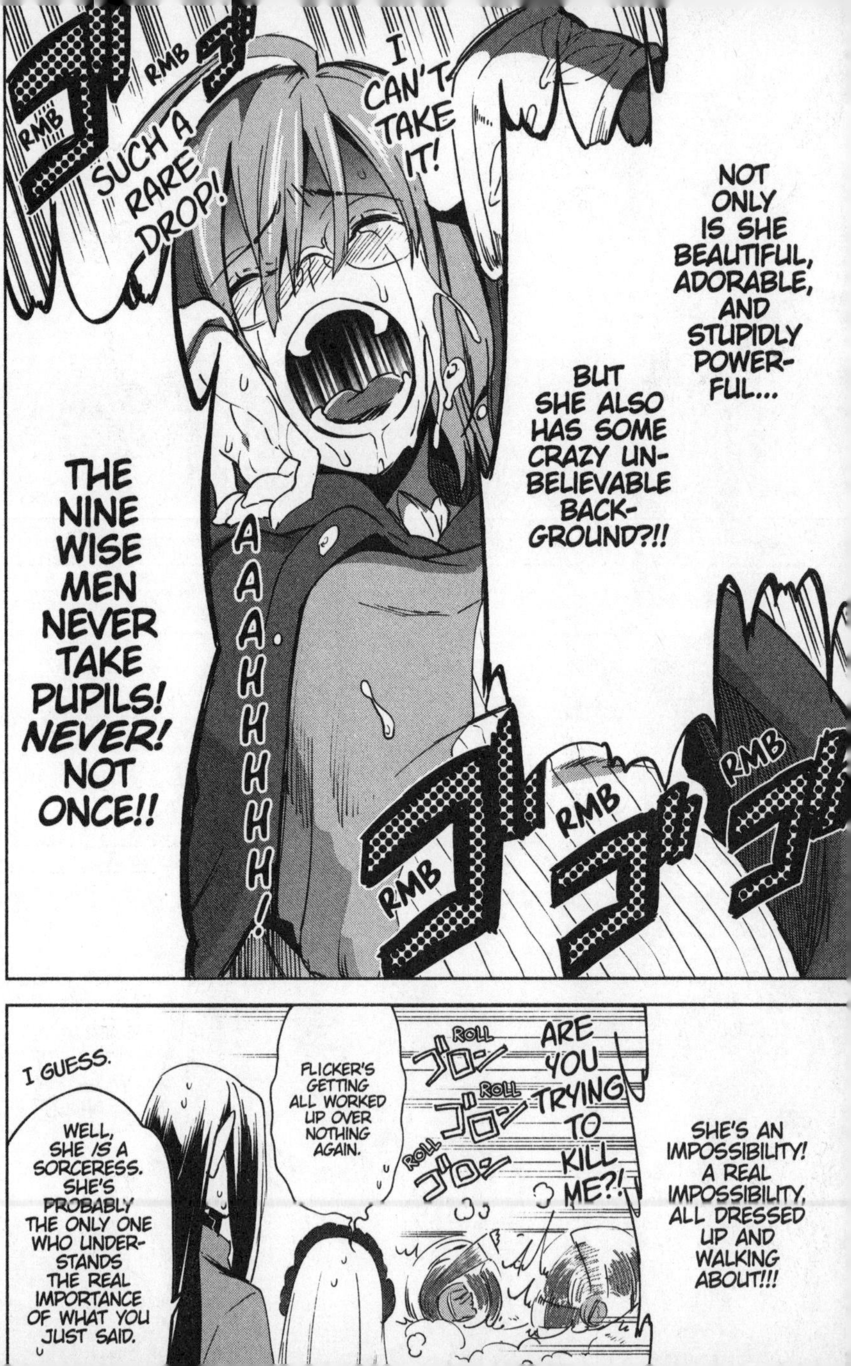
NOT ONLY IS SHE BEAUTIFUL, ADORABLE, AND STUPIDLY POWER-FUL...
BUT SHE ALSO HAS SOME CRAZY UN-BELIEVABLE BACK-GROUND?!!
I CAN'T TAKE IT!
RMB
RMB
SUCH A RARE DROP!
RMB
RMB
RMB
THE NINE WISE MEN NEVER TAKE PUPILS! *NEVER!* NOT ONCE!!
AAAAHHHHHH!
SHE'S AN IMPOSSIBILITY! A REAL IMPOSSIBILITY, ALL DRESSED UP AND WALKING ABOUT!!!
ARE YOU TRYING TO KILL ME?!
ROLL
ROLL
ROLL
FLICKER'S GETTING ALL WORKED UP OVER NOTHING AGAIN.
I GUESS.
WELL, SHE *IS* A SORCERESS. SHE'S PROBABLY THE ONLY ONE WHO UNDER-STANDS THE REAL IMPORTANCE OF WHAT YOU JUST SAID.

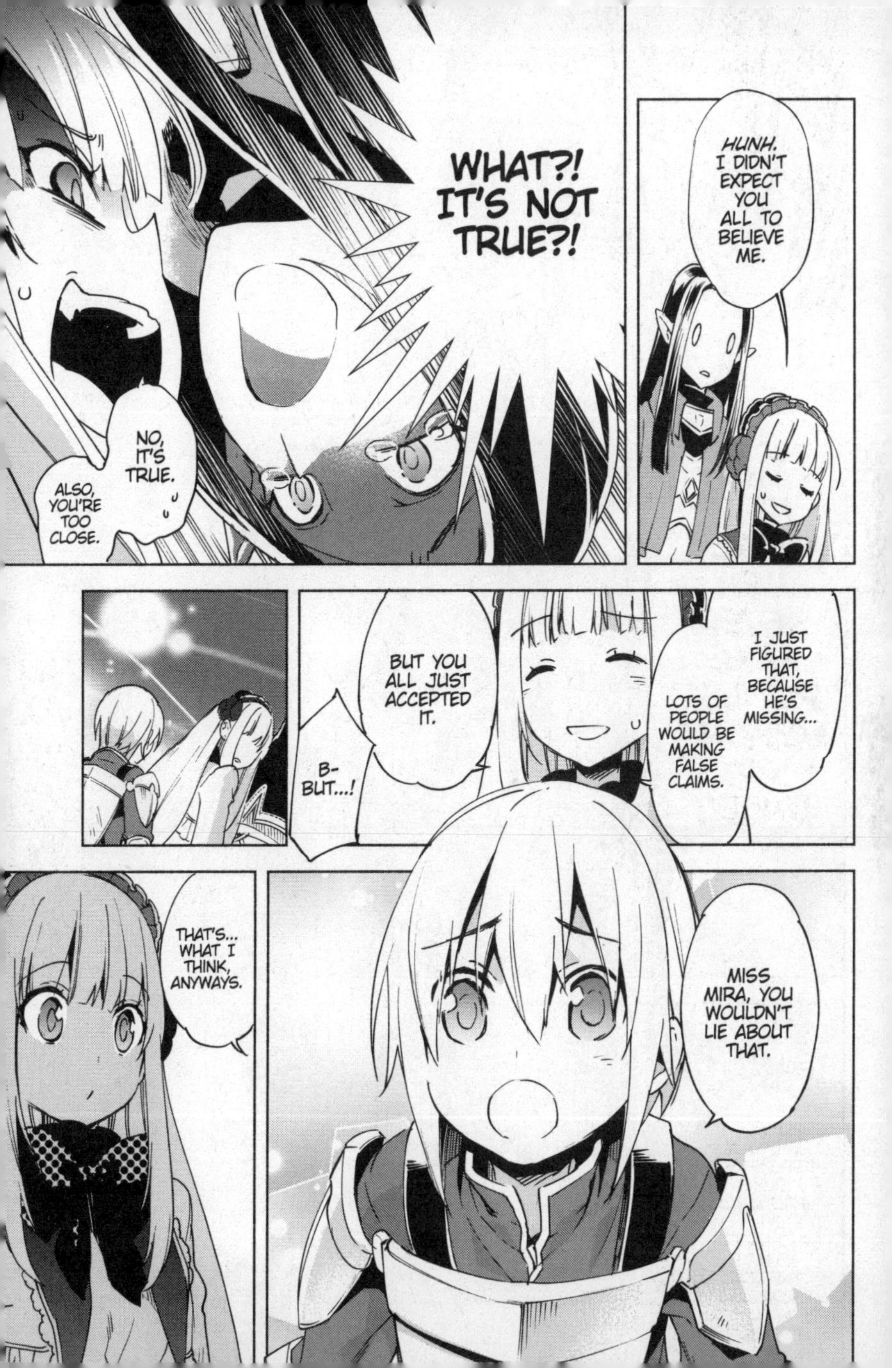
HUNH. I DIDN'T EXPECT YOU ALL TO BELIEVE ME.
WHAT?! IT'S NOT TRUE?!
NO, IT'S TRUE.
ALSO, YOU'RE TOO CLOSE.
I JUST FIGURED THAT, BECAUSE HE'S MISSING...
LOTS OF PEOPLE WOULD BE MAKING FALSE CLAIMS.
BUT YOU ALL JUST ACCEPTED IT.
B- BUT...!
MISS MIRA, YOU WOULDN'T LIE ABOUT THAT.
THAT'S... WHAT I THINK, ANYWAYS.

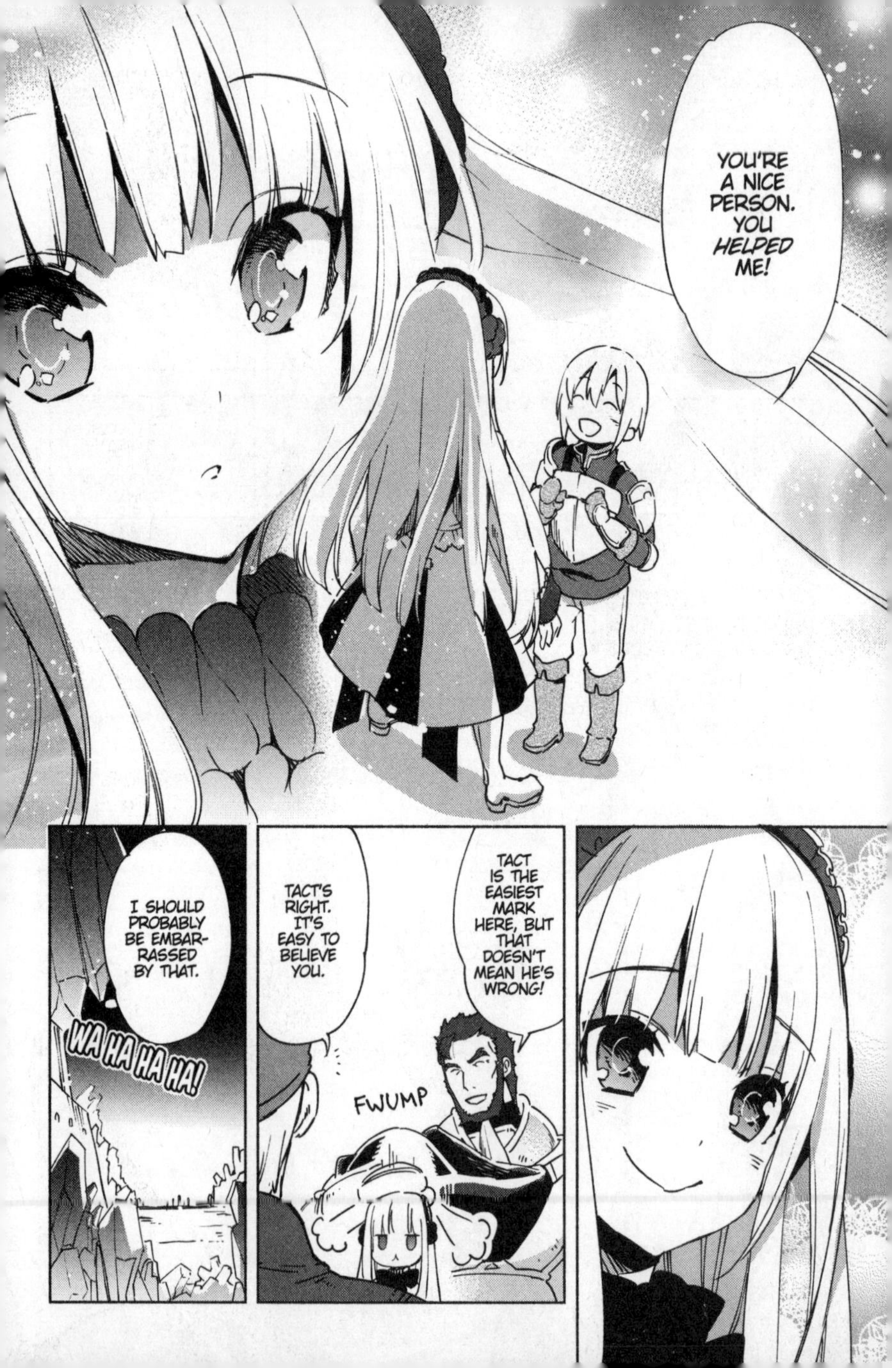
YOU'RE A NICE PERSON. YOU HELPED ME!
TACT IS THE EASIEST MARK HERE, BUT THAT DOESN'T MEAN HE'S WRONG!
TACT'S RIGHT. IT'S EASY TO BELIEVE YOU.
FWUMP
I SHOULD PROBABLY BE EMBARRASSED BY THAT.
WA HA HA HA!

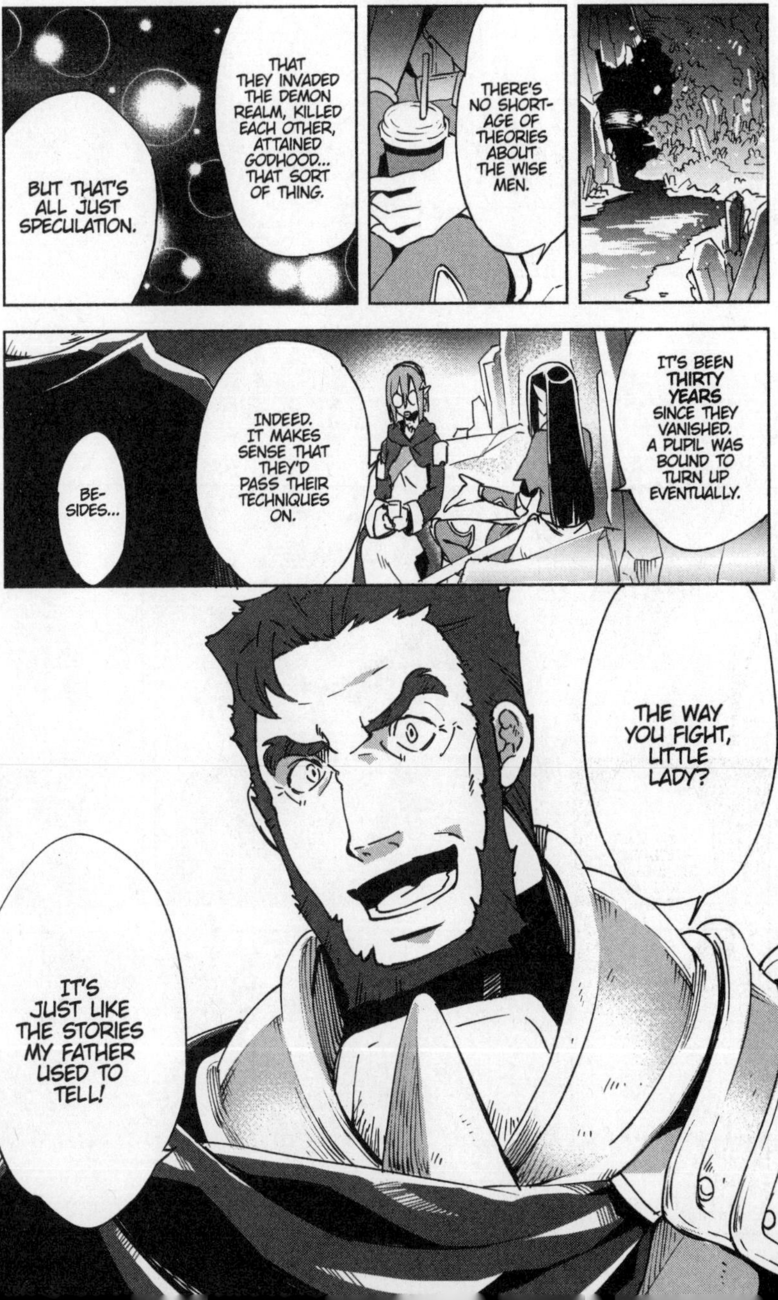
THERE'S NO SHORTAGE OF THEORIES ABOUT THE WISE MEN.
THAT THEY INVADED THE DEMON REALM, KILLED EACH OTHER, ATTAINED GODHOOD... THAT SORT OF THING.
BUT THAT'S ALL JUST SPECULATION.
IT'S BEEN **THIRTY YEARS** SINCE THEY VANISHED. A PUPIL WAS BOUND TO TURN UP EVENTUALLY.
INDEED. IT MAKES SENSE THAT THEY'D PASS THEIR TECHNIQUES ON.
BESIDES...
THE WAY YOU FIGHT, LITTLE LADY?
IT'S JUST LIKE THE STORIES MY FATHER USED TO TELL!

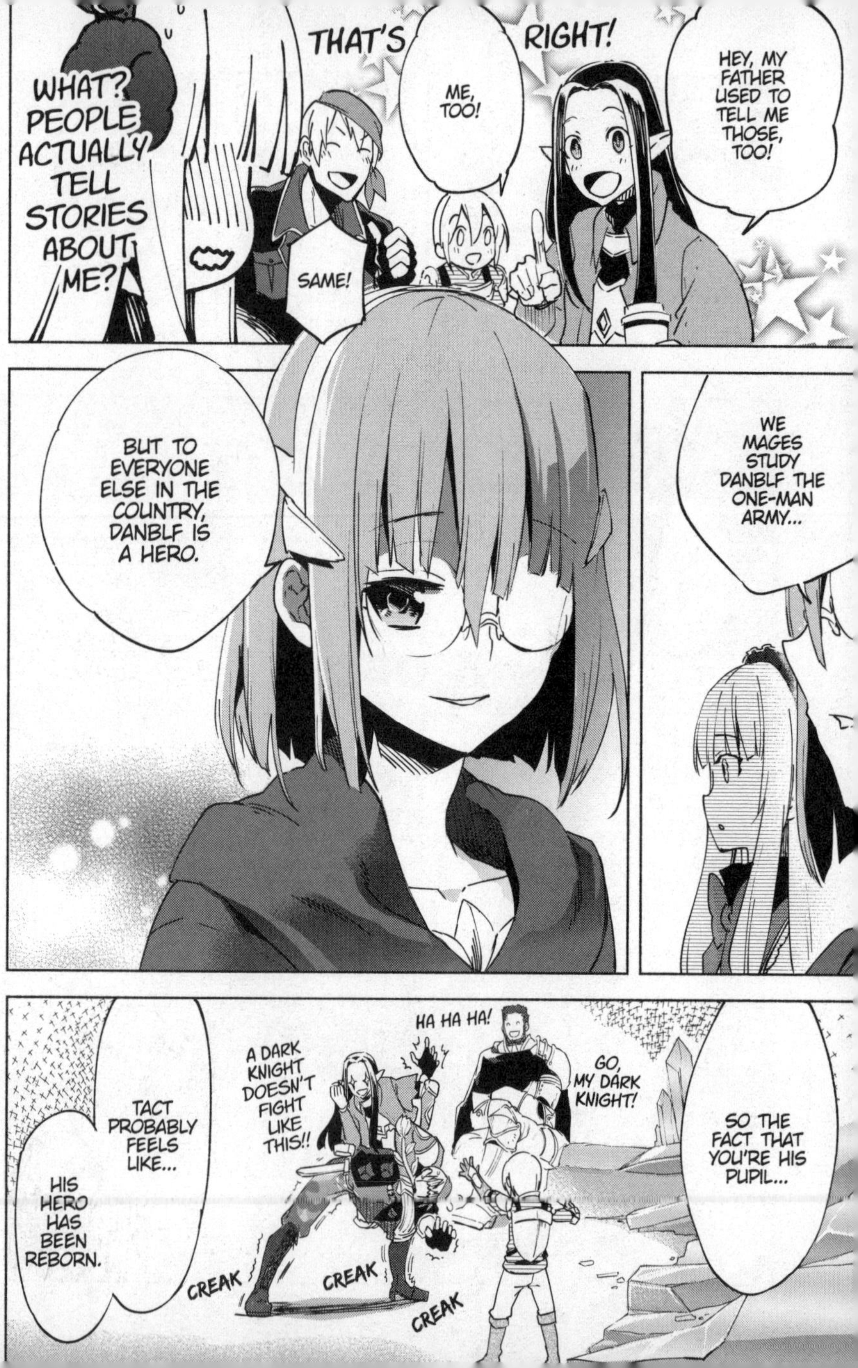
HEY, MY FATHER USED TO TELL ME THOSE, TOO!
THAT'S RIGHT!
ME, TOO!
SAME!
WHAT? PEOPLE ACTUALLY TELL STORIES ABOUT ME?
WE MAGES STUDY DANBLF THE ONE-MAN ARMY...
BUT TO EVERYONE ELSE IN THE COUNTRY, DANBLF IS A HERO.
SO THE FACT THAT YOU'RE HIS PUPIL...
GO, MY DARK KNIGHT!
HA HA HA!
A DARK KNIGHT DOESN'T FIGHT LIKE THIS!!
TACT PROBABLY FEELS LIKE...
HIS HERO HAS BEEN REBORN.
CREAK
CREAK
CREAK

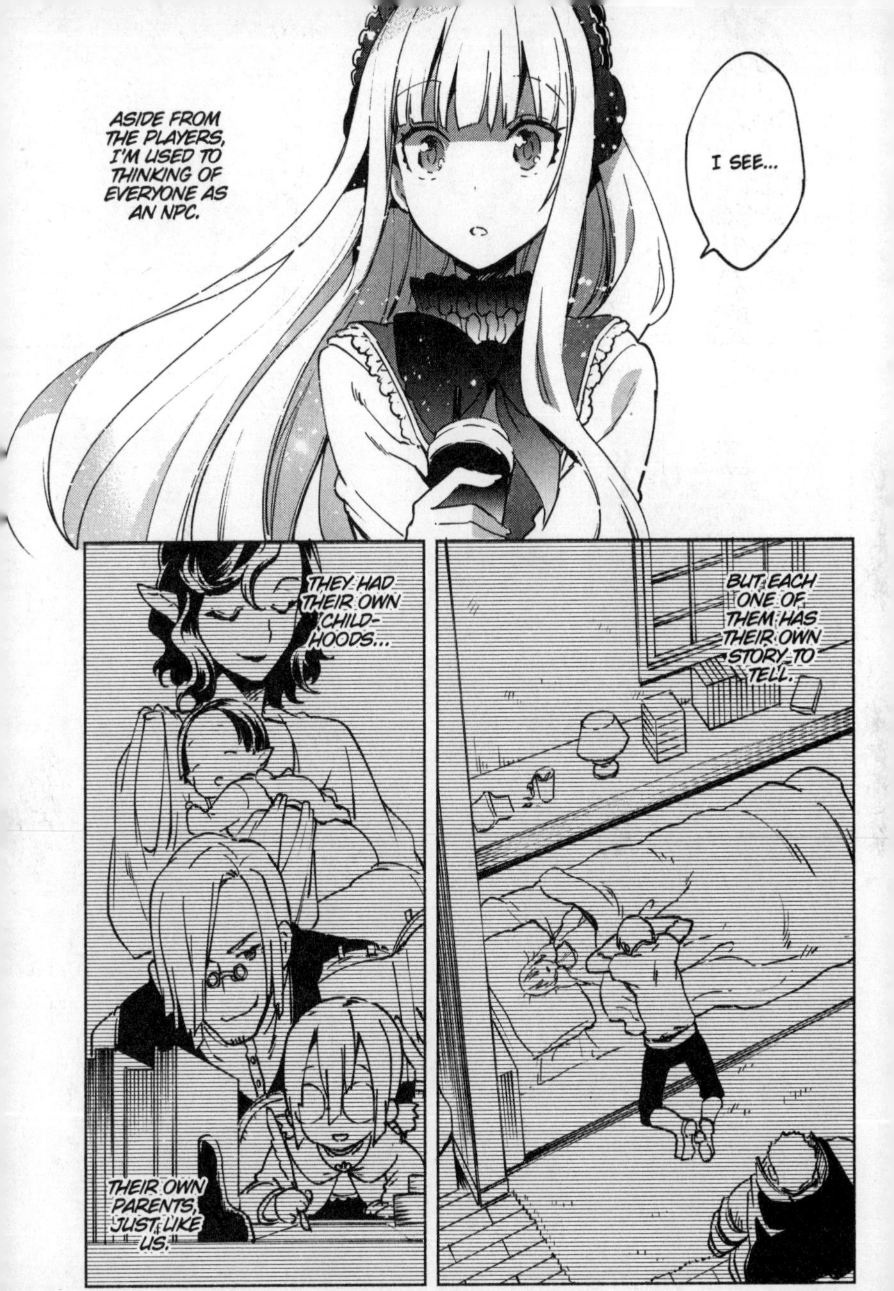
I SEE...
ASIDE FROM THE PLAYERS, I'M USED TO THINKING OF EVERYONE AS AN NPC.
BUT EACH ONE OF THEM HAS THEIR OWN STORY TO TELL.
THEY HAD THEIR OWN CHILDHOODS...
THEIR OWN PARENTS, JUST LIKE US.

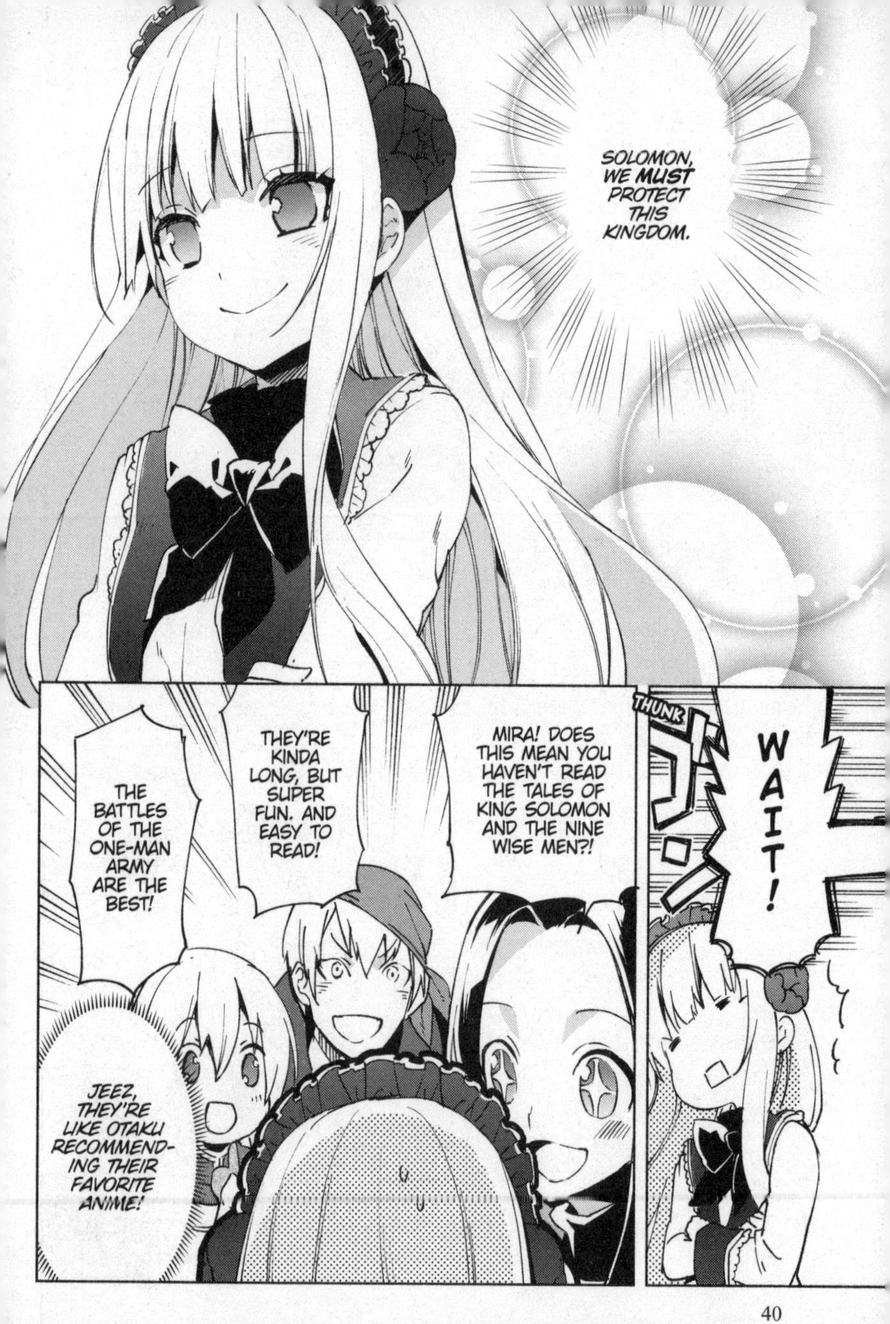
SOLOMON, WE MUST PROTECT THIS KINGDOM.
THUNK
WAIT!
MIRA! DOES THIS MEAN YOU HAVEN'T READ THE TALES OF KING SOLOMON AND THE NINE WISE MEN?!
THEY'RE KINDA LONG, BUT SUPER FUN. AND EASY TO READ!
THE BATTLES OF THE ONE-MAN ARMY ARE THE BEST!
JEEZ, THEY'RE LIKE OTAKU RECOMMEND-ING THEIR FAVORITE ANIME!

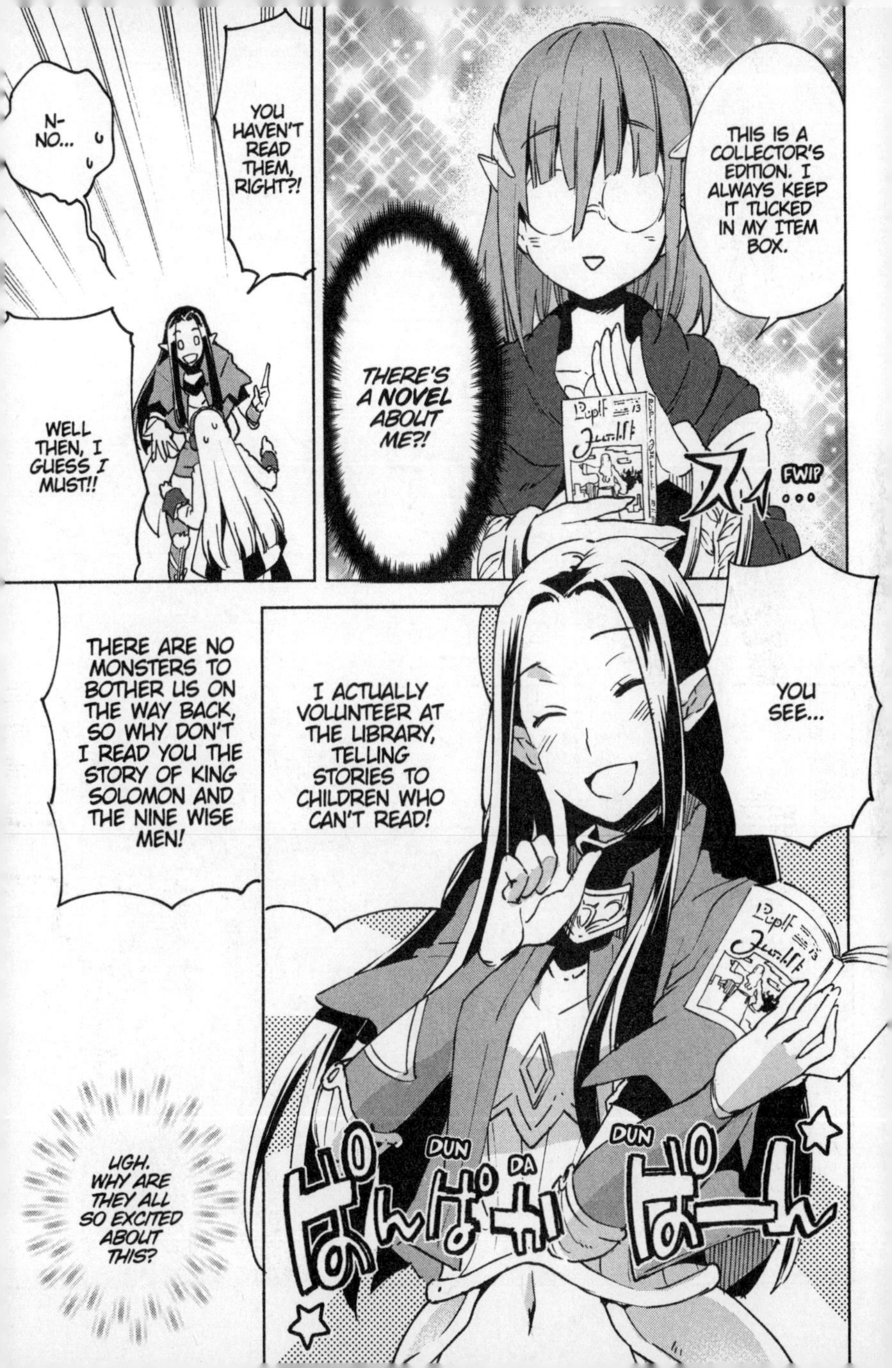
THIS IS A COLLECTOR'S EDITION. I ALWAYS KEEP IT TUCKED IN MY ITEM BOX.
スィ
FWIP...
THERE'S A NOVEL ABOUT ME?!
YOU HAVEN'T READ THEM, RIGHT?!
N- NO...
WELL THEN, I GUESS I MUST!!
YOU SEE...
I ACTUALLY VOLUNTEER AT THE LIBRARY, TELLING STORIES TO CHILDREN WHO CAN'T READ!
THERE ARE NO MONSTERS TO BOTHER US ON THE WAY BACK, SO WHY DON'T I READ YOU THE STORY OF KING SOLOMON AND THE NINE WISE MEN!
ぱんぱかぱーん
DUN DA DUN
UGH. WHY ARE THEY ALL SO EXCITED ABOUT THIS?

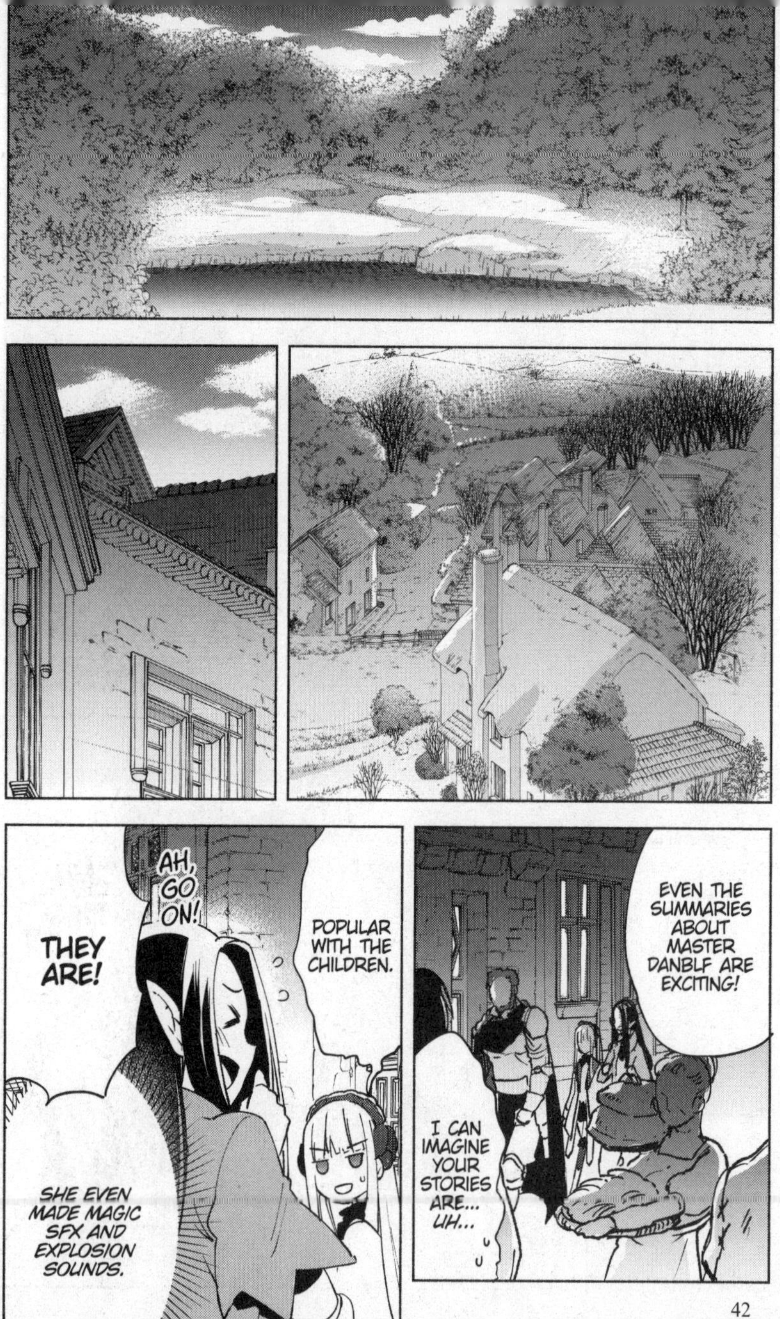
EVEN THE SUMMARIES ABOUT MASTER DANBLF ARE EXCITING!
I CAN IMAGINE YOUR STORIES ARE... UH...
POPULAR WITH THE CHILDREN.
AH, GO ON!
THEY ARE!
SHE EVEN MADE MAGIC SFX AND EXPLOSION SOUNDS.

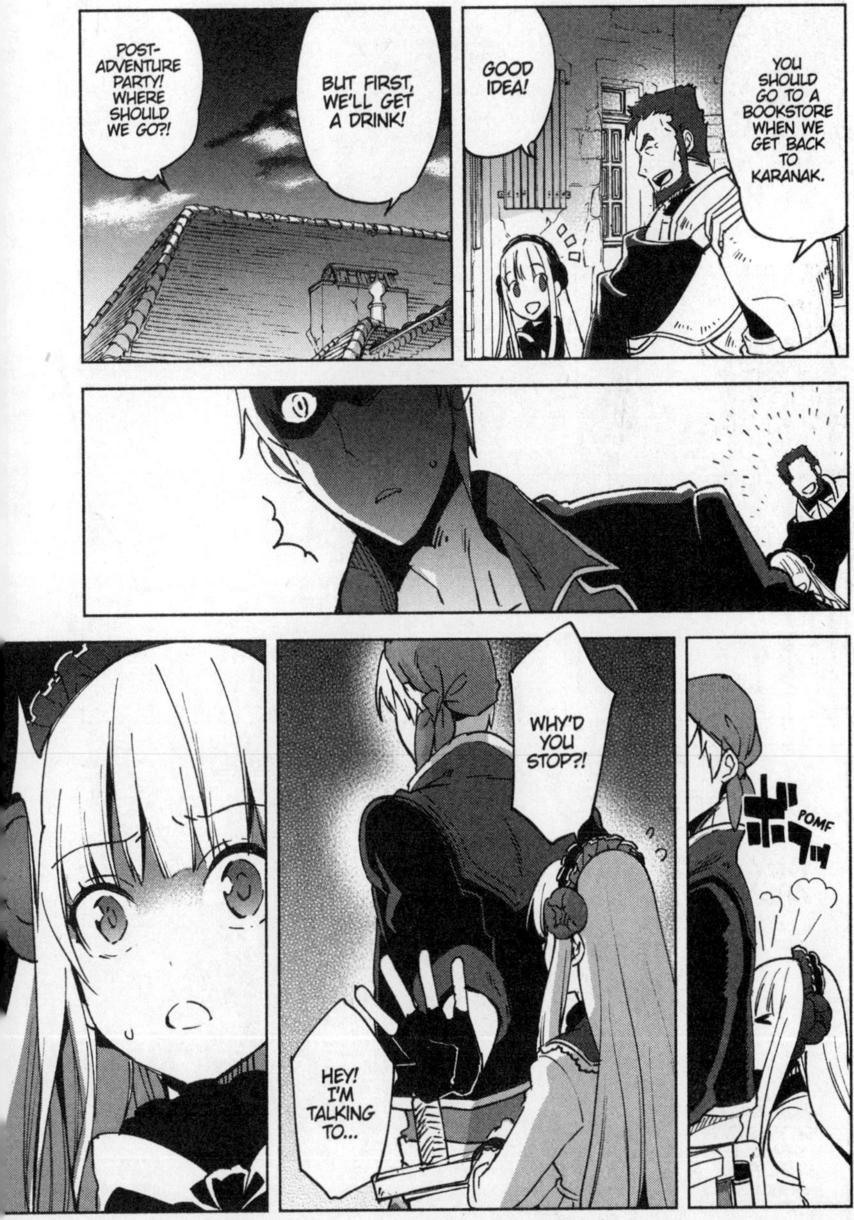
YOU SHOULD GO TO A BOOKSTORE WHEN WE GET BACK TO KARANAK.
GOOD IDEA!
BUT FIRST, WE'LL GET A DRINK!
POST-ADVENTURE PARTY! WHERE SHOULD WE GO?!
POMF
WHY'D YOU STOP?!
HEY! I'M TALKING TO...

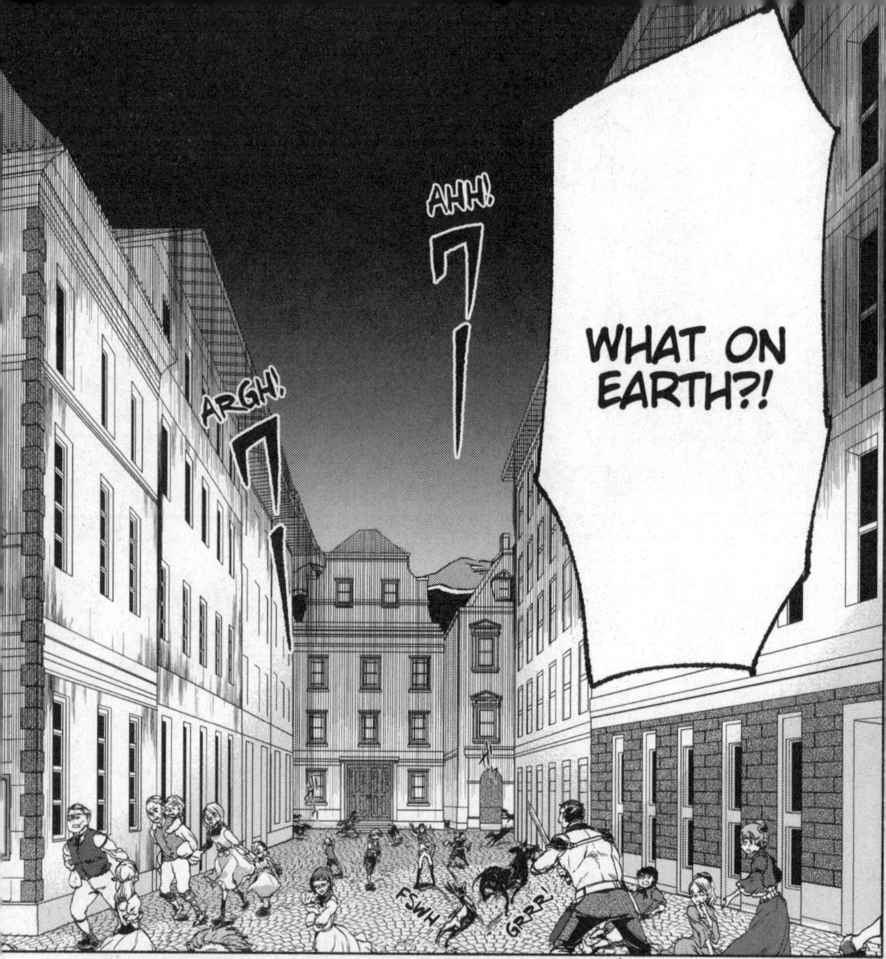
WHAT ON EARTH?!
AHH!
ARGH!
GRRR!
FSWH

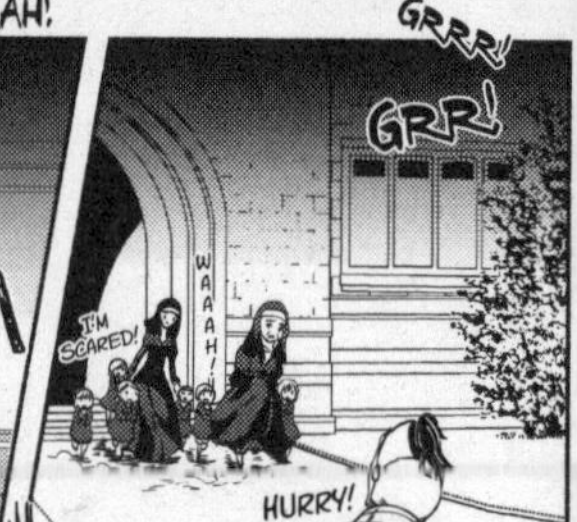
GRRR!
GRR!
WAAAH!
I'M SCARED!
HURRY!
WHOOSH

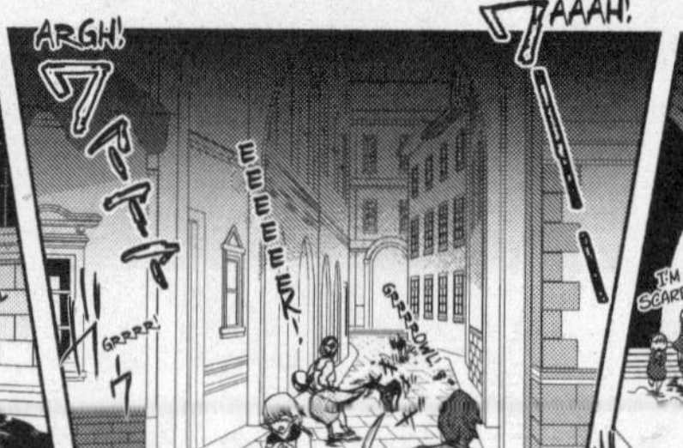
AAAH!
EEEEEEER!
ARGH!
GRRRR
WHOOSH

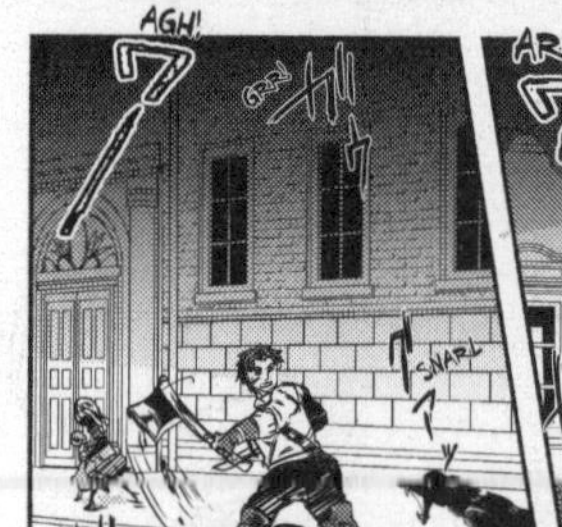
AGH!
SNARL
WHOOSH

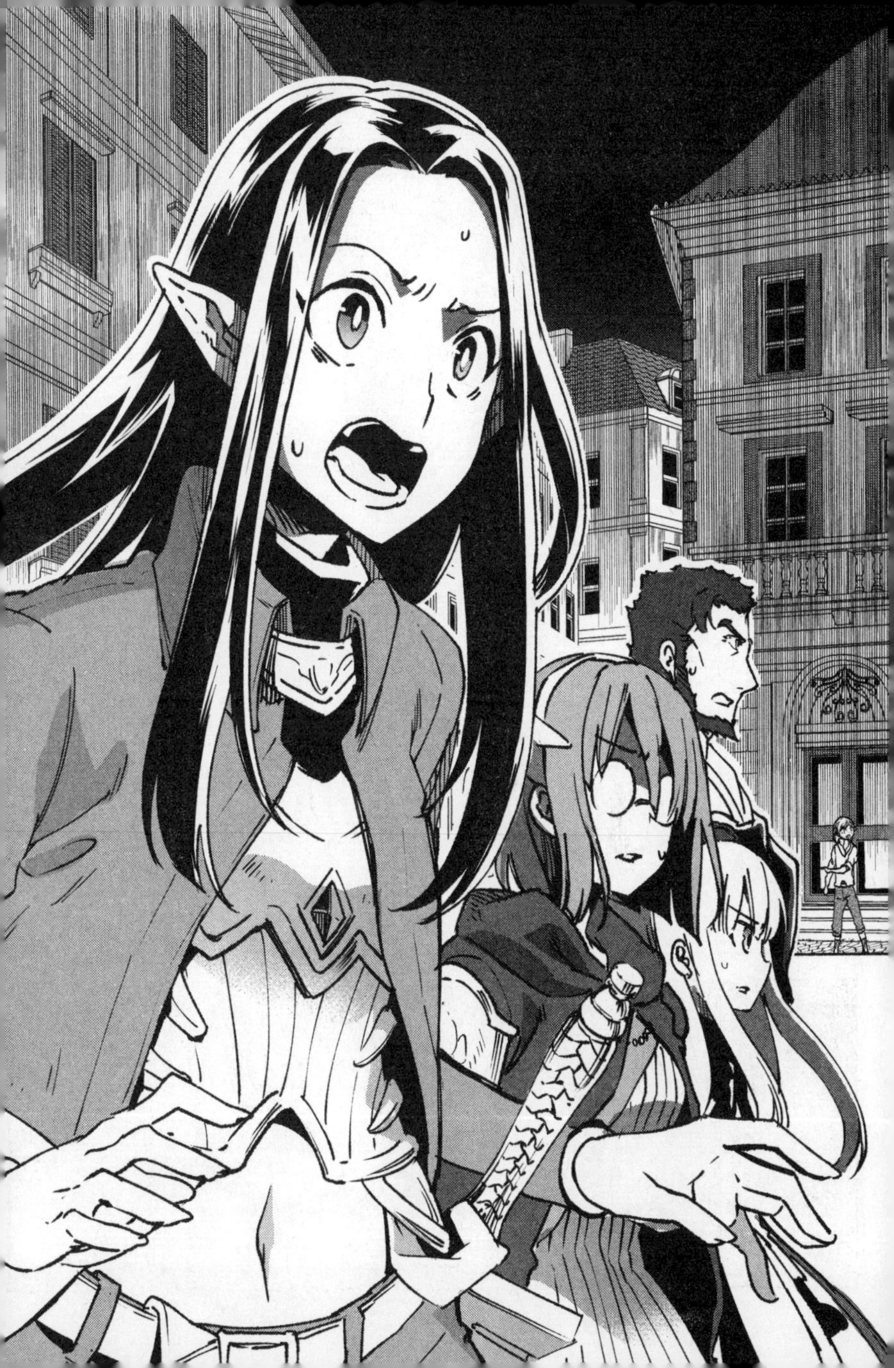

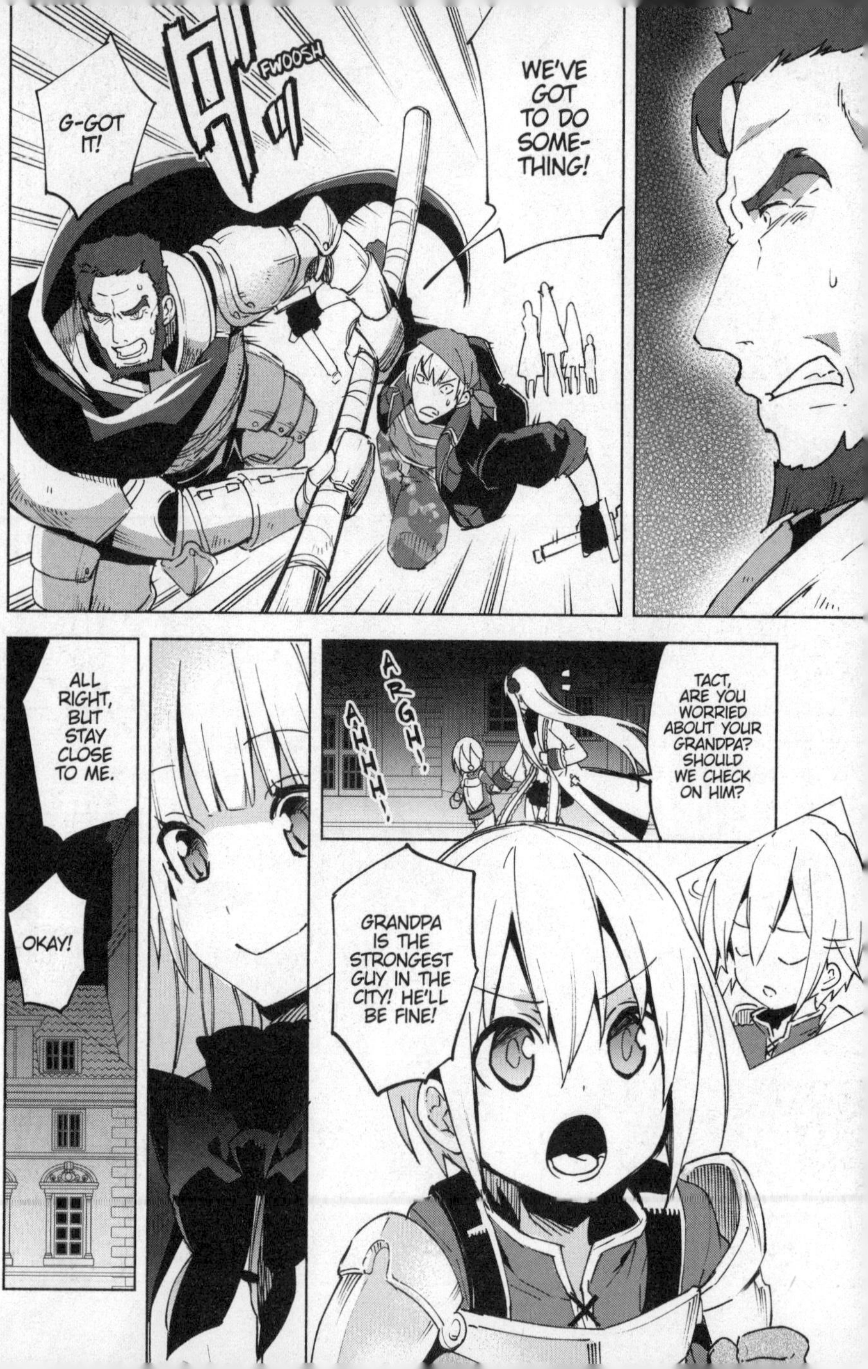
WE'VE GOT TO DO SOME-THING!
FWOOSH
G-GOT IT!
TACT, ARE YOU WORRIED ABOUT YOUR GRANDPA? SHOULD WE CHECK ON HIM?
ARGH!
AHHH!
GRANDPA IS THE STRONGEST GUY IN THE CITY! HE'LL BE FINE!
ALL RIGHT, BUT STAY CLOSE TO ME.
OKAY!

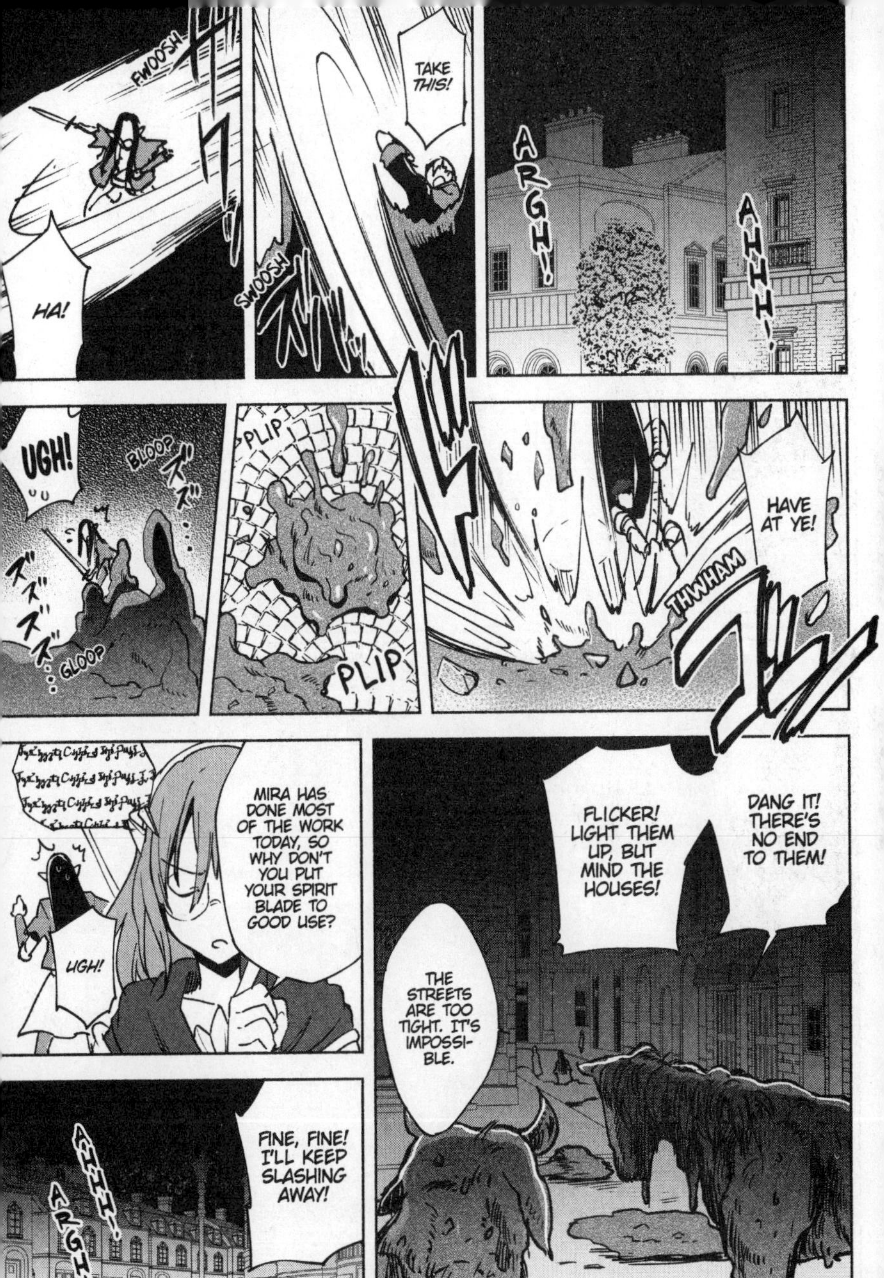
ARGH!
AHHH!
TAKE THIS!
SWOOSH
FWOOSH
HA!
HAVE AT YE!
THWHAM
PLIP
PLIP
UGH!
BLOOP
GLOOP
DANG IT! THERE'S NO END TO THEM!
FLICKER! LIGHT THEM UP, BUT MIND THE HOUSES!
THE STREETS ARE TOO TIGHT. IT'S IMPOSSI-BLE.
MIRA HAS DONE MOST OF THE WORK TODAY, SO WHY DON'T YOU PUT YOUR SPIRIT BLADE TO GOOD USE?
UGH!
FINE, FINE! I'LL KEEP SLASHING AWAY!
AHHH!
ARGH!

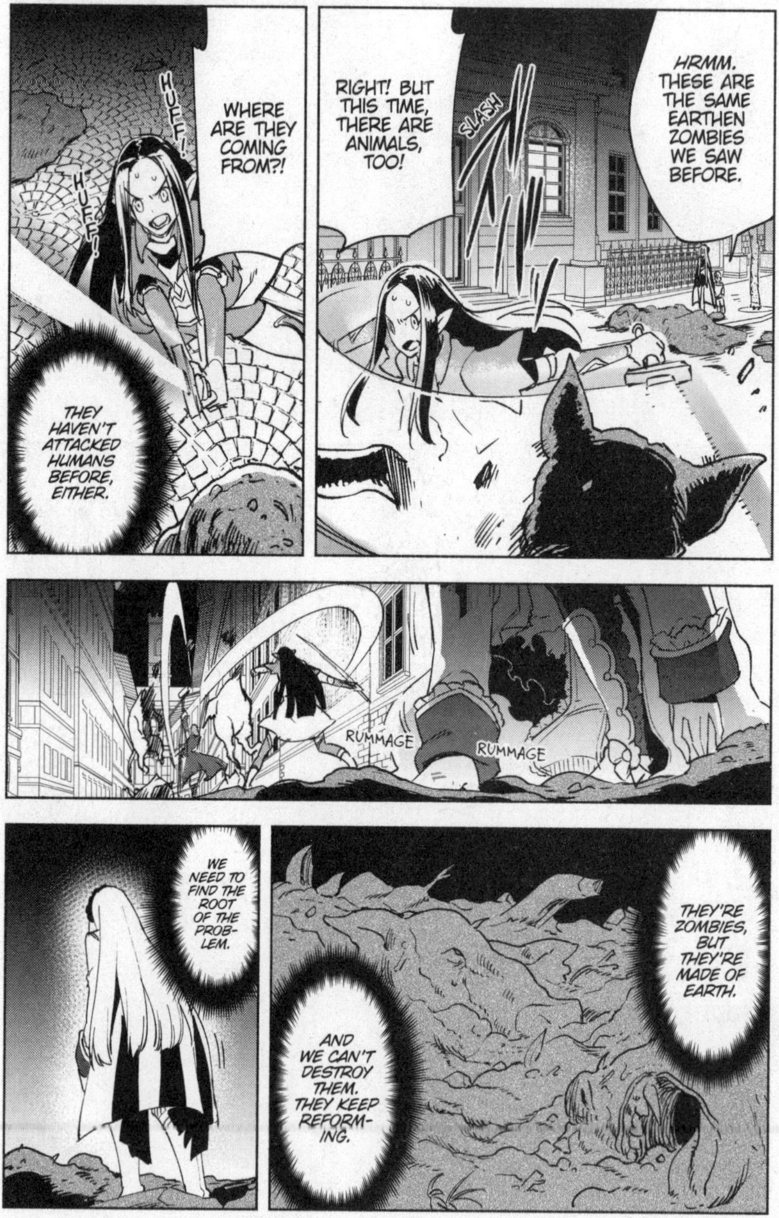
HRMM. THESE ARE THE SAME EARTHEN ZOMBIES WE SAW BEFORE.
RIGHT! BUT THIS TIME, THERE ARE ANIMALS, TOO!
SLASH
HUFF! HUFF!
WHERE ARE THEY COMING FROM?!
THEY HAVEN'T ATTACKED HUMANS BEFORE, EITHER.
RUMMAGE
RUMMAGE
THEY'RE ZOMBIES, BUT THEY'RE MADE OF EARTH.
AND WE CAN'T DESTROY THEM. THEY KEEP REFORM-ING.
WE NEED TO FIND THE ROOT OF THE PROB-LEM.

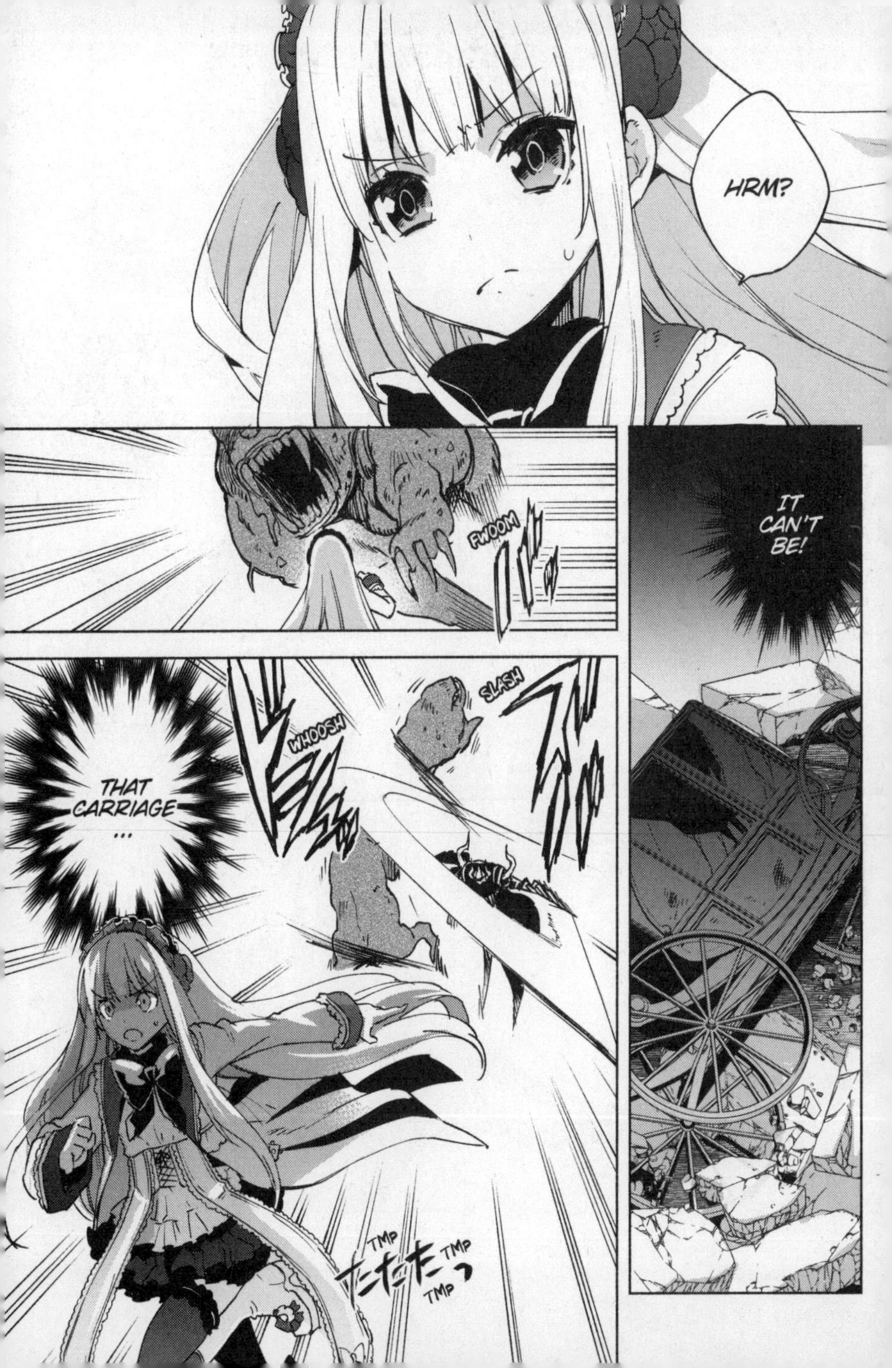
HRM?
IT CAN'T BE!
FWOOM
SLASH
WHOOSH
THAT CARRIAGE ...
TMP TMP TMP TMP

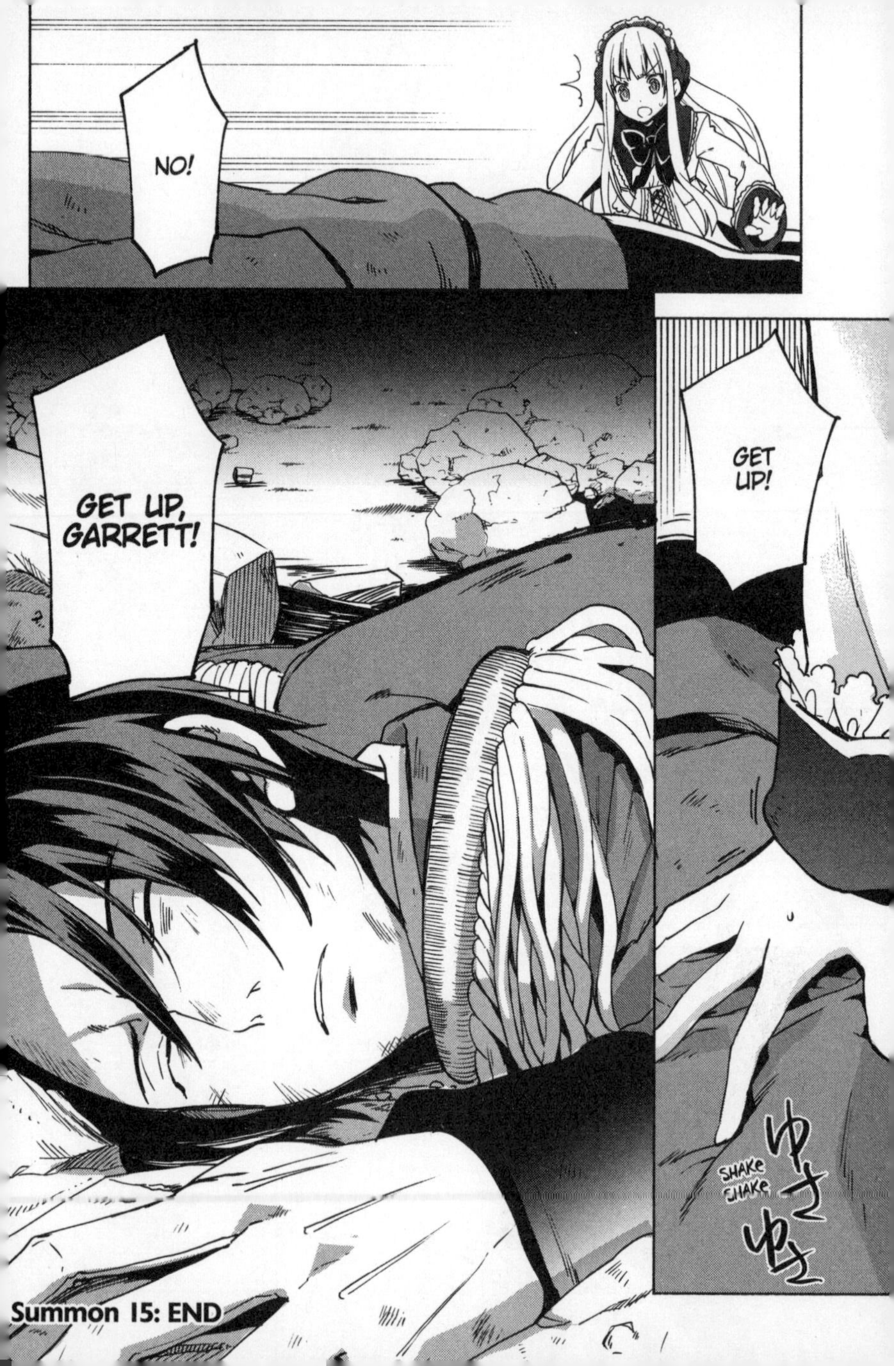
NO!
GET UP!
SHAKE SHAKE
ゆさゆさ
GET UP, GARRETT!

Summon 15: END

She
Professed
Herself
Pupil of the
Wise Man

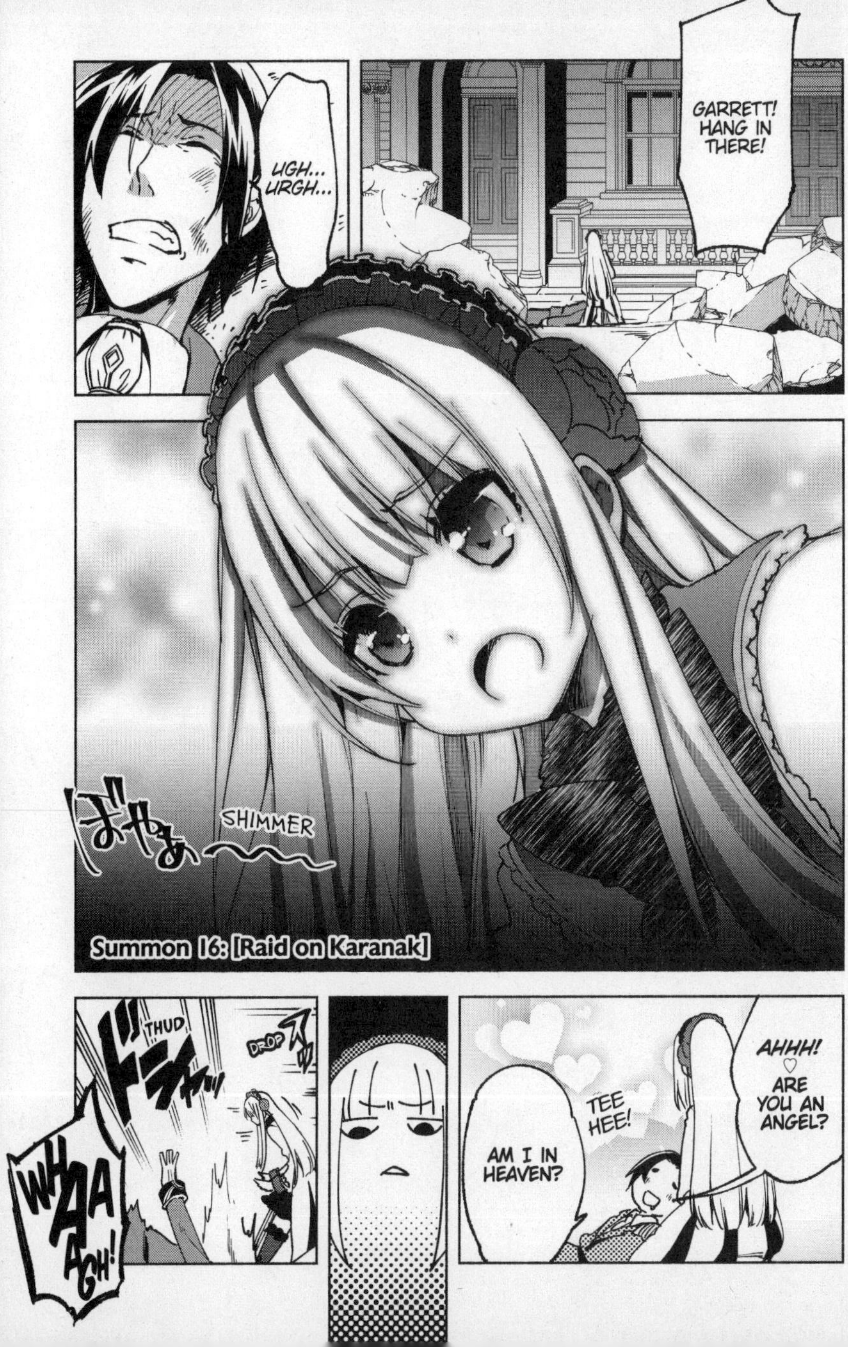
GARRETT! HANG IN THERE!
UGH... URGH...
SHIMMER
Summon 16: [Raid on Karanak]
AHHH! ♡ ARE YOU AN ANGEL?
TEE HEE!
AM I IN HEAVEN?
DROP
THUD
WHOAAAGH!

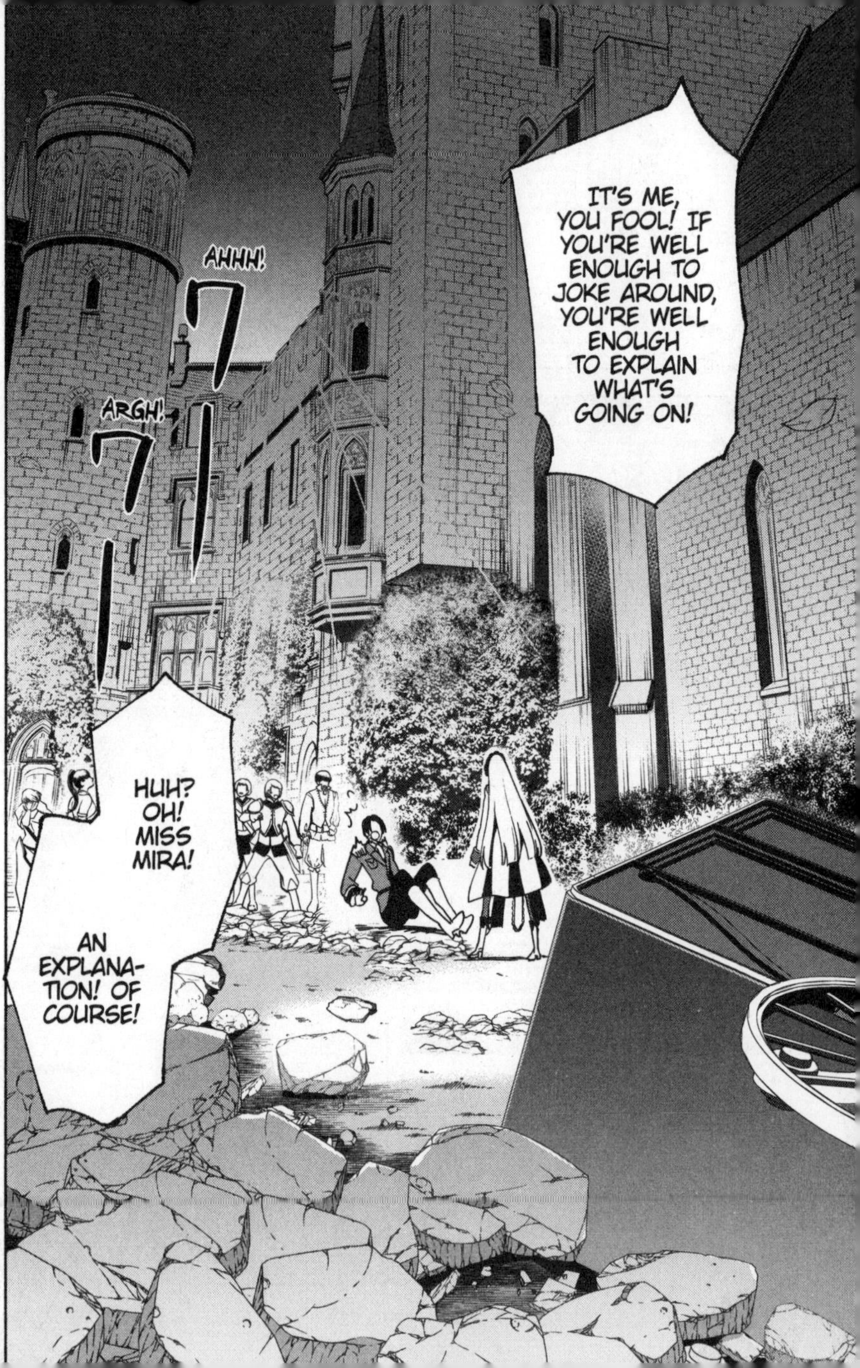
IT'S ME, YOU FOOL! IF YOU'RE WELL ENOUGH TO JOKE AROUND, YOU'RE WELL ENOUGH TO EXPLAIN WHAT'S GOING ON!
AHHH!
ARGH!
HUH? OH! MISS MIRA!
AN EXPLANATION! OF COURSE!

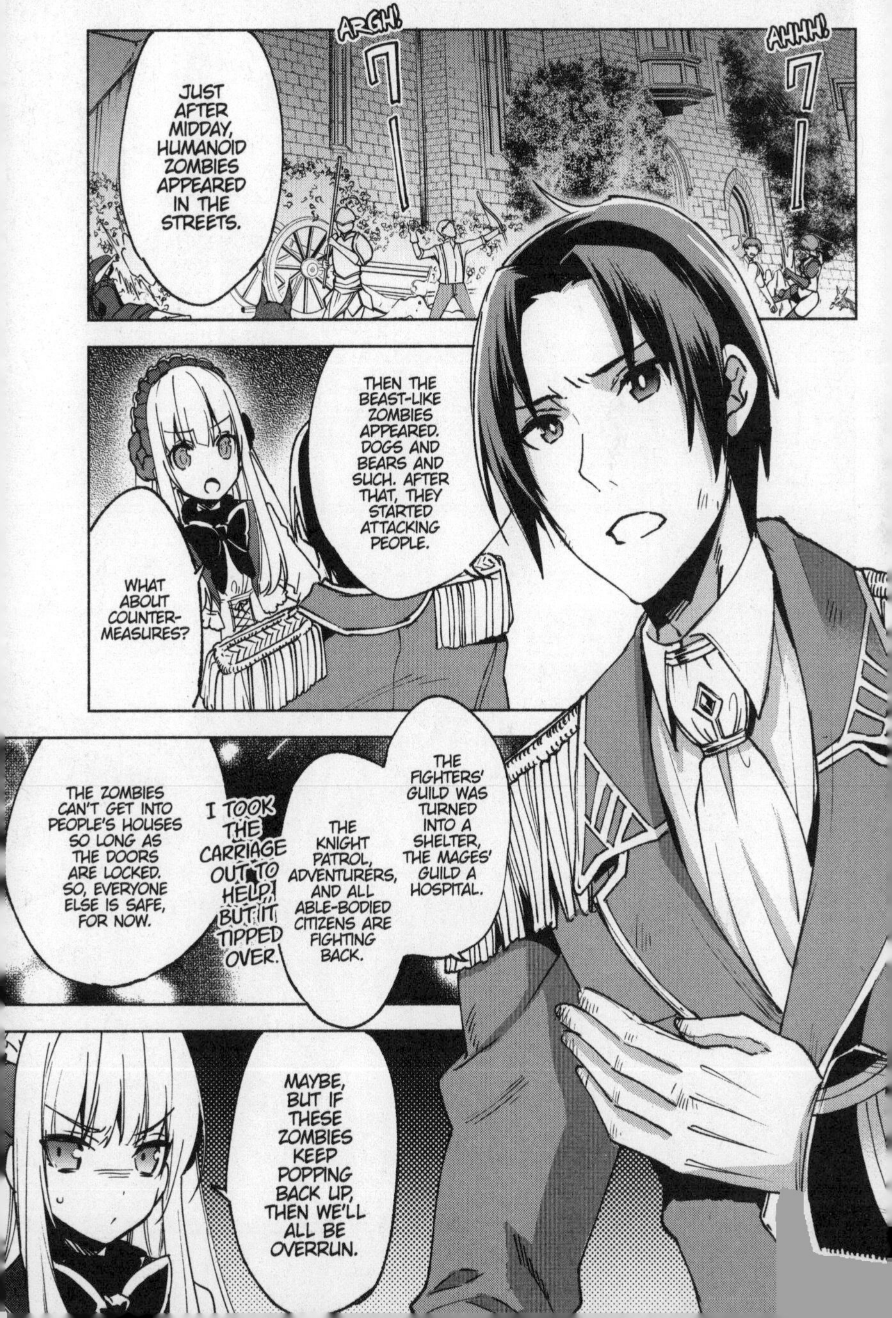
AHHH!
ARGH!
JUST AFTER MIDDAY, HUMANOID ZOMBIES APPEARED IN THE STREETS.
THEN THE BEAST-LIKE ZOMBIES APPEARED. DOGS AND BEARS AND SUCH. AFTER THAT, THEY STARTED ATTACKING PEOPLE.
WHAT ABOUT COUNTER-MEASURES?
THE FIGHTERS' GUILD WAS TURNED INTO A SHELTER, THE MAGES' GUILD A HOSPITAL.
THE KNIGHT PATROL, ADVENTURERS, AND ALL ABLE-BODIED CITIZENS ARE FIGHTING BACK.
I TOOK THE CARRIAGE OUT TO HELP, BUT IT TIPPED OVER.
THE ZOMBIES CAN'T GET INTO PEOPLE'S HOUSES SO LONG AS THE DOORS ARE LOCKED. SO, EVERYONE ELSE IS SAFE, FOR NOW.
MAYBE, BUT IF THESE ZOMBIES KEEP POPPING BACK UP, THEN WE'LL ALL BE OVERRUN.

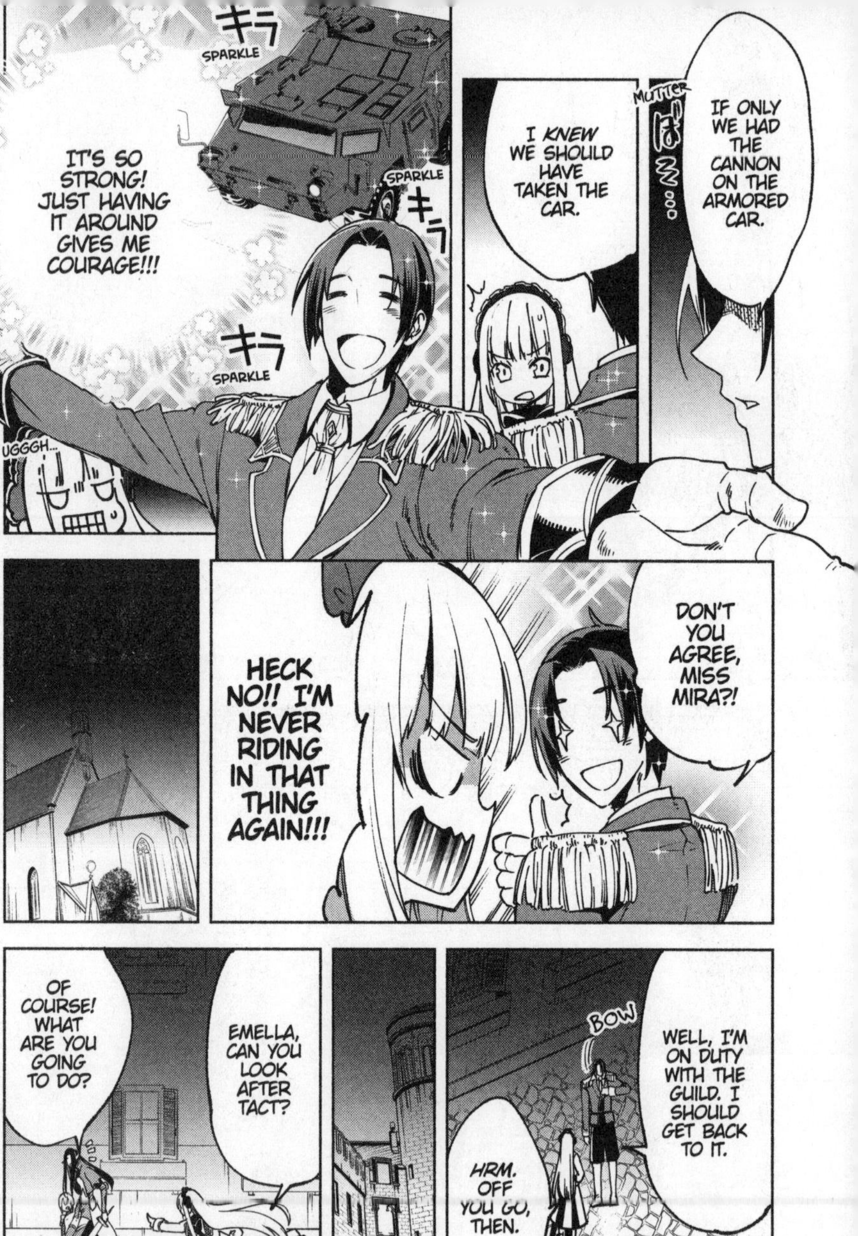
MUTTER
ぼそ...
IF ONLY WE HAD THE CANNON ON THE ARMORED CAR.
I KNEW WE SHOULD HAVE TAKEN THE CAR.
キラ
SPARKLE
キラ
SPARKLE
IT'S SO STRONG! JUST HAVING IT AROUND GIVES ME COURAGE!!!
キラ
SPARKLE
UGGGH...
DON'T YOU AGREE, MISS MIRA?!
HECK NO!! I'M NEVER RIDING IN THAT THING AGAIN!!!
WELL, I'M ON DUTY WITH THE GUILD. I SHOULD GET BACK TO IT.
BOW
HRM. OFF YOU GO, THEN.
EMELLA, CAN YOU LOOK AFTER TACT?
OF COURSE! WHAT ARE YOU GOING TO DO?

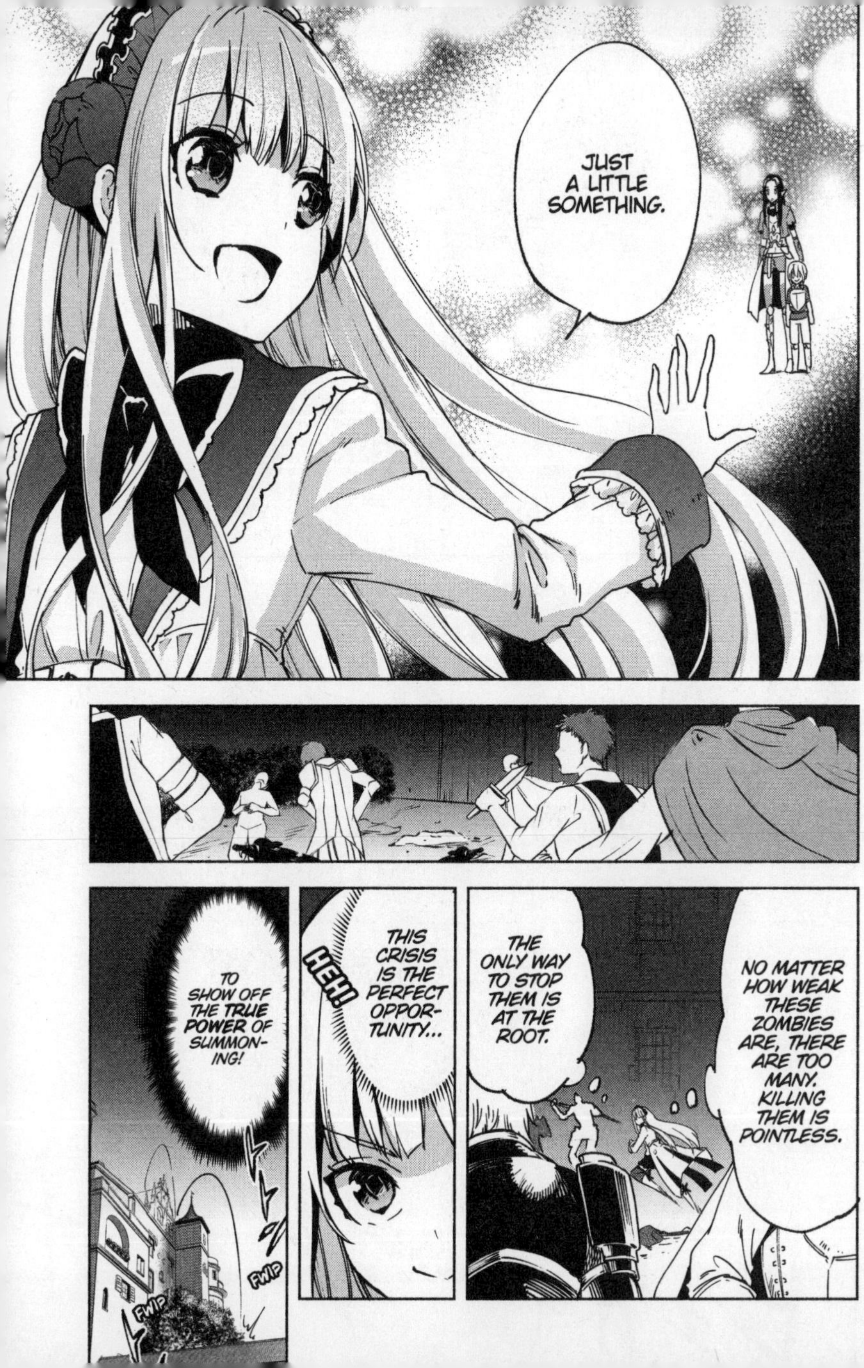
JUST A LITTLE SOMETHING.
NO MATTER HOW WEAK THESE ZOMBIES ARE, THERE ARE TOO MANY. KILLING THEM IS POINTLESS.
THE ONLY WAY TO STOP THEM IS AT THE ROOT.
THIS CRISIS IS THE PERFECT OPPOR-TUNITY...
HEH!
TO SHOW OFF THE TRUE POWER OF SUMMON-ING!
FWIP
FWIP

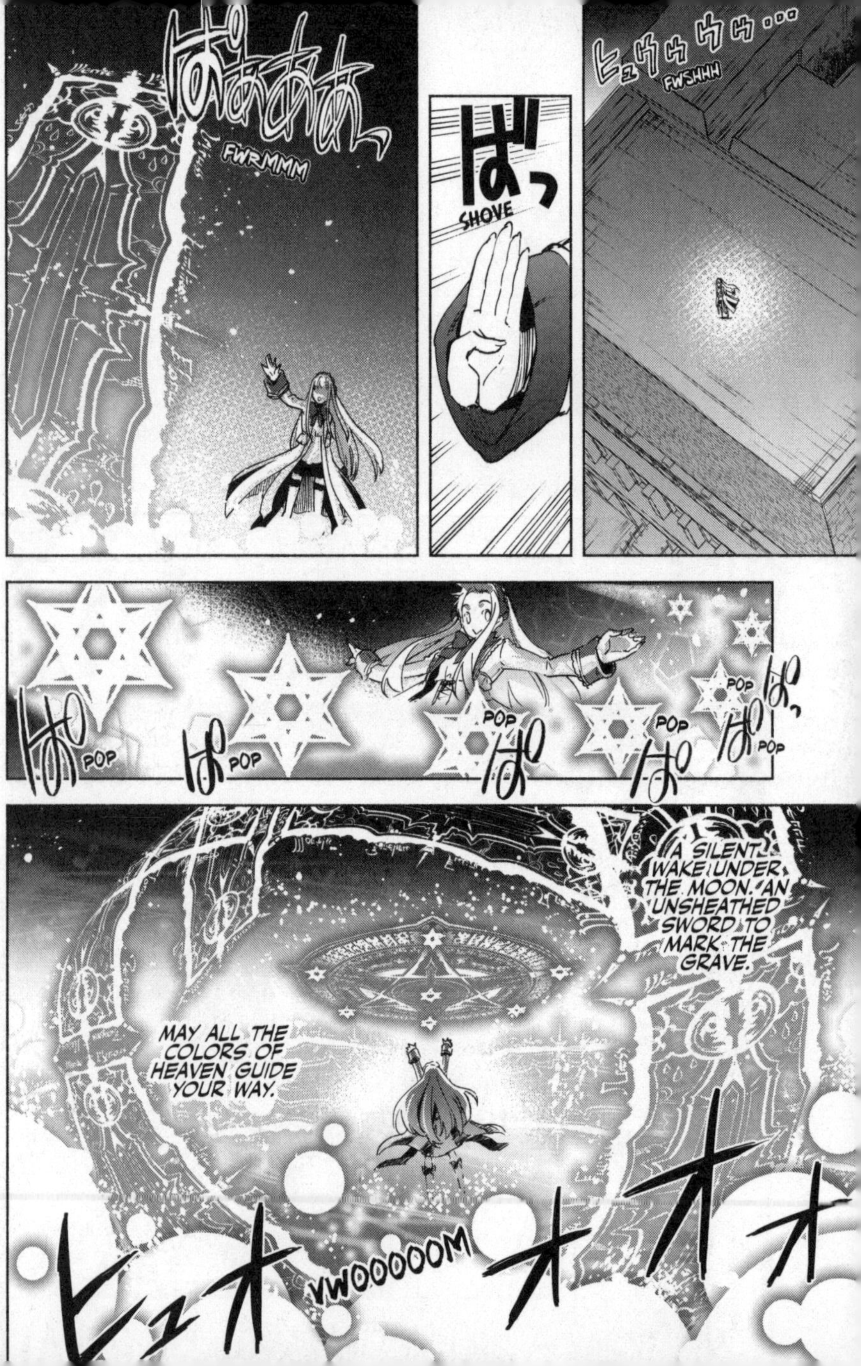
ヒュウゥウゥ…
FWSHHH
ばっ
SHOVE
ぱあああ
FWRMMM
ぱっ
POP
POP
ぱ
POP
ぱ
POP
ぱ
POP
ぱ
POP
A SILENT WAKE UNDER THE MOON. AN UNSHEATHED SWORD TO MARK THE GRAVE.
MAY ALL THE COLORS OF HEAVEN GUIDE YOUR WAY.
ヒュオオオ
VWOOOOOM

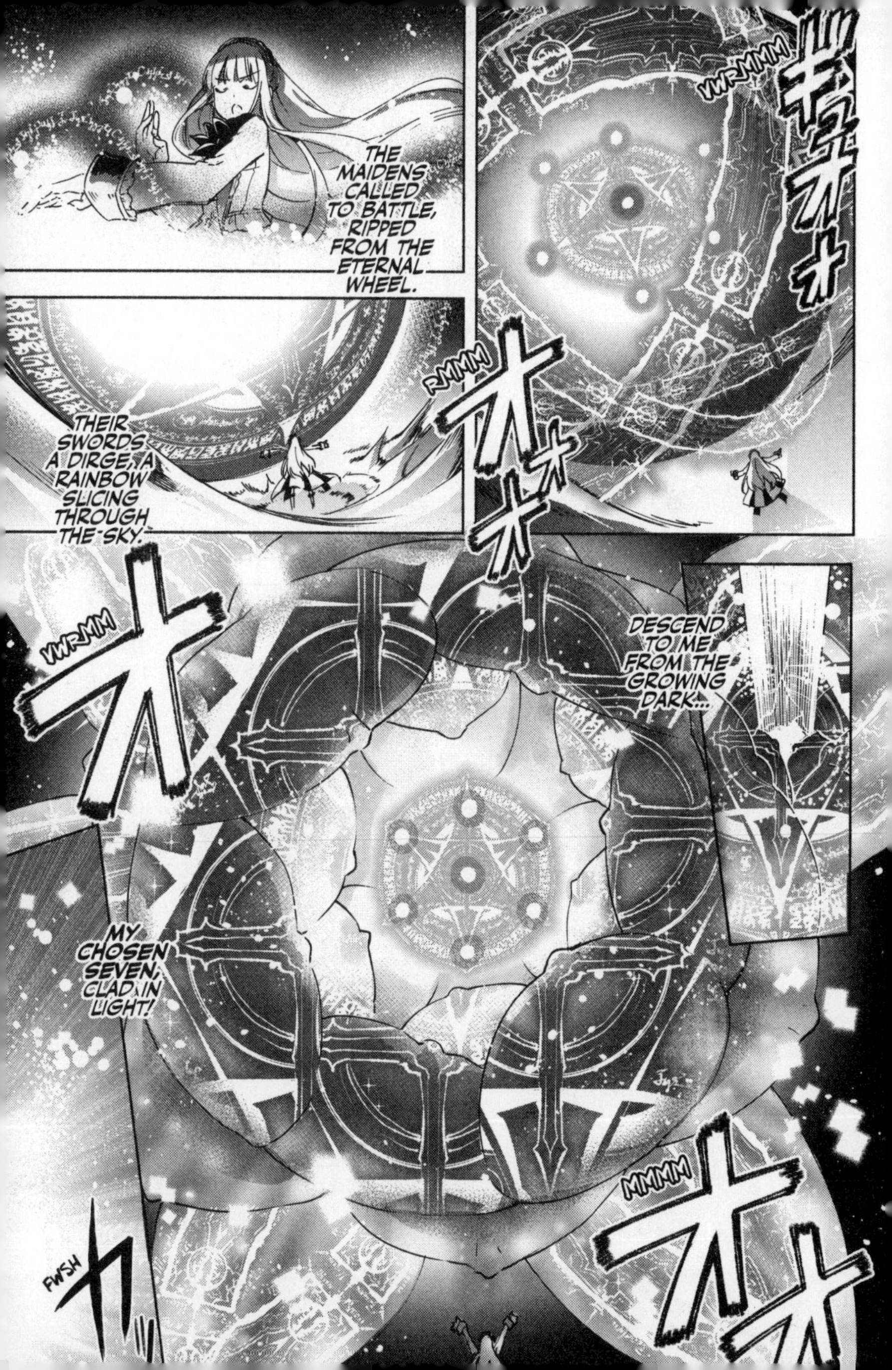
VWRMMM
RMMM
THE MAIDENS CALLED TO BATTLE, RIPPED FROM THE ETERNAL WHEEL.
THEIR SWORDS A DIRGE, A RAINBOW SLICING THROUGH THE SKY.
DESCEND TO ME FROM THE GROWING DARK...
VWRMMM
MY CHOSEN SEVEN, CLAD IN LIGHT!
MMMM
FWSH

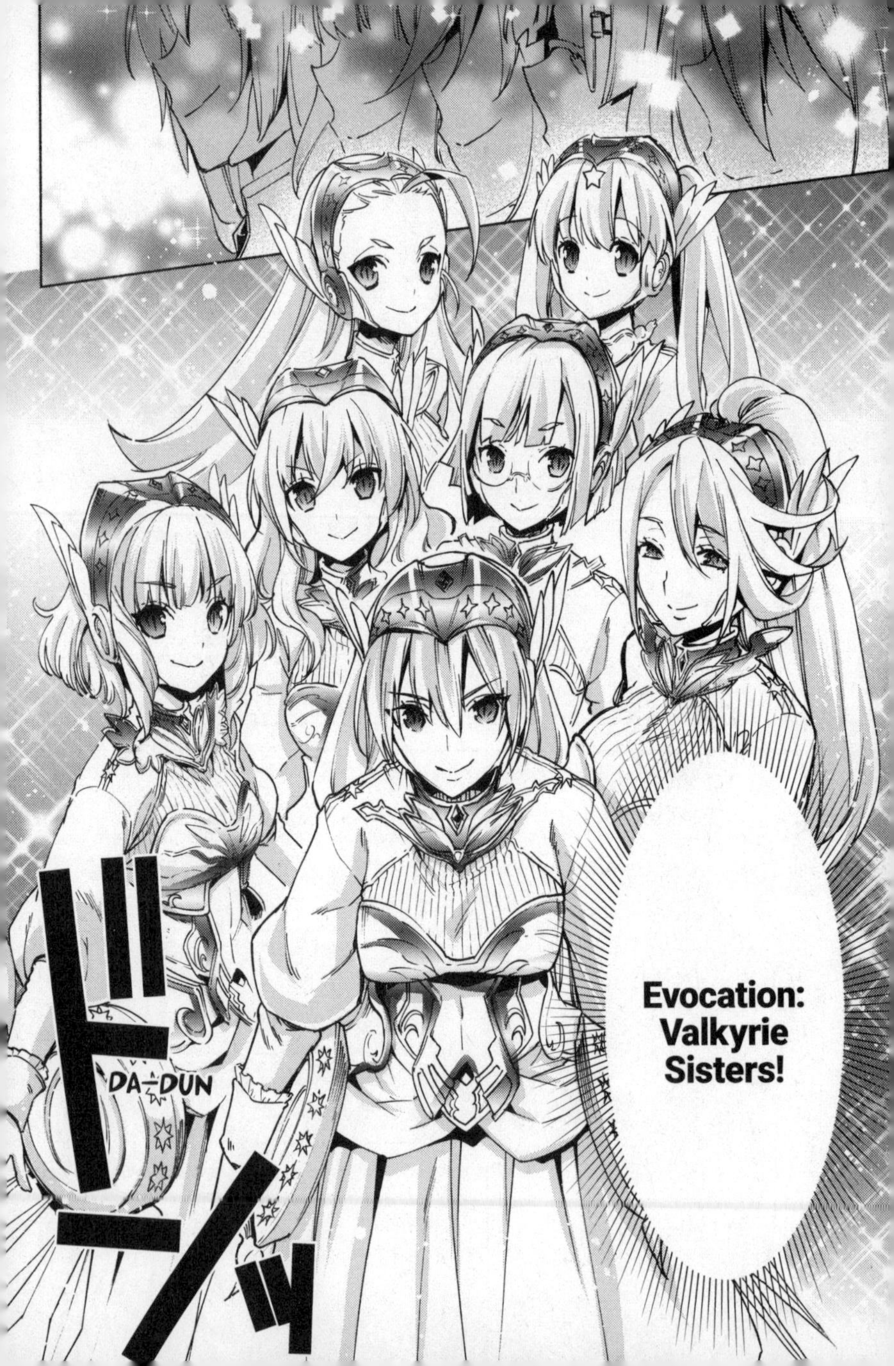
Evocation: Valkyrie Sisters!
DA-DUN

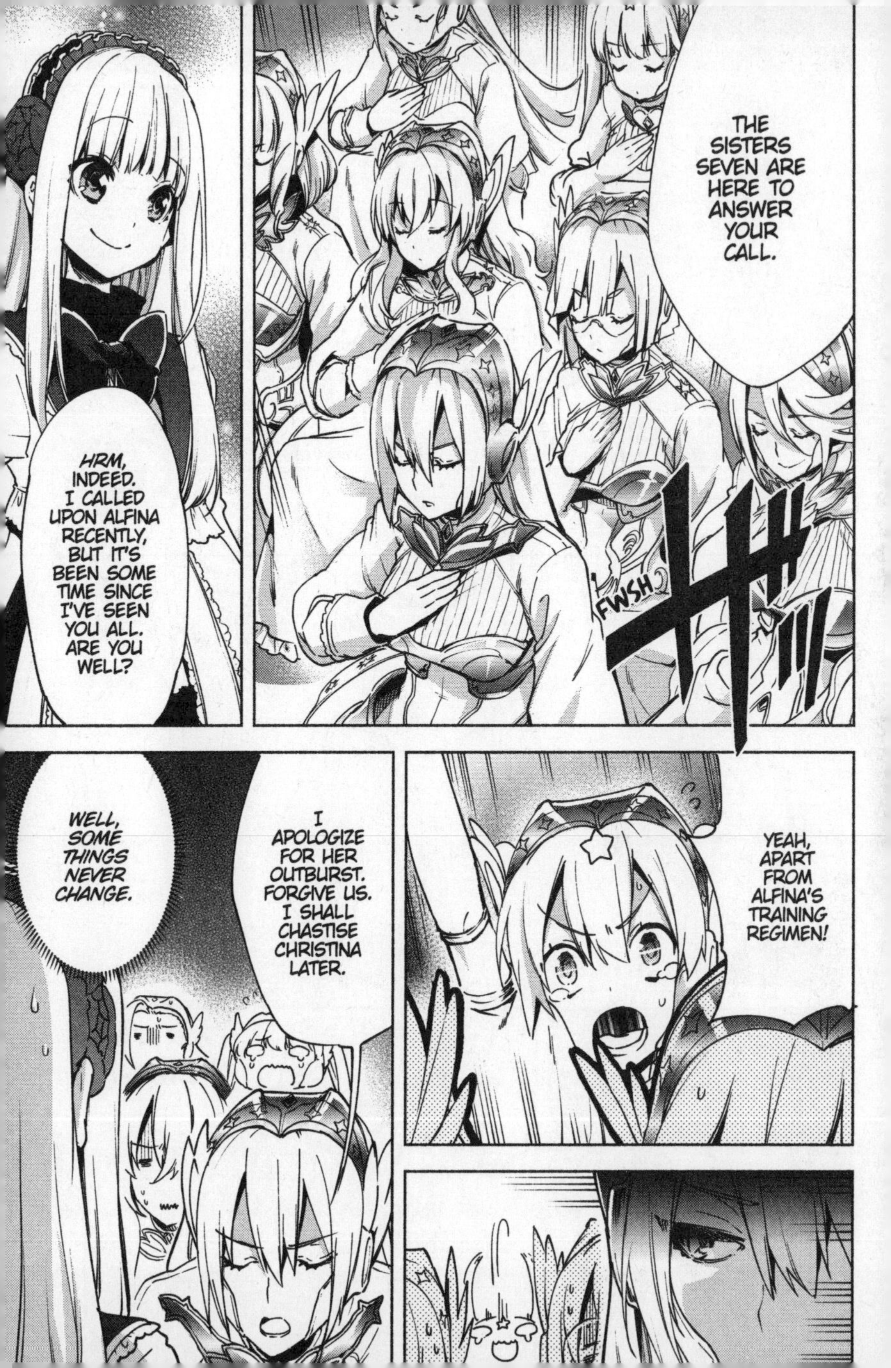
THE SISTERS SEVEN ARE HERE TO ANSWER YOUR CALL.
FWSH
HRM, INDEED. I CALLED UPON ALFINA RECENTLY, BUT IT'S BEEN SOME TIME SINCE I'VE SEEN YOU ALL. ARE YOU WELL?
YEAH, APART FROM ALFINA'S TRAINING REGIMEN!
I APOLOGIZE FOR HER OUTBURST. FORGIVE US. I SHALL CHASTISE CHRISTINA LATER.
WELL, SOME THINGS NEVER CHANGE.

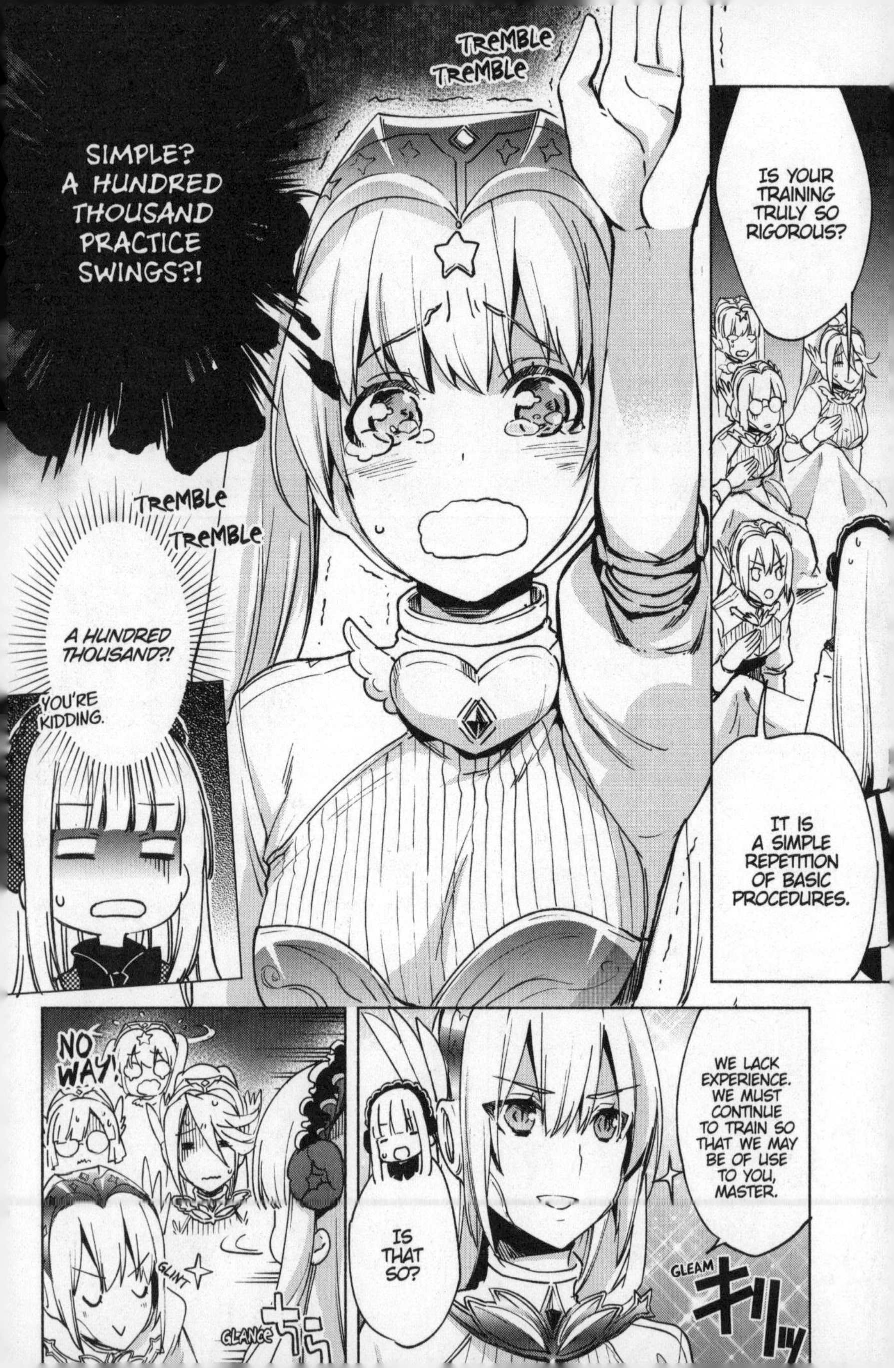
IS YOUR TRAINING TRULY SO RIGOROUS?
IT IS A SIMPLE REPETITION OF BASIC PROCEDURES.
TREMBLE TREMBLE
SIMPLE? A HUNDRED THOUSAND PRACTICE SWINGS?!
TREMBLE TREMBLE
A HUNDRED THOUSAND?!
YOU'RE KIDDING.
WE LACK EXPERIENCE. WE MUST CONTINUE TO TRAIN SO THAT WE MAY BE OF USE TO YOU, MASTER.
GLEAM キリッ
IS THAT SO?
GLANCE ちら
NO WAY!
GLINT

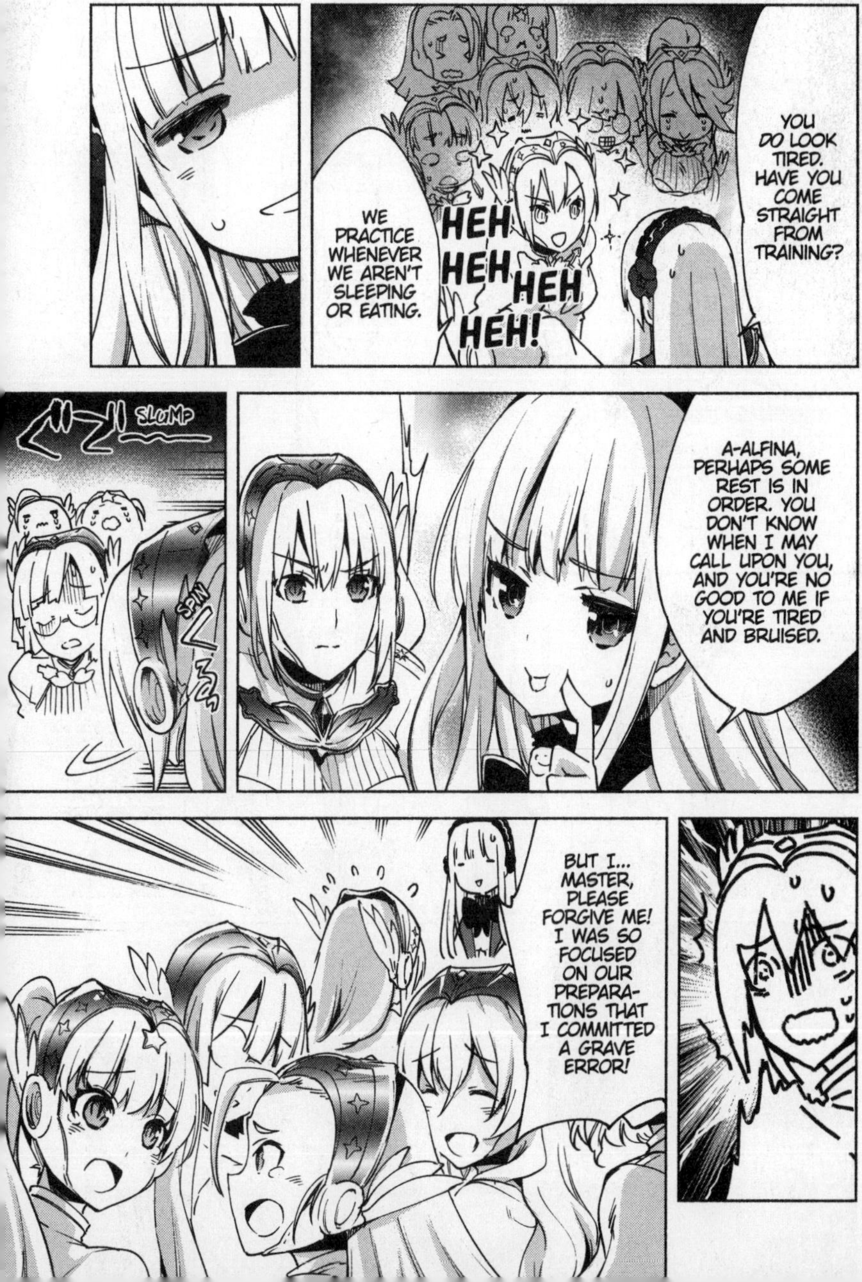
YOU DO LOOK TIRED. HAVE YOU COME STRAIGHT FROM TRAINING?
HEH HEH HEH HEH!
WE PRACTICE WHENEVER WE AREN'T SLEEPING OR EATING.
A-ALFINA, PERHAPS SOME REST IS IN ORDER. YOU DON'T KNOW WHEN I MAY CALL UPON YOU, AND YOU'RE NO GOOD TO ME IF YOU'RE TIRED AND BRUISED.
SLUMP
SPIN
BUT I... MASTER, PLEASE FORGIVE ME! I WAS SO FOCUSED ON OUR PREPARATIONS THAT I COMMITTED A GRAVE ERROR!

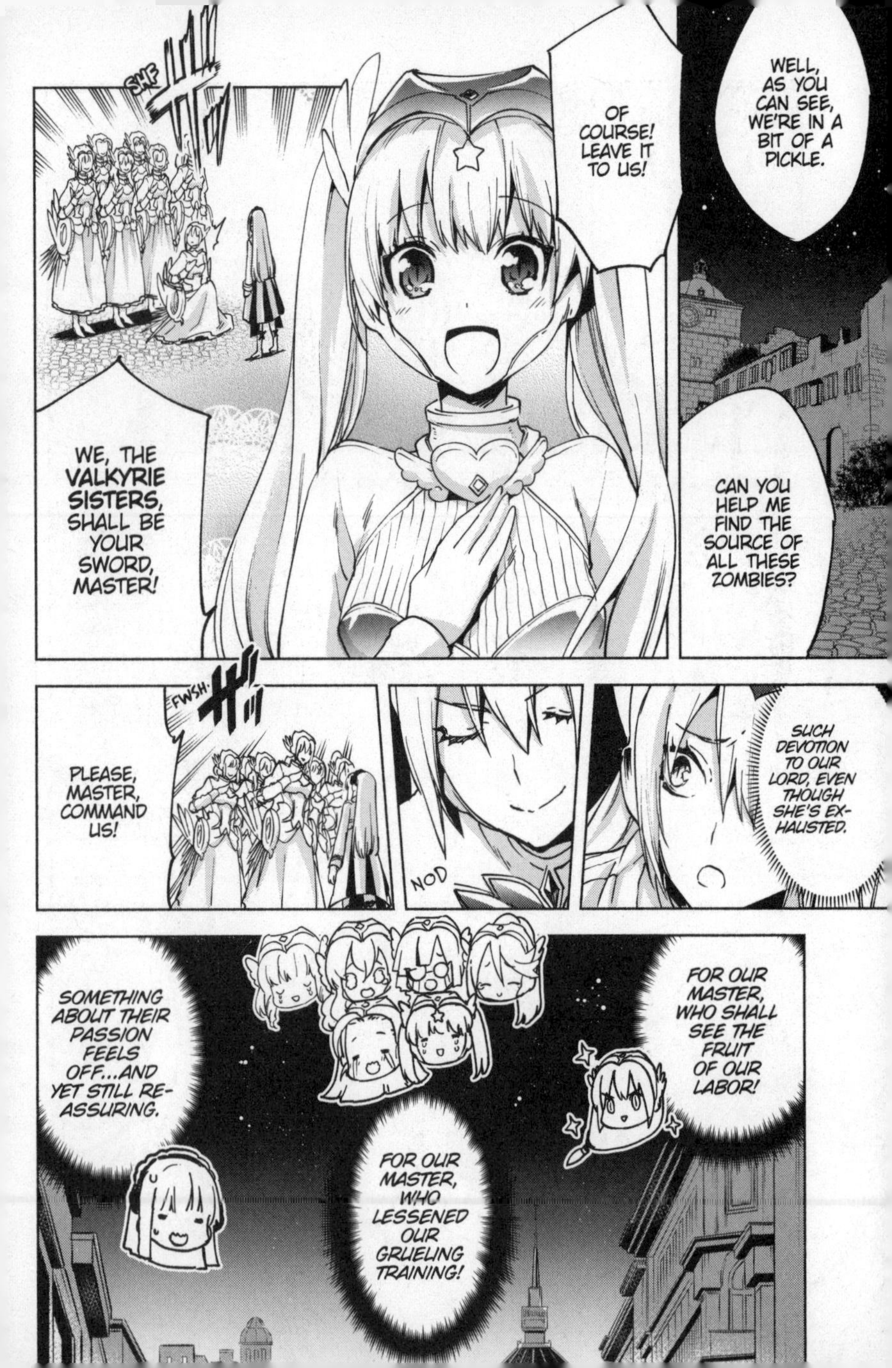
WELL, AS YOU CAN SEE, WE'RE IN A BIT OF A PICKLE.
CAN YOU HELP ME FIND THE SOURCE OF ALL THESE ZOMBIES?
OF COURSE! LEAVE IT TO US!
SHF
WE, THE VALKYRIE SISTERS, SHALL BE YOUR SWORD, MASTER!
SUCH DEVOTION TO OUR LORD, EVEN THOUGH SHE'S EX-HAUSTED.
NOD
FWSH.
PLEASE, MASTER, COMMAND US!
FOR OUR MASTER, WHO SHALL SEE THE FRUIT OF OUR LABOR!
FOR OUR MASTER, WHO LESSENED OUR GRUELING TRAINING!
SOMETHING ABOUT THEIR PASSION FEELS OFF...AND YET STILL RE-ASSURING.

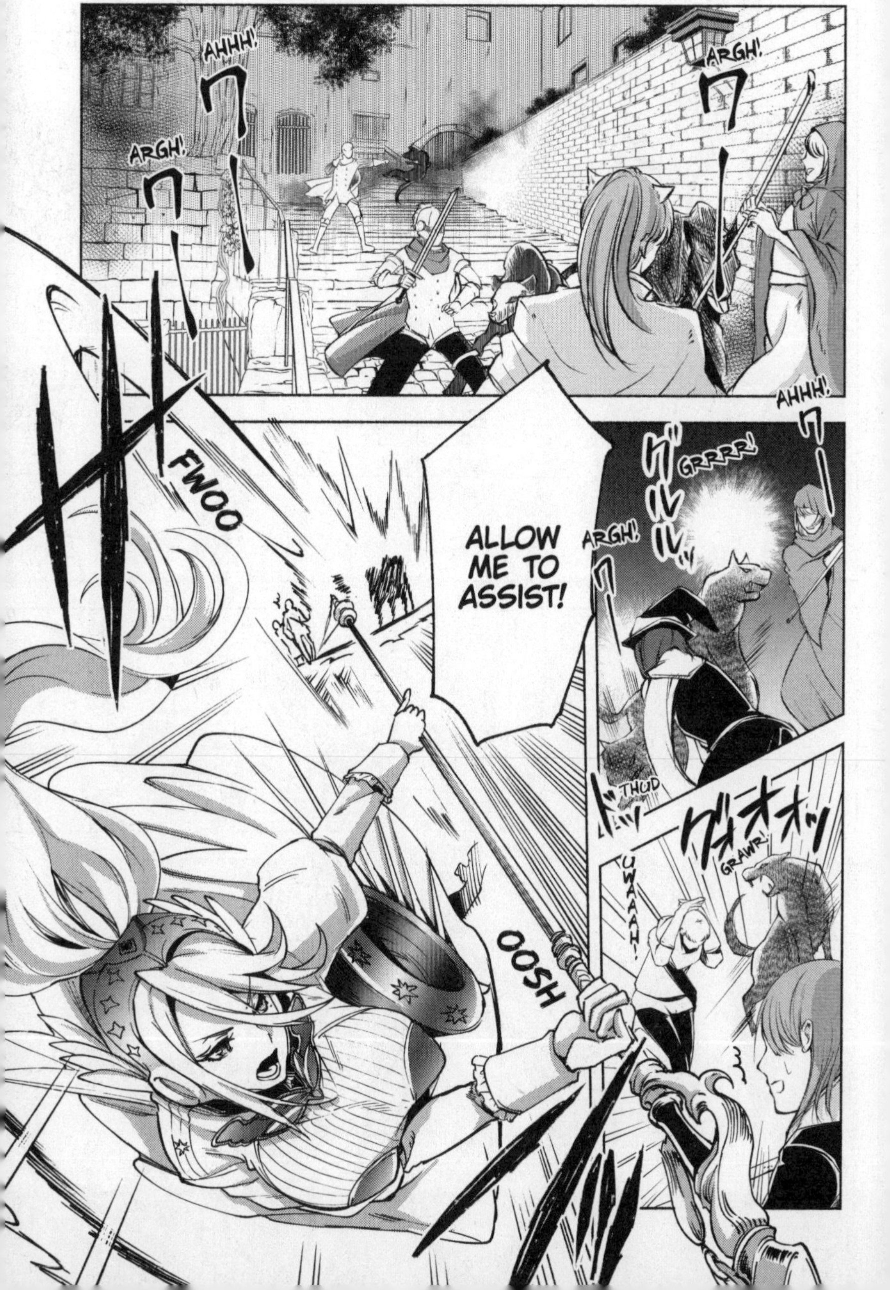

ワー
ARGH!
ワー
AHHH!
ワー
ARGH!
ワー
AHHH!
グルルル
GRRRR!
ワー
ARGH!
ドッ
THUD
グオオオッ
GRAWR!
UWAAAH!
FWOO
ALLOW ME TO ASSIST!
OOSH

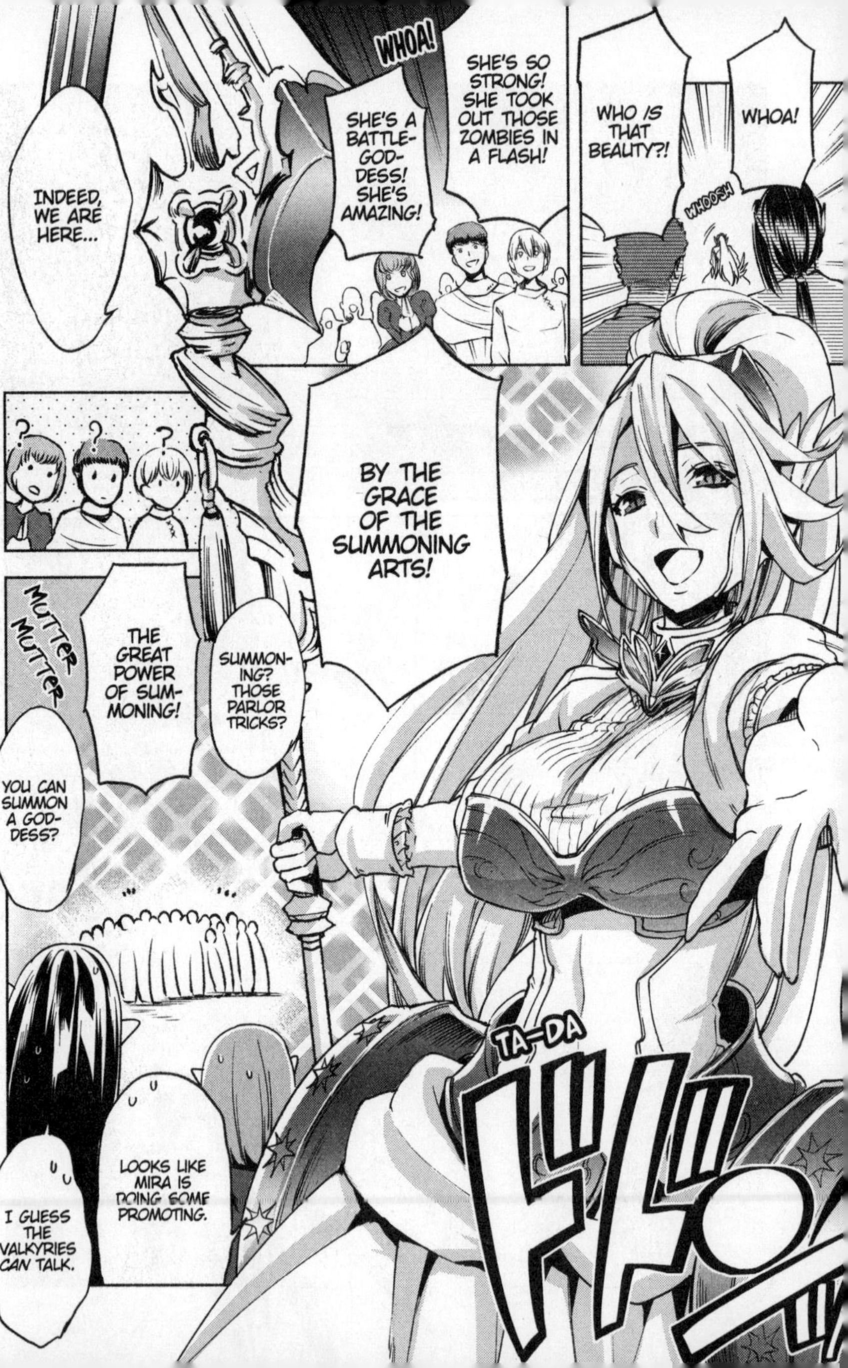
WHOA!
WHO IS THAT BEAUTY?!
WHOOSH
WHOA!
SHE'S SO STRONG! SHE TOOK OUT THOSE ZOMBIES IN A FLASH!
SHE'S A BATTLE-GODDESS! SHE'S AMAZING!
INDEED, WE ARE HERE...
BY THE GRACE OF THE SUMMONING ARTS!
TA-DA
SUMMONING? THOSE PARLOR TRICKS?
THE GREAT POWER OF SUMMONING!
MUTTER MUTTER
YOU CAN SUMMON A GODDESS?
LOOKS LIKE MIRA IS DOING SOME PROMOTING.
I GUESS THE VALKYRIES CAN TALK.

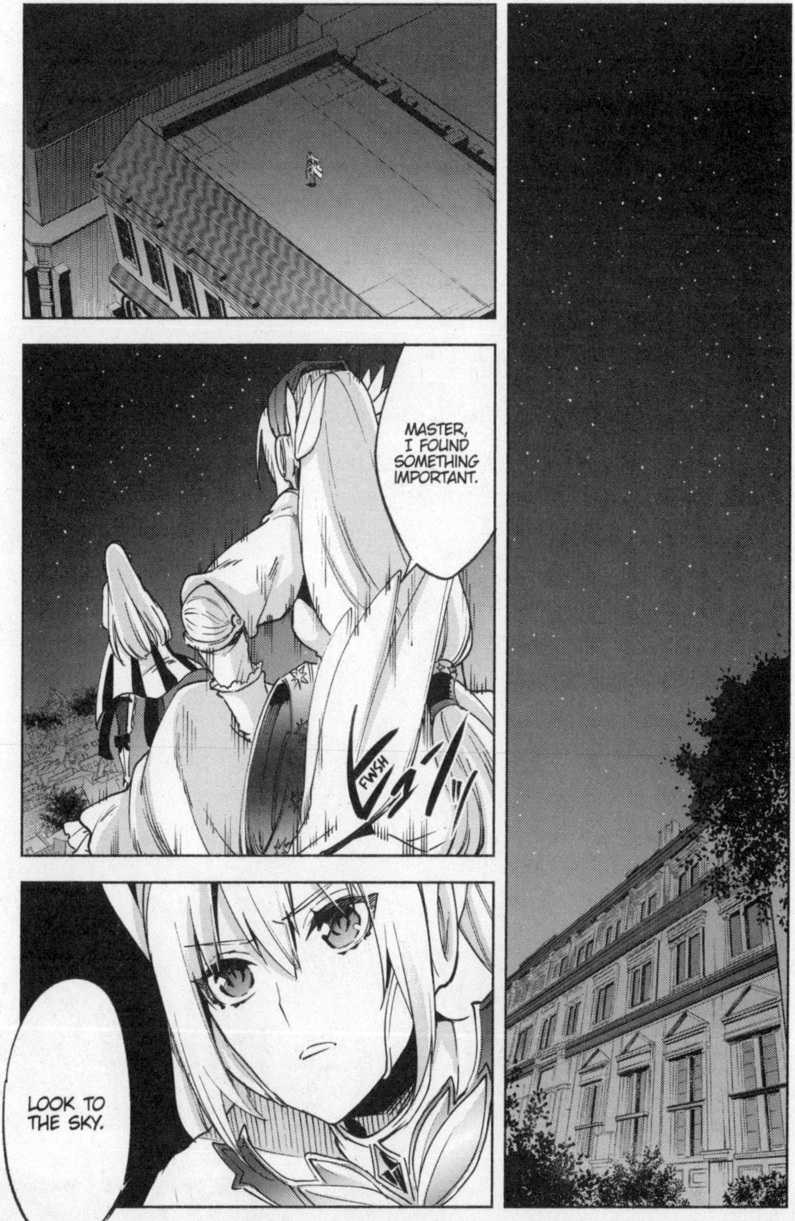
MASTER, I FOUND SOMETHING IMPORTANT.
FWSH
LOOK TO THE SKY.

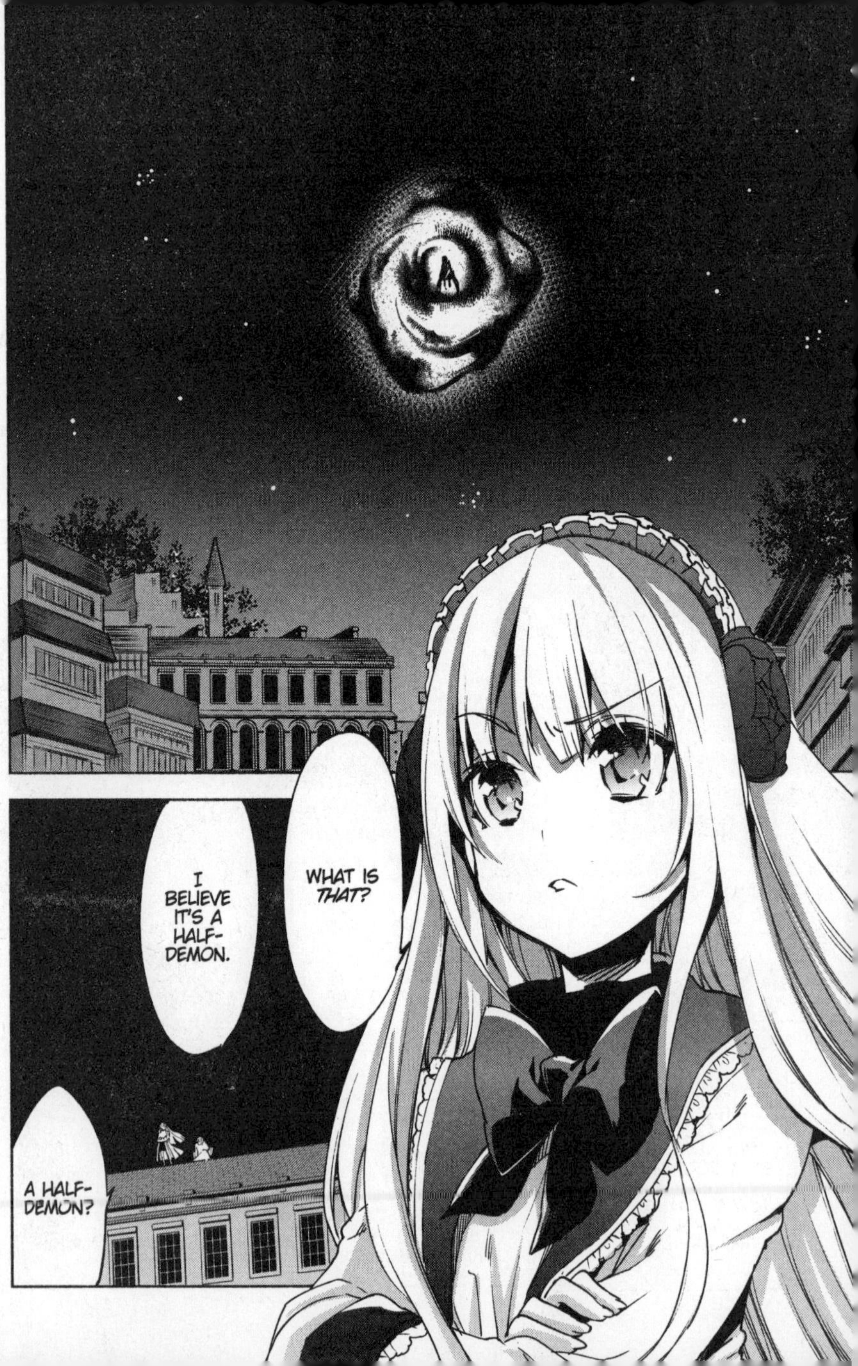
WHAT IS *THAT?*
I BELIEVE IT'S A HALF-DEMON.
A HALF-DEMON?

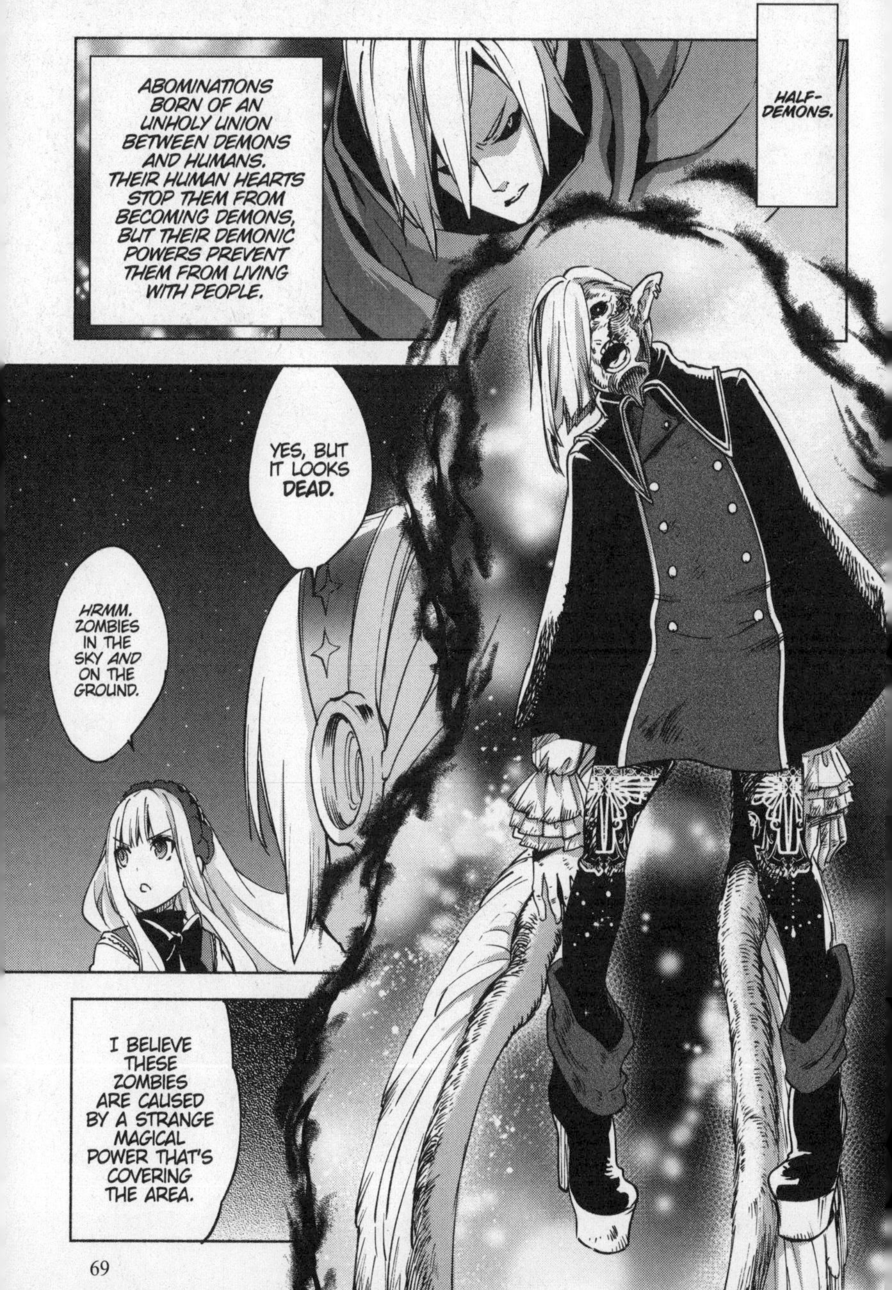
HALF-DEMONS.
ABOMINATIONS BORN OF AN UNHOLY UNION BETWEEN DEMONS AND HUMANS. THEIR HUMAN HEARTS STOP THEM FROM BECOMING DEMONS, BUT THEIR DEMONIC POWERS PREVENT THEM FROM LIVING WITH PEOPLE.
YES, BUT IT LOOKS DEAD.
HRMM. ZOMBIES IN THE SKY AND ON THE GROUND.
I BELIEVE THESE ZOMBIES ARE CAUSED BY A STRANGE MAGICAL POWER THAT'S COVERING THE AREA.

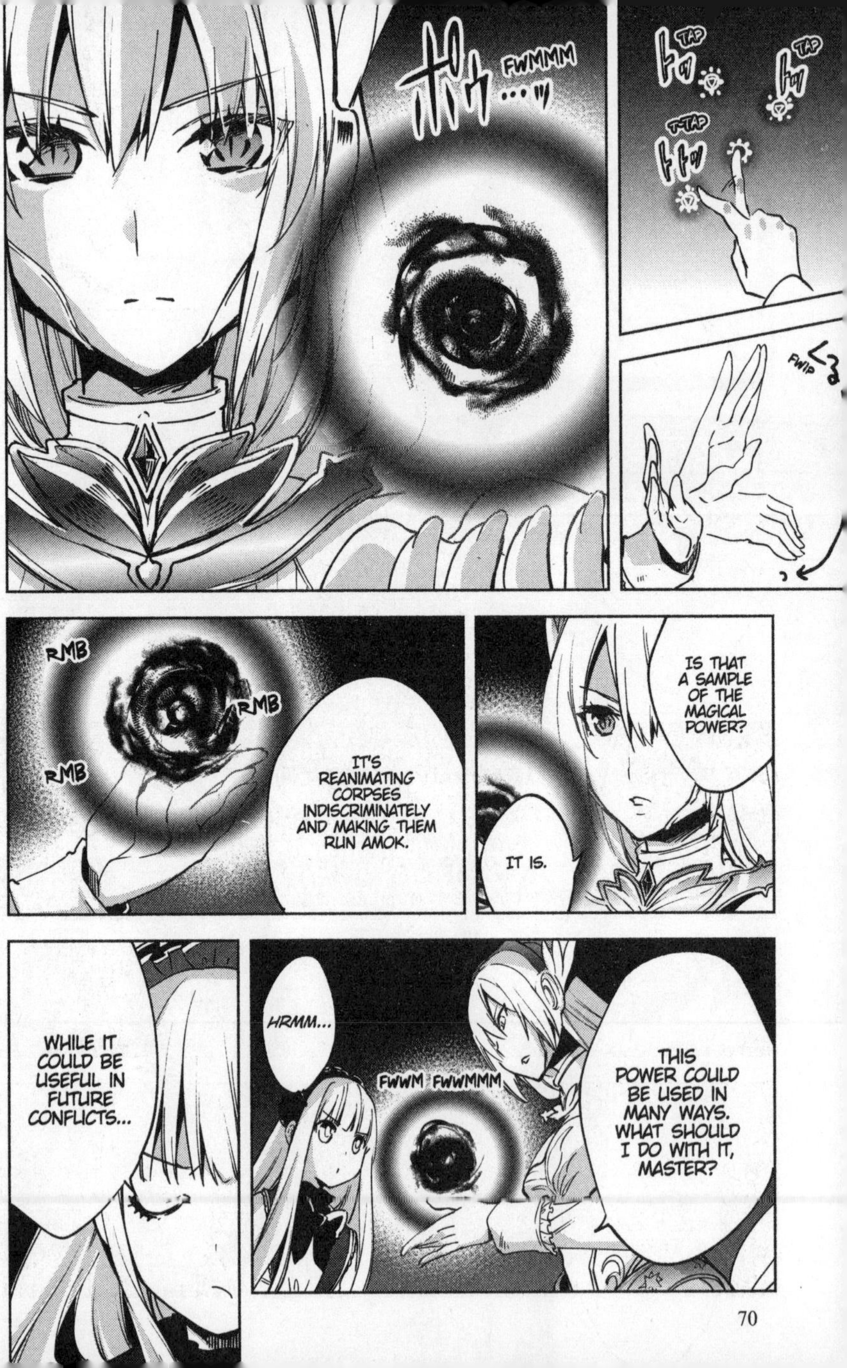

TAP
TAP
T-TAP
FWIP
FWMMM
IS THAT A SAMPLE OF THE MAGICAL POWER?
IT IS.
RMB
RMB
RMB
IT'S REANIMATING CORPSES INDISCRIMINATELY AND MAKING THEM RUN AMOK.
THIS POWER COULD BE USED IN MANY WAYS. WHAT SHOULD I DO WITH IT, MASTER?
HRMM...
FWWM FWWMMM
WHILE IT COULD BE USEFUL IN FUTURE CONFLICTS...

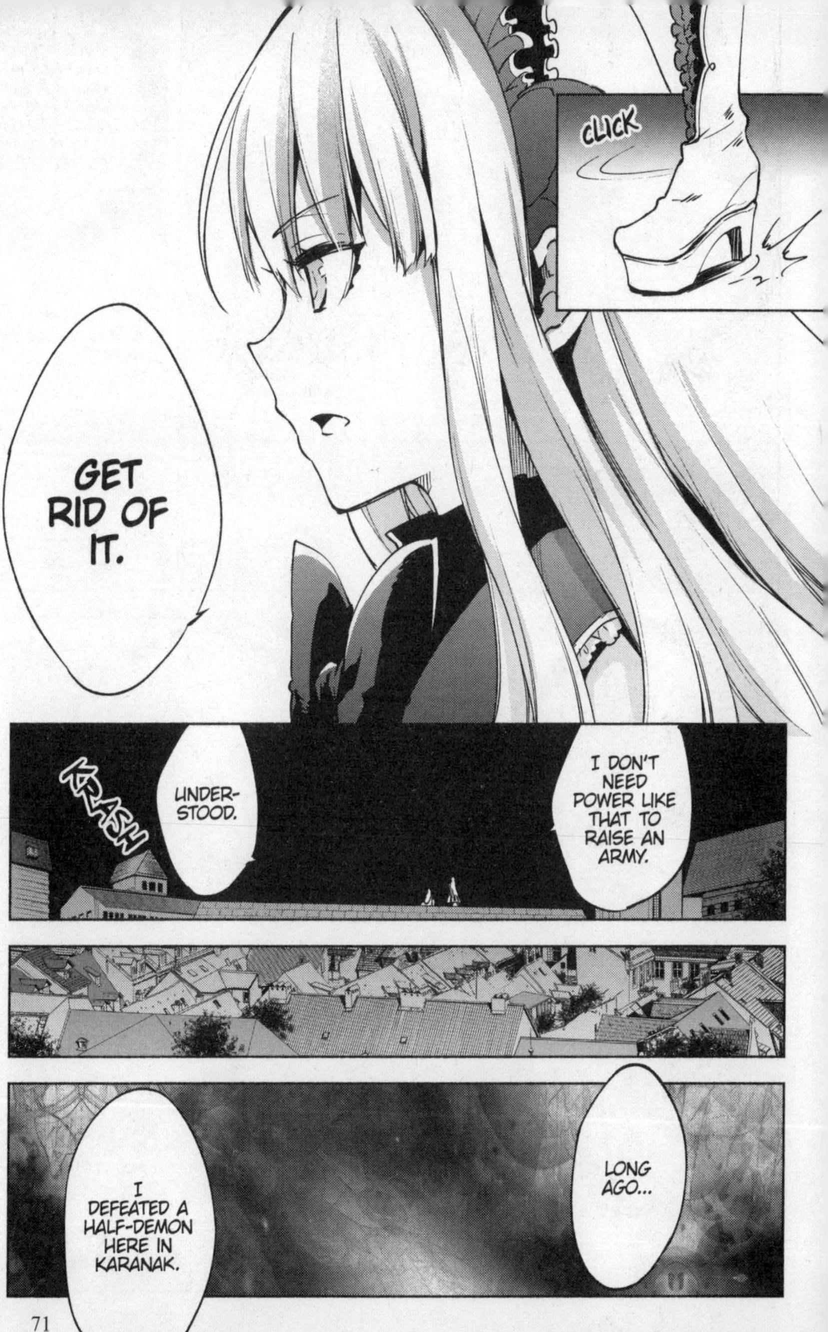
CLICK
GET RID OF IT.
I DON'T NEED POWER LIKE THAT TO RAISE AN ARMY.
UNDER-STOOD.
KRASH
LONG AGO...
I DEFEATED A HALF-DEMON HERE IN KARANAK.

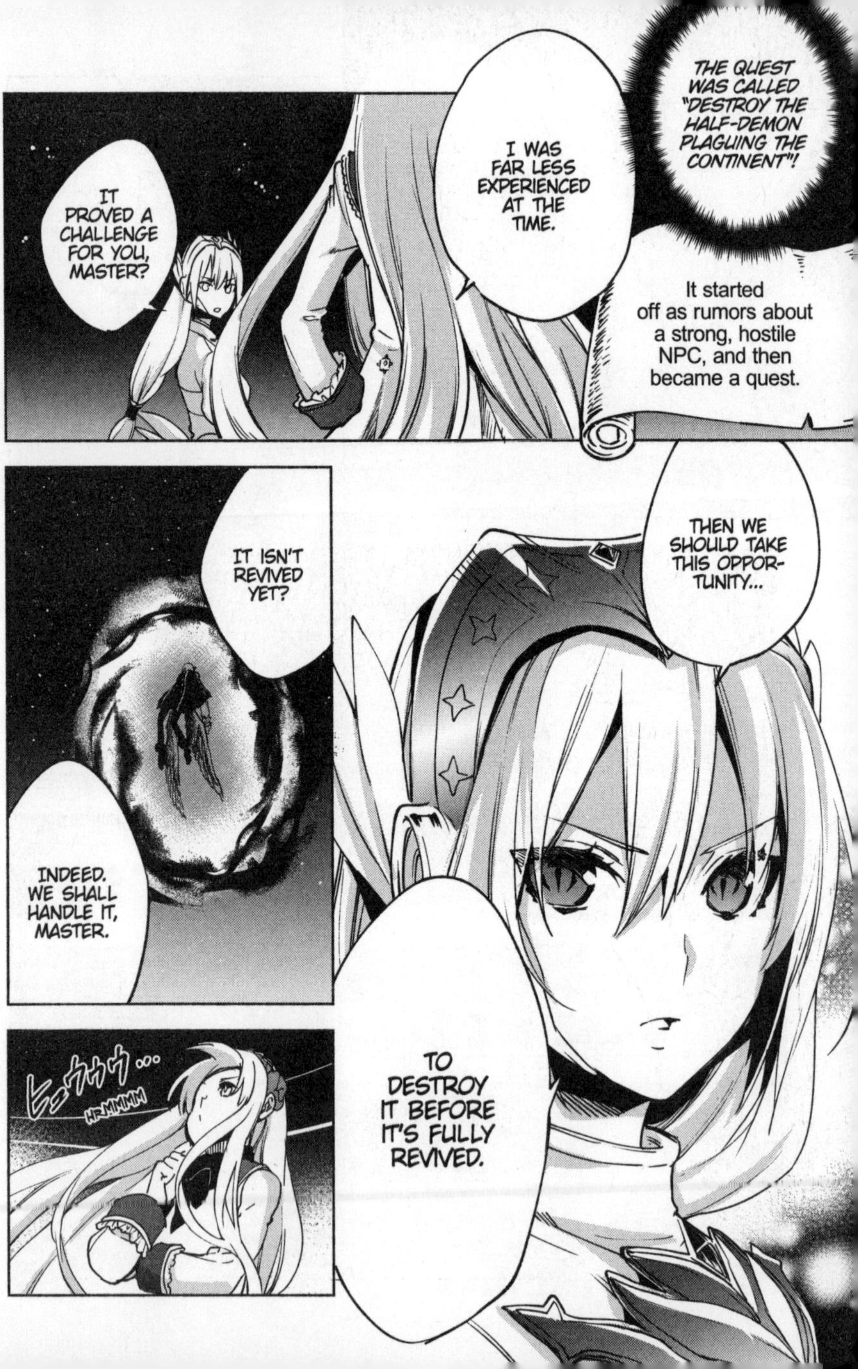
THE QUEST WAS CALLED "DESTROY THE HALF-DEMON PLAGUING THE CONTINENT"!
It started off as rumors about a strong, hostile NPC, and then became a quest.
I WAS FAR LESS EXPERIENCED AT THE TIME.
IT PROVED A CHALLENGE FOR YOU, MASTER?
THEN WE SHOULD TAKE THIS OPPORTUNITY...
TO DESTROY IT BEFORE IT'S FULLY REVIVED.
IT ISN'T REVIVED YET?
INDEED. WE SHALL HANDLE IT, MASTER.
ヒュウウウ…
HRMMMM

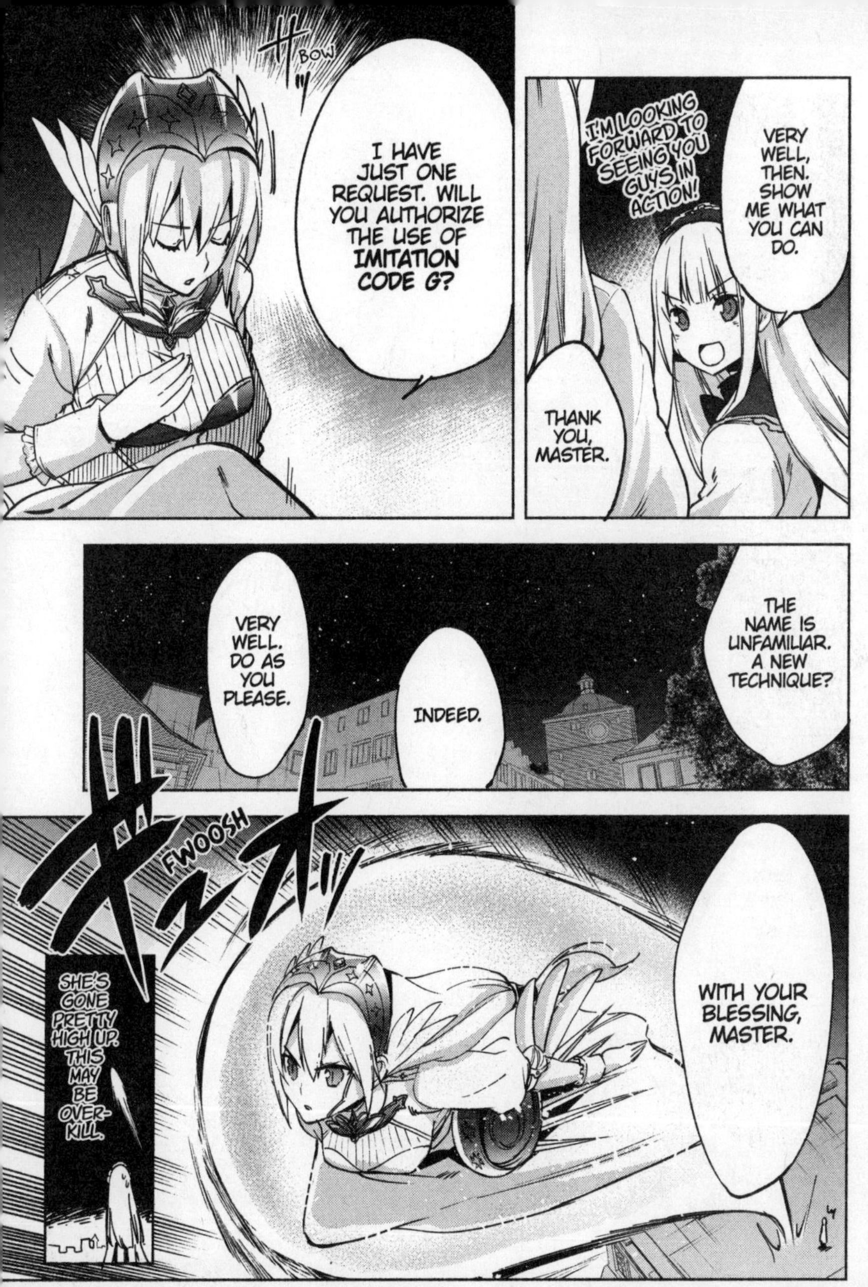
VERY WELL, THEN. SHOW ME WHAT YOU CAN DO.
I'M LOOKING FORWARD TO SEEING YOU GUYS IN ACTION!
THANK YOU, MASTER.
BOW
I HAVE JUST ONE REQUEST. WILL YOU AUTHORIZE THE USE OF IMITATION CODE G?
THE NAME IS UNFAMILIAR. A NEW TECHNIQUE?
INDEED.
VERY WELL. DO AS YOU PLEASE.
WITH YOUR BLESSING, MASTER.
FWOOSH
SHE'S GONE PRETTY HIGH UP. THIS MAY BE OVER-KILL.

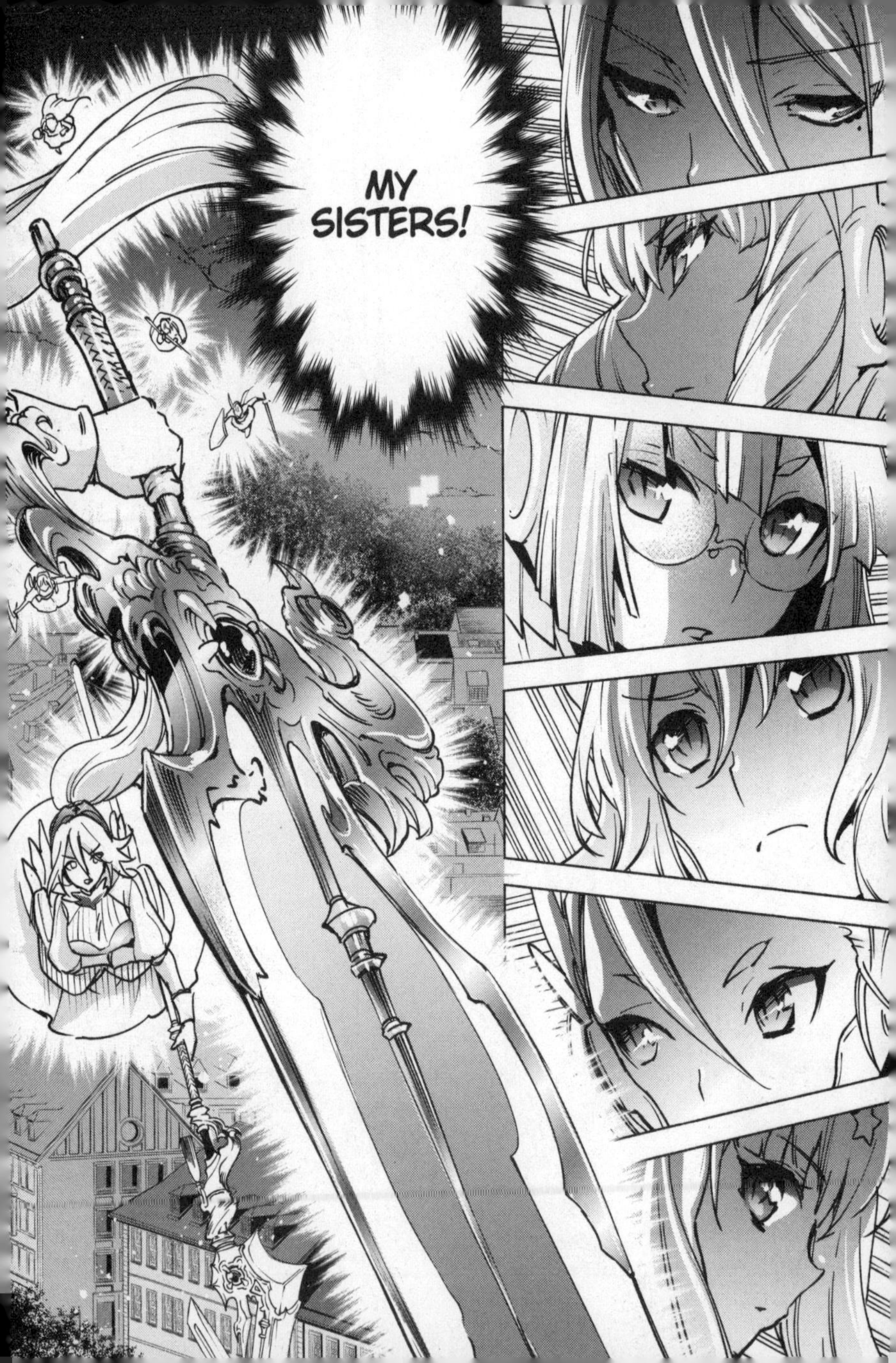
MY SISTERS!

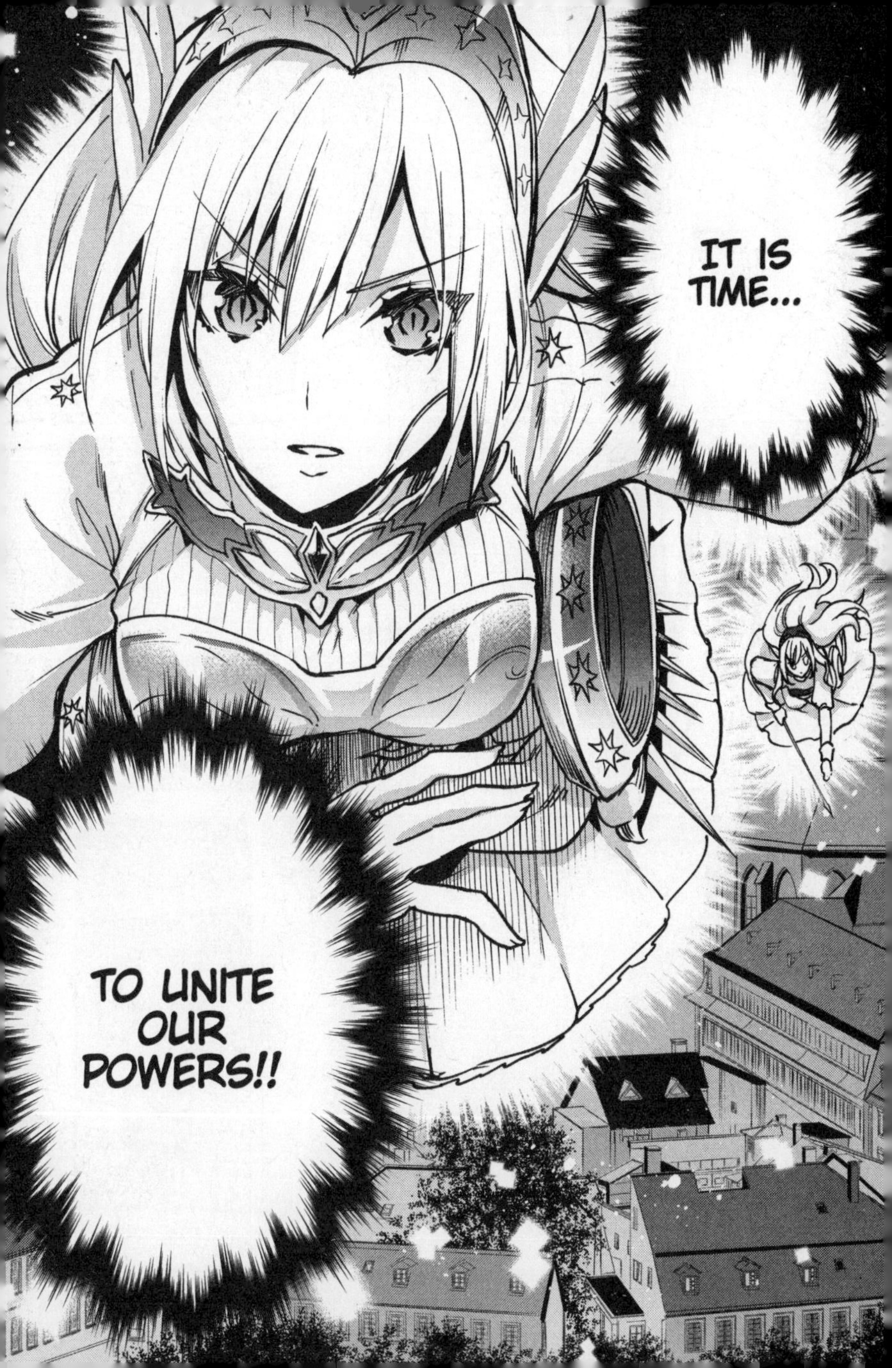
IT IS TIME...
TO UNITE OUR POWERS!!

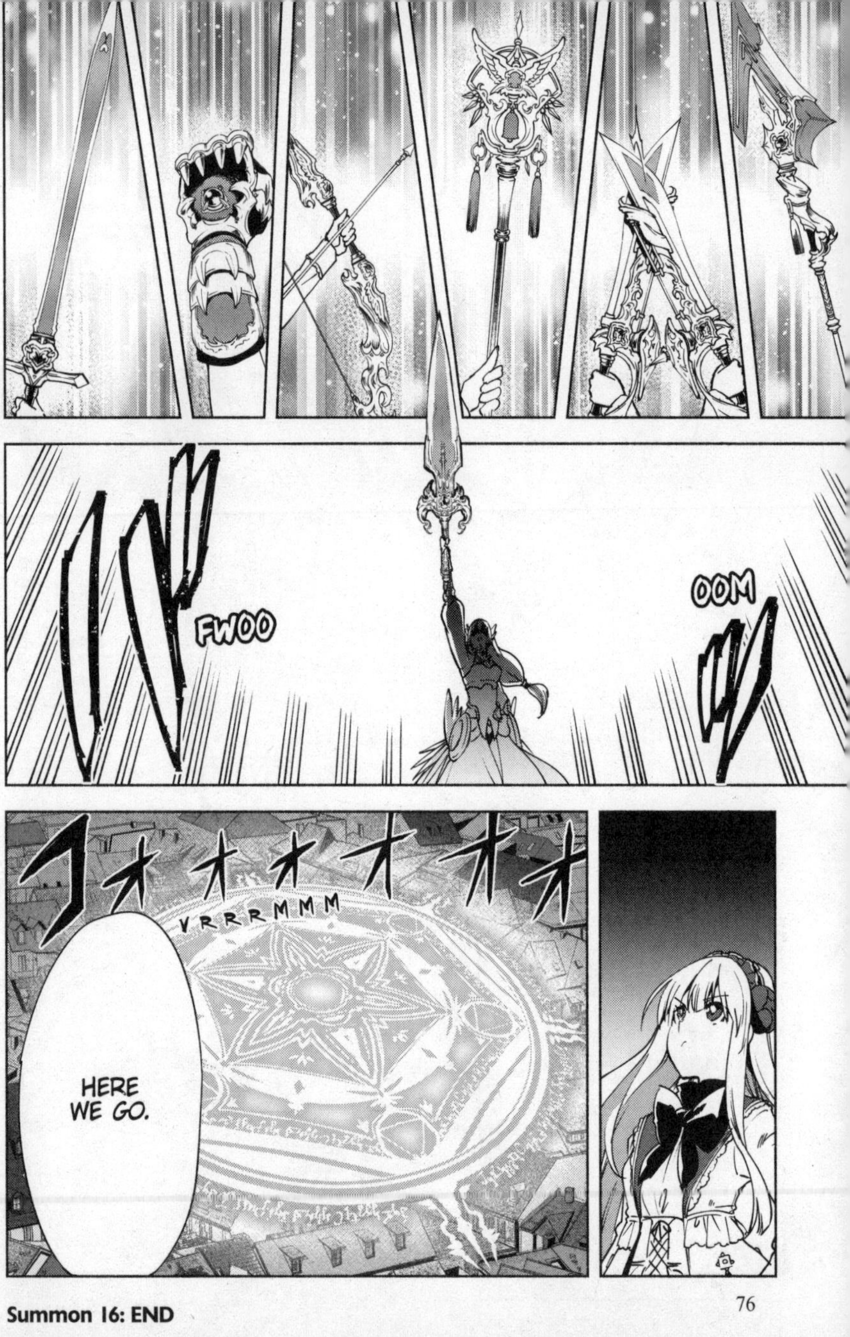
OOM
FWOO
コオオオオオオ
VRRRMMM
HERE WE GO.

Summon 16: END

THE SISTERS SEVEN ARE HERE TO ANSWER YOUR CALL.

FWSH!

She
Professed
Herself
Pupil of the
Wise Man

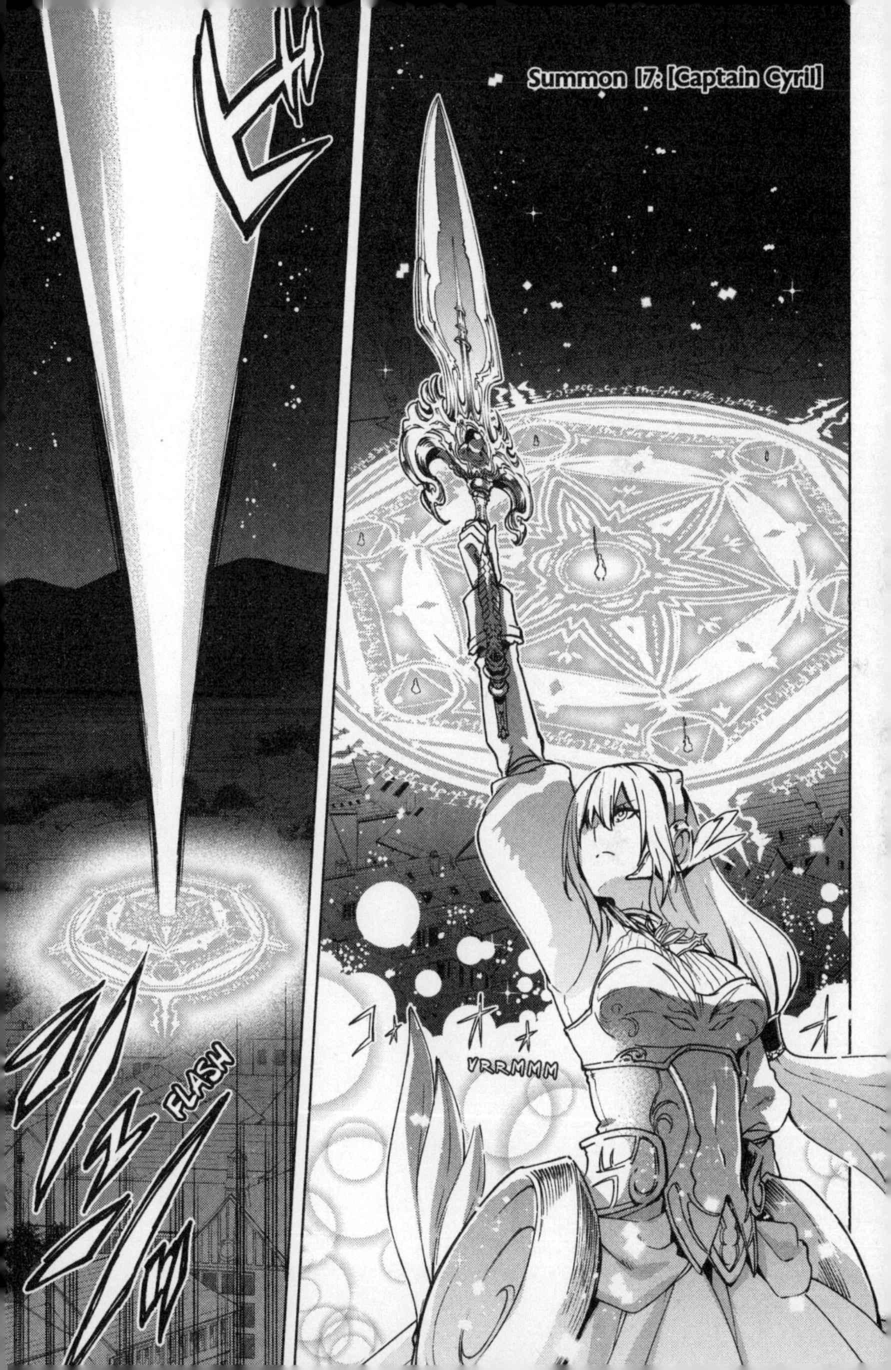
Summon 17: [Captain Cyril]
VRRMMM
FLASH

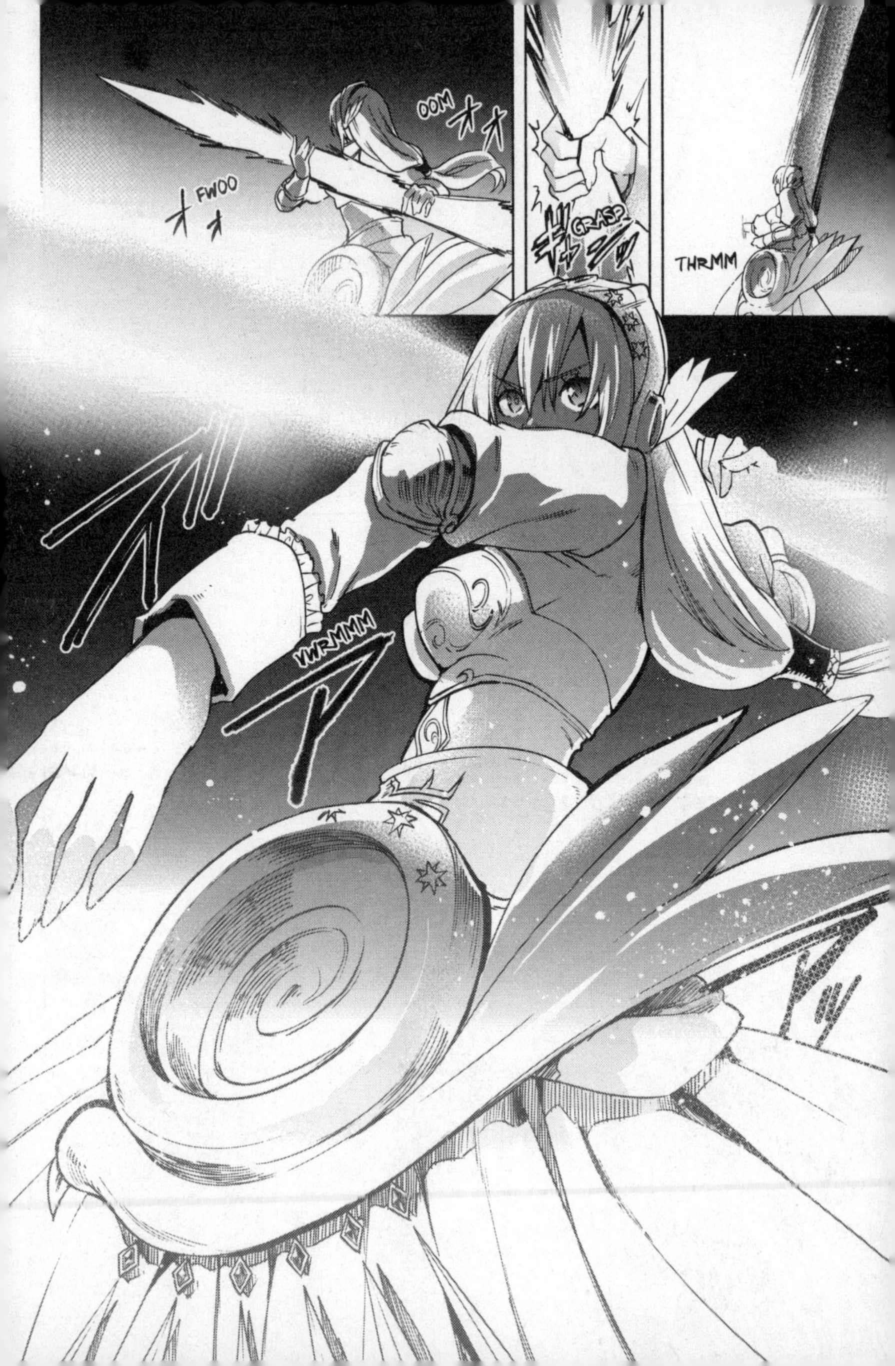
THRMM
GRASP
OOM オオ
FWOO オオ
YWRMMM

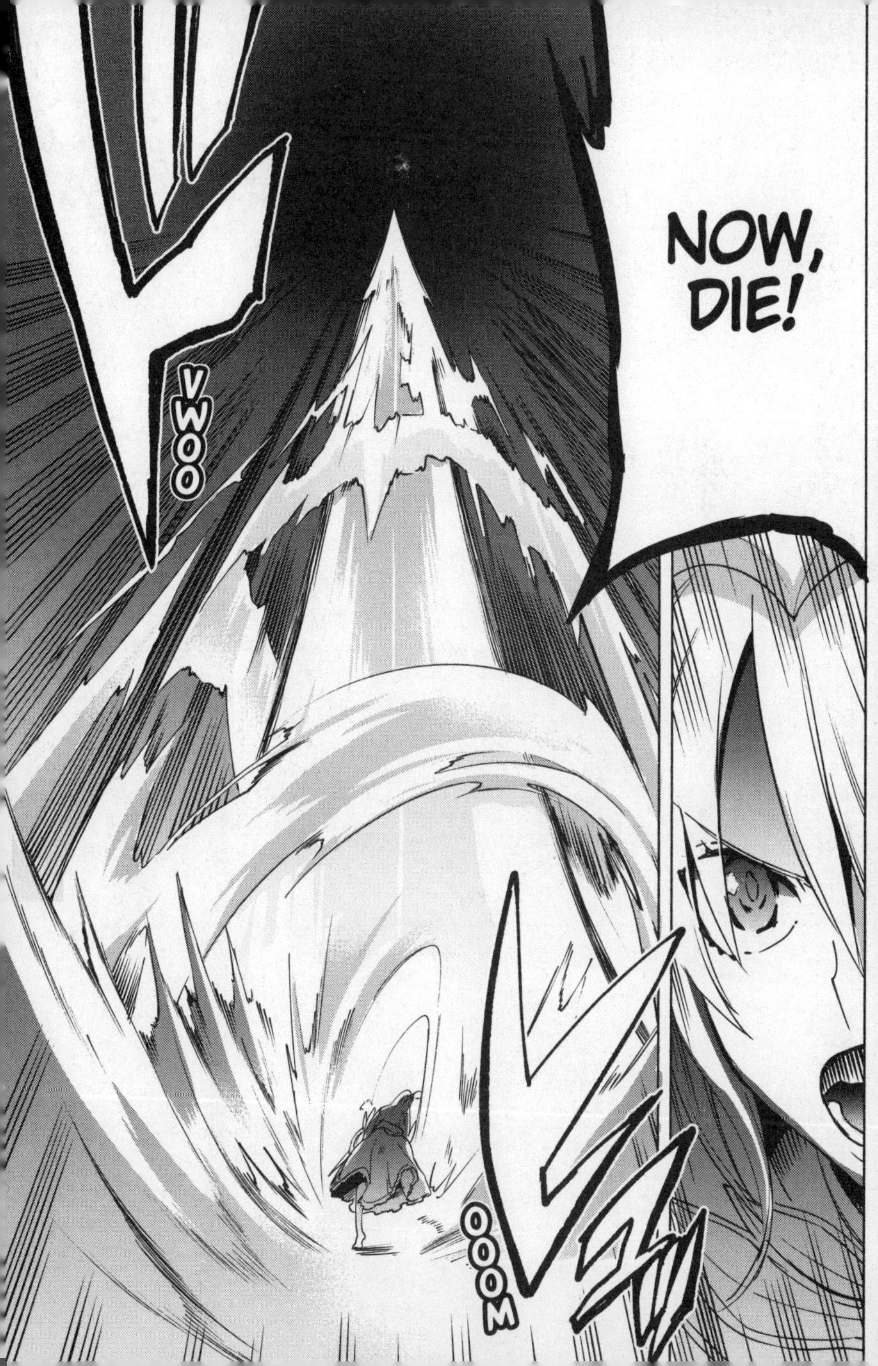
NOW, DIE!
VWOO
OOOM

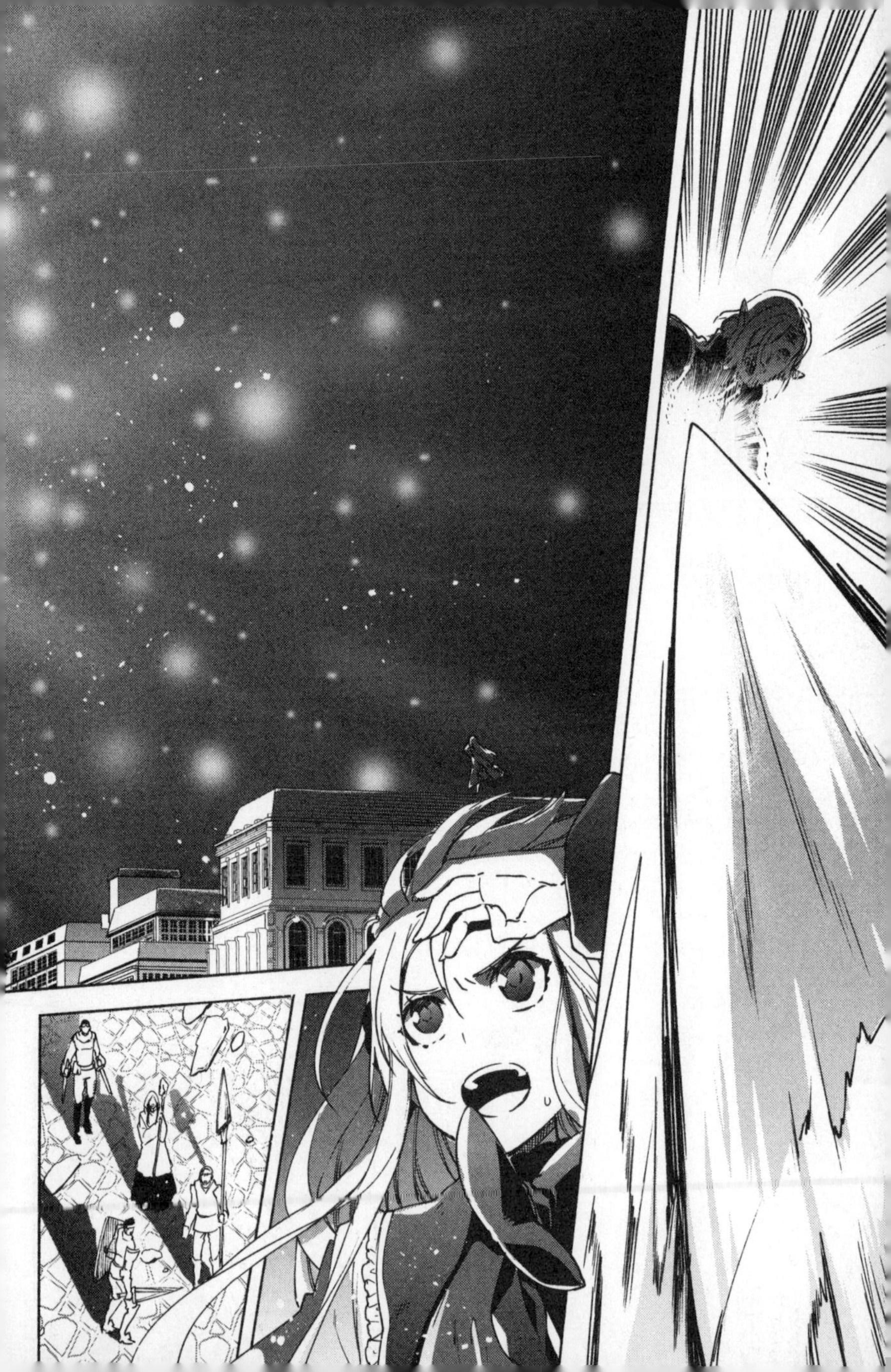

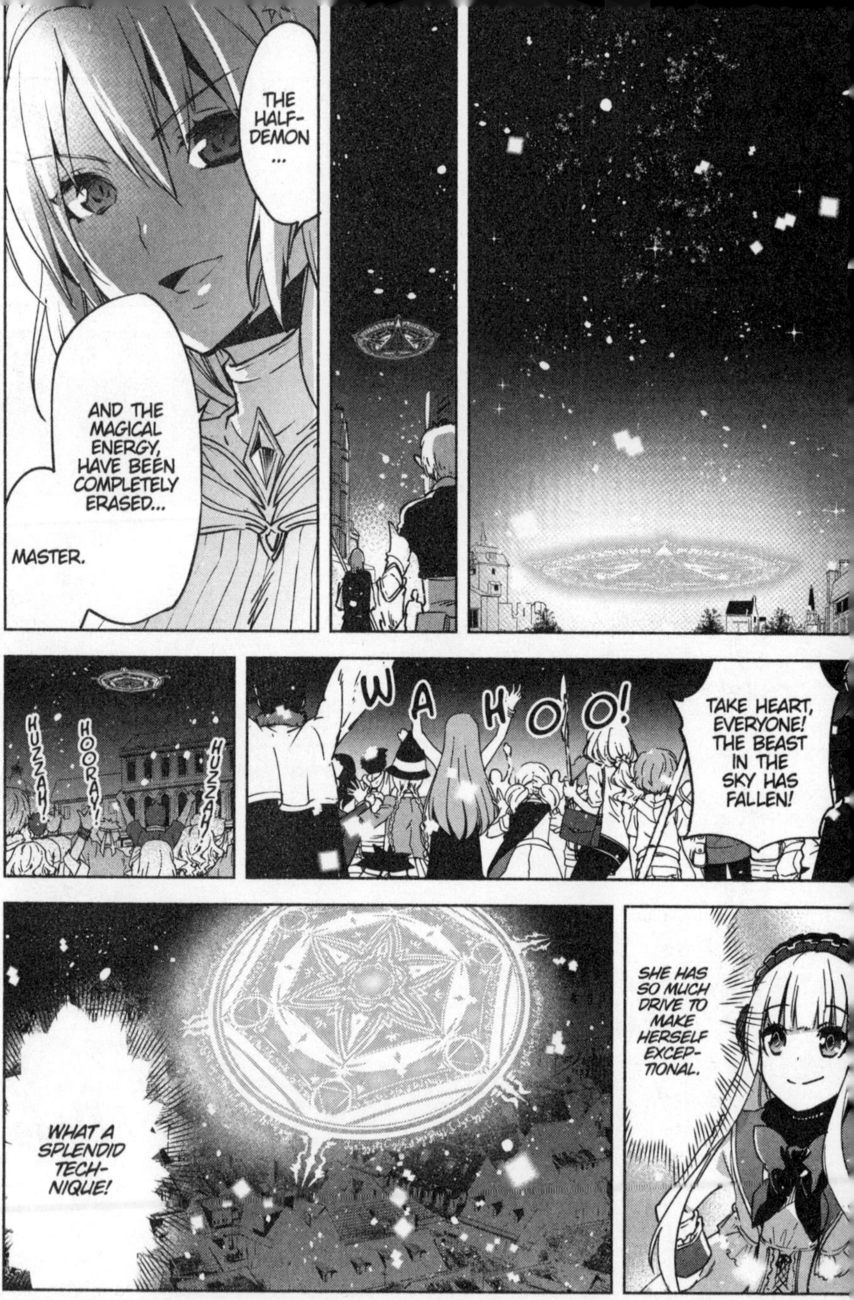
THE HALF-DEMON...
AND THE MAGICAL ENERGY, HAVE BEEN COMPLETELY ERASED...
MASTER.
TAKE HEART, EVERYONE! THE BEAST IN THE SKY HAS FALLEN!
WAHOO!
HUZZAH!
HOORAY!
HUZZAH!
SHE HAS SO MUCH DRIVE TO MAKE HERSELF EXCEP-TIONAL.
WHAT A SPLENDID TECH-NIQUE!

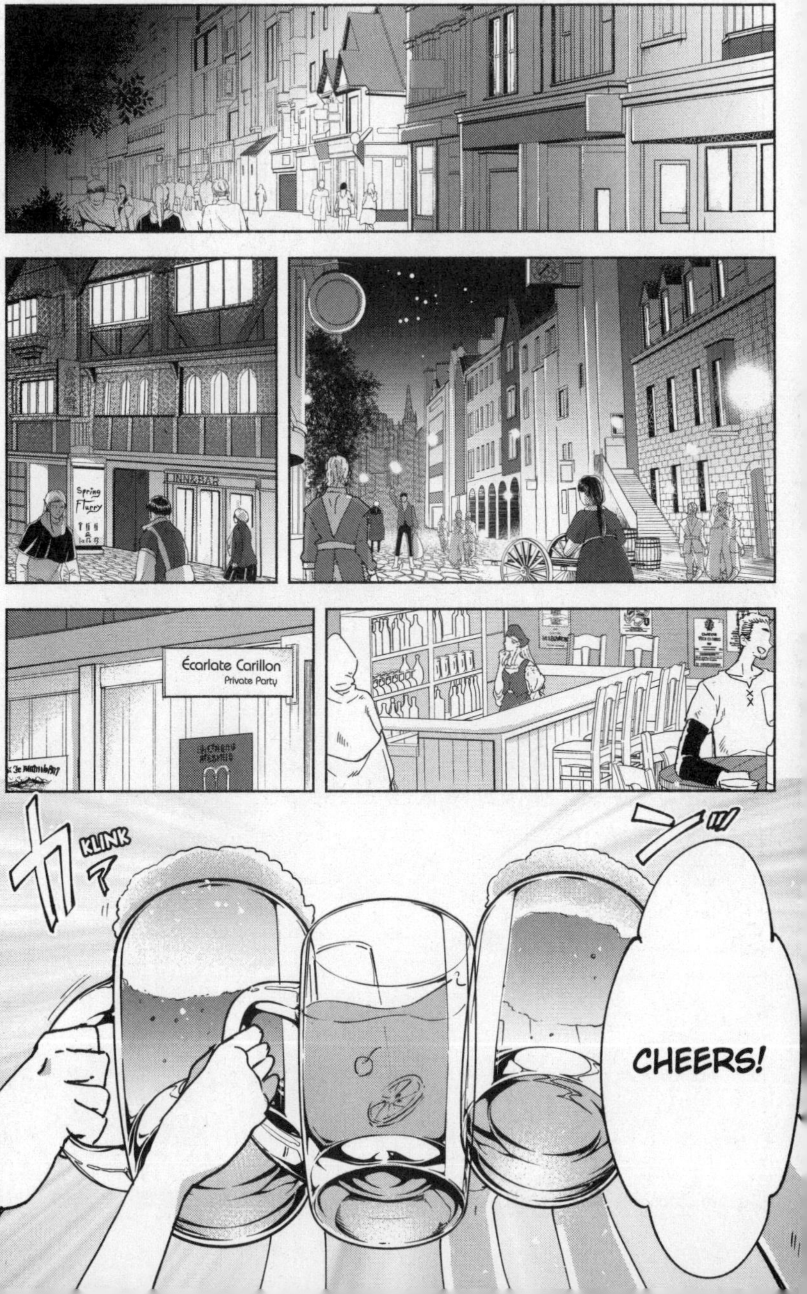
Spring Flurry
INN&BAR
Écarlate Carillon
Private Party
CHEERS!
KLINK

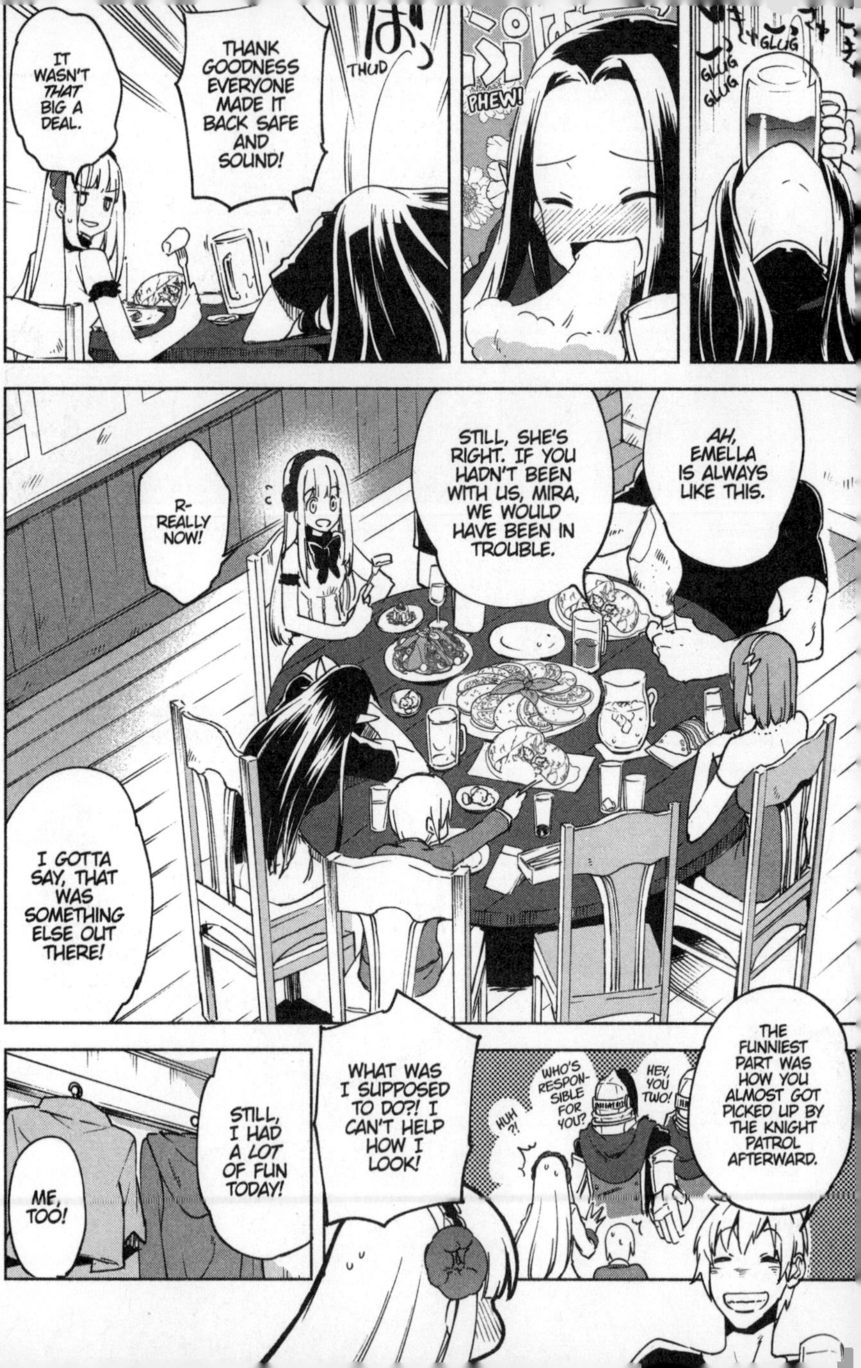

GLUG GLUG
GLUG GLUG
PHEW!
THUD
THANK GOODNESS EVERYONE MADE IT BACK SAFE AND SOUND!
IT WASN'T *THAT* BIG A DEAL.
AH, EMELLA IS ALWAYS LIKE THIS.
STILL, SHE'S RIGHT. IF YOU HADN'T BEEN WITH US, MIRA, WE WOULD HAVE BEEN IN TROUBLE.
R-REALLY NOW!
I GOTTA SAY, THAT WAS SOMETHING ELSE OUT THERE!
THE FUNNIEST PART WAS HOW YOU ALMOST GOT PICKED UP BY THE KNIGHT PATROL AFTERWARD.
HEY, YOU TWO!
WHO'S RESPON-SIBLE FOR YOU?
HUH?!
WHAT WAS I SUPPOSED TO DO?! I CAN'T HELP HOW I LOOK!
STILL, I HAD A *LOT* OF FUN TODAY!
ME, TOO!

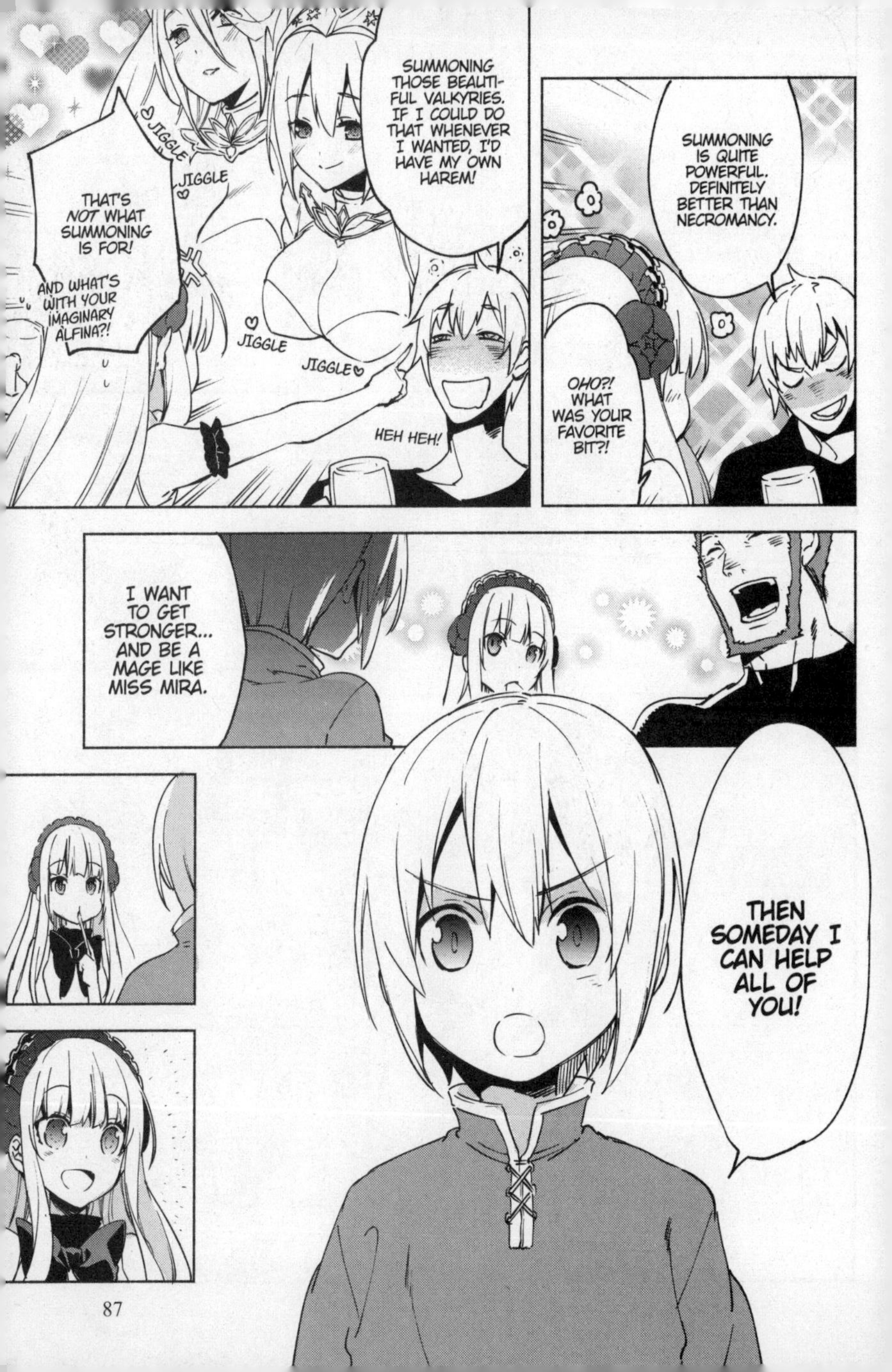

SUMMONING IS QUITE POWERFUL. DEFINITELY BETTER THAN NECROMANCY.
OHO?! WHAT WAS YOUR FAVORITE BIT?!
SUMMONING THOSE BEAUTIFUL VALKYRIES. IF I COULD DO THAT WHENEVER I WANTED, I'D HAVE MY OWN HAREM!
JIGGLE
JIGGLE
THAT'S *NOT* WHAT SUMMONING IS FOR!
AND WHAT'S WITH YOUR IMAGINARY ALFINA?!
JIGGLE
JIGGLE
HEH HEH!
I WANT TO GET STRONGER... AND BE A MAGE LIKE MISS MIRA.
THEN SOMEDAY I CAN HELP ALL OF YOU!

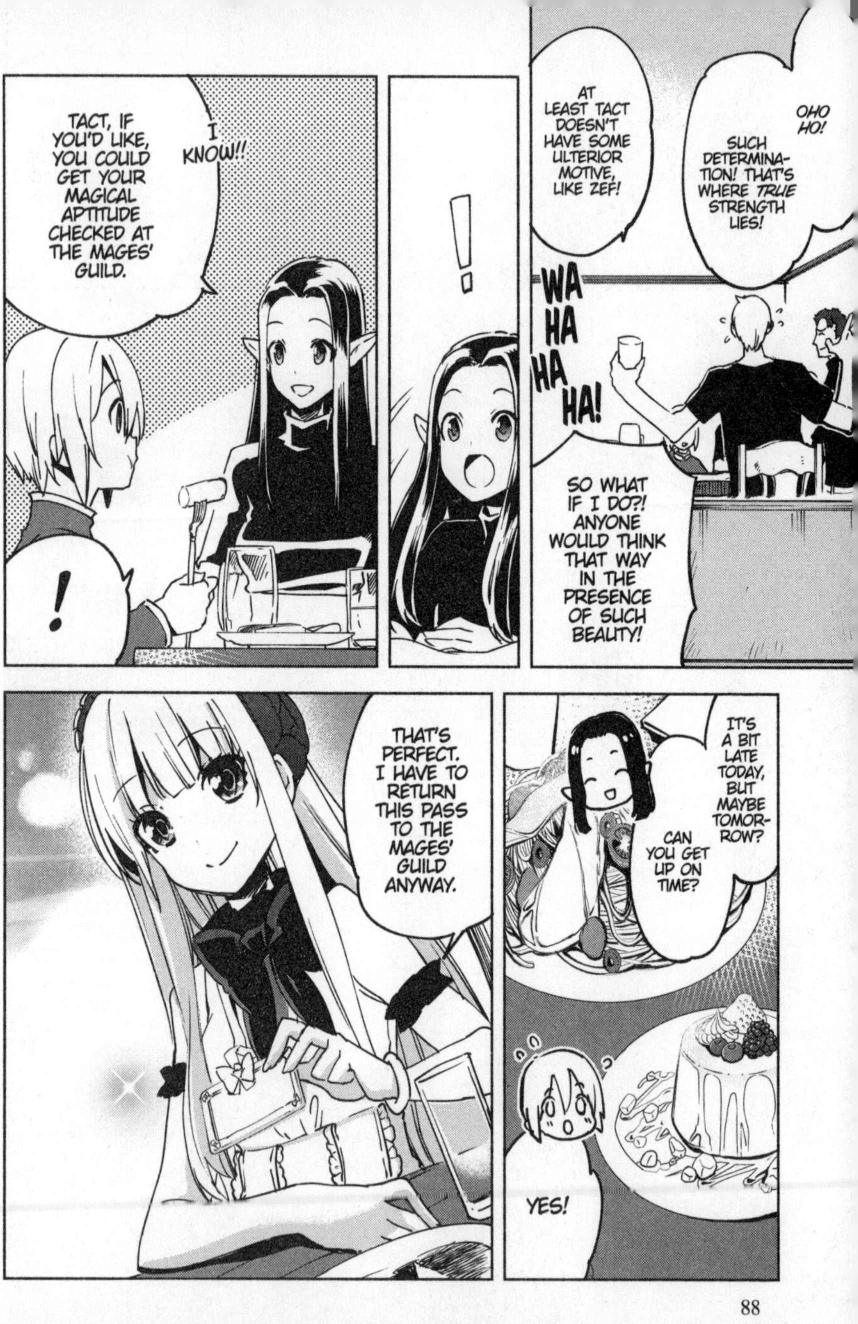
OHO HO!
SUCH DETERMINATION! THAT'S WHERE TRUE STRENGTH LIES!
AT LEAST TACT DOESN'T HAVE SOME ULTERIOR MOTIVE, LIKE ZEF!
WA HA HA HA!
SO WHAT IF I DO?! ANYONE WOULD THINK THAT WAY IN THE PRESENCE OF SUCH BEAUTY!
!
I KNOW!!
TACT, IF YOU'D LIKE, YOU COULD GET YOUR MAGICAL APTITUDE CHECKED AT THE MAGES' GUILD.
!
IT'S A BIT LATE TODAY, BUT MAYBE TOMORROW?
CAN YOU GET UP ON TIME?
YES!
THAT'S PERFECT. I HAVE TO RETURN THIS PASS TO THE MAGES' GUILD ANYWAY.

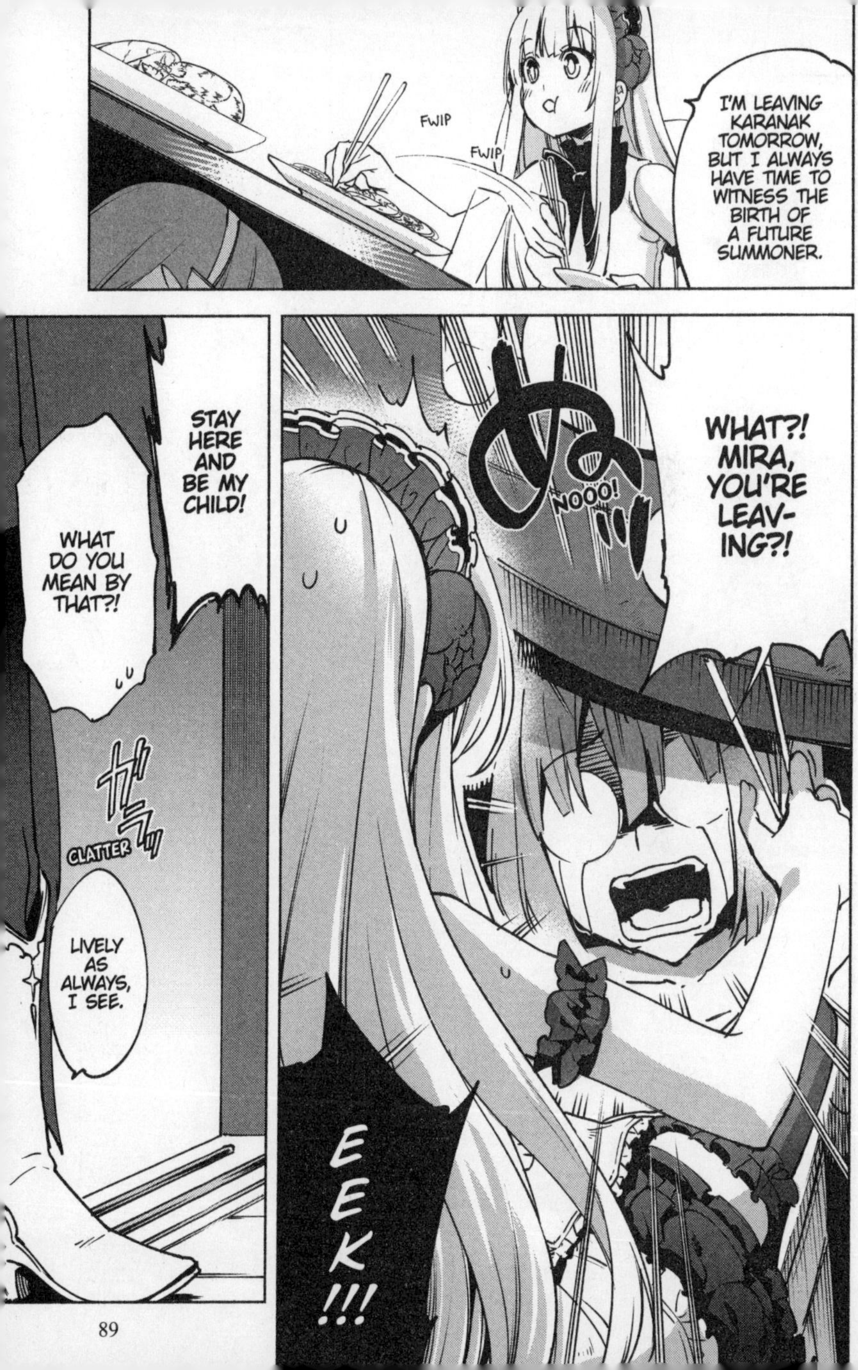
I'M LEAVING KARANAK TOMORROW, BUT I ALWAYS HAVE TIME TO WITNESS THE BIRTH OF A FUTURE SUMMONER.
FWIP
FWIP
WHAT?! MIRA, YOU'RE LEAV-ING?!
NOOO!
EEK!!!
STAY HERE AND BE MY CHILD!
WHAT DO YOU MEAN BY THAT?!
CLATTER
LIVELY AS ALWAYS, I SEE.

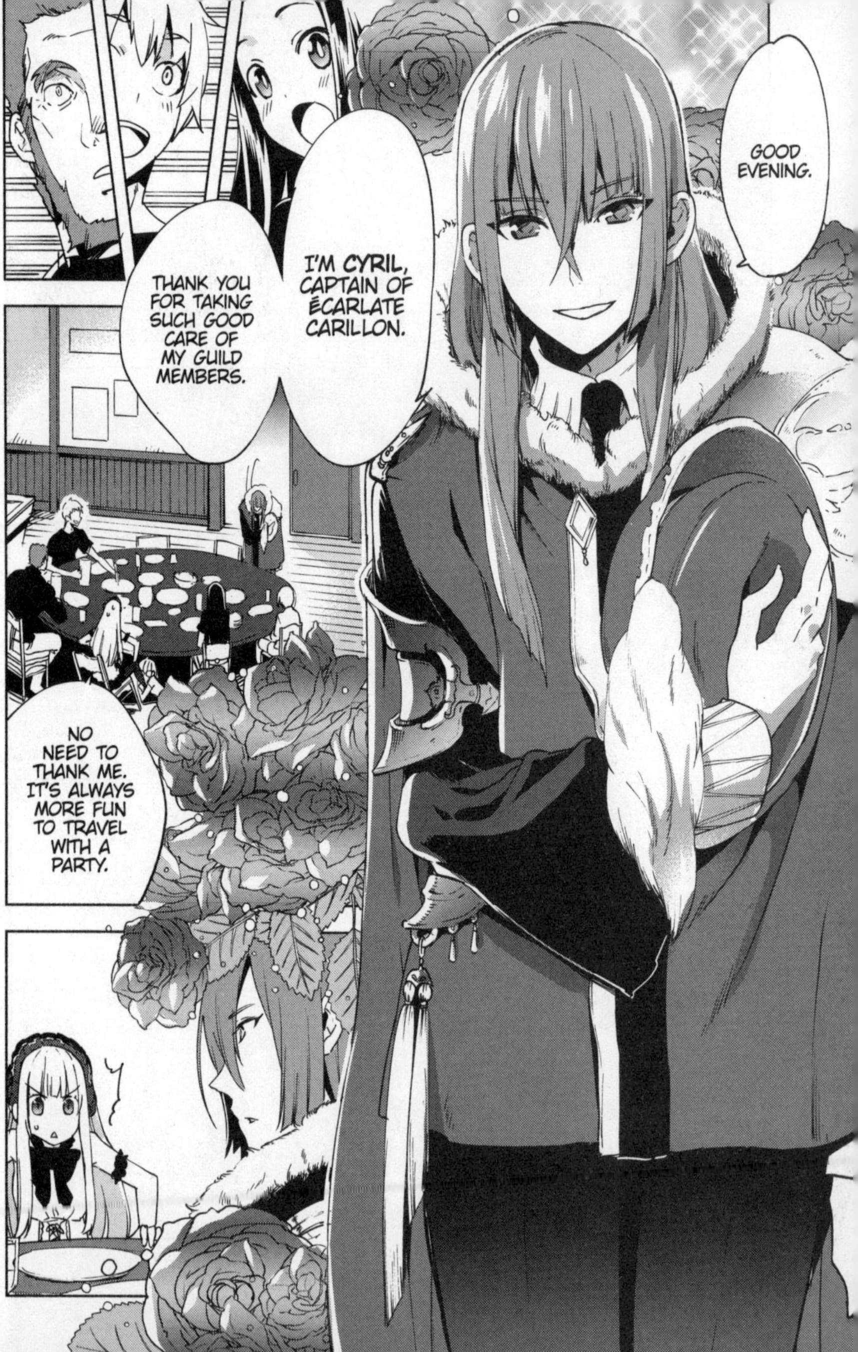
GOOD EVENING.
I'M CYRIL, CAPTAIN OF ÉCARLATE CARILLON.
THANK YOU FOR TAKING SUCH GOOD CARE OF MY GUILD MEMBERS.
NO NEED TO THANK ME. IT'S ALWAYS MORE FUN TO TRAVEL WITH A PARTY.

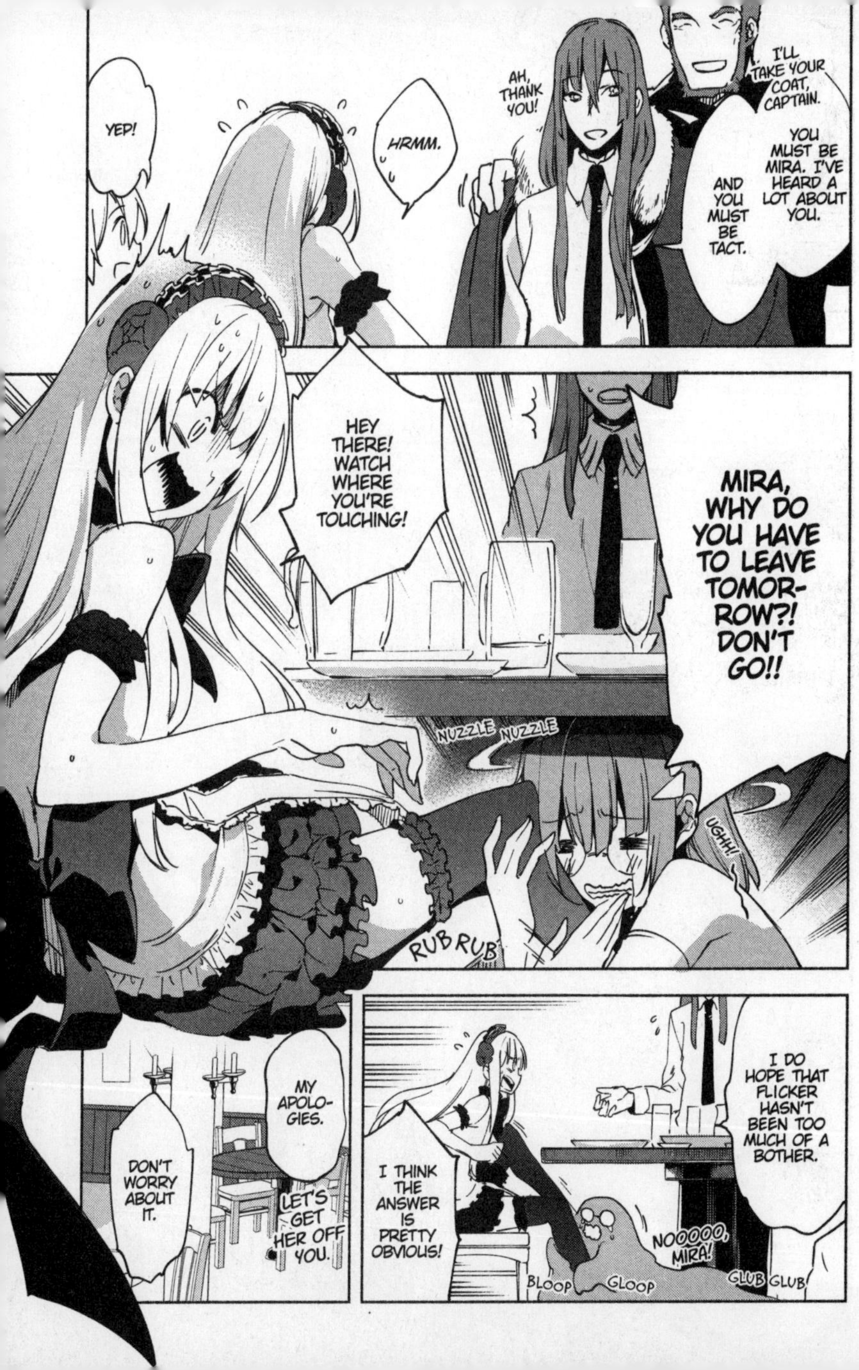
I'LL TAKE YOUR COAT, CAPTAIN.
AH, THANK YOU!
YOU MUST BE MIRA. I'VE HEARD A LOT ABOUT YOU.
AND YOU MUST BE TACT.
HRMM.
YEP!
MIRA, WHY DO YOU HAVE TO LEAVE TOMOR-ROW?! DON'T GO!!
HEY THERE! WATCH WHERE YOU'RE TOUCHING!
NUZZLE NUZZLE
UGHH!
RUB RUB
I DO HOPE THAT FLICKER HASN'T BEEN TOO MUCH OF A BOTHER.
NOOOOO, MIRA!
I THINK THE ANSWER IS PRETTY OBVIOUS!
GLUB GLUB
GLOOP
BLOOP
MY APOLO-GIES.
LET'S GET HER OFF YOU.
DON'T WORRY ABOUT IT.

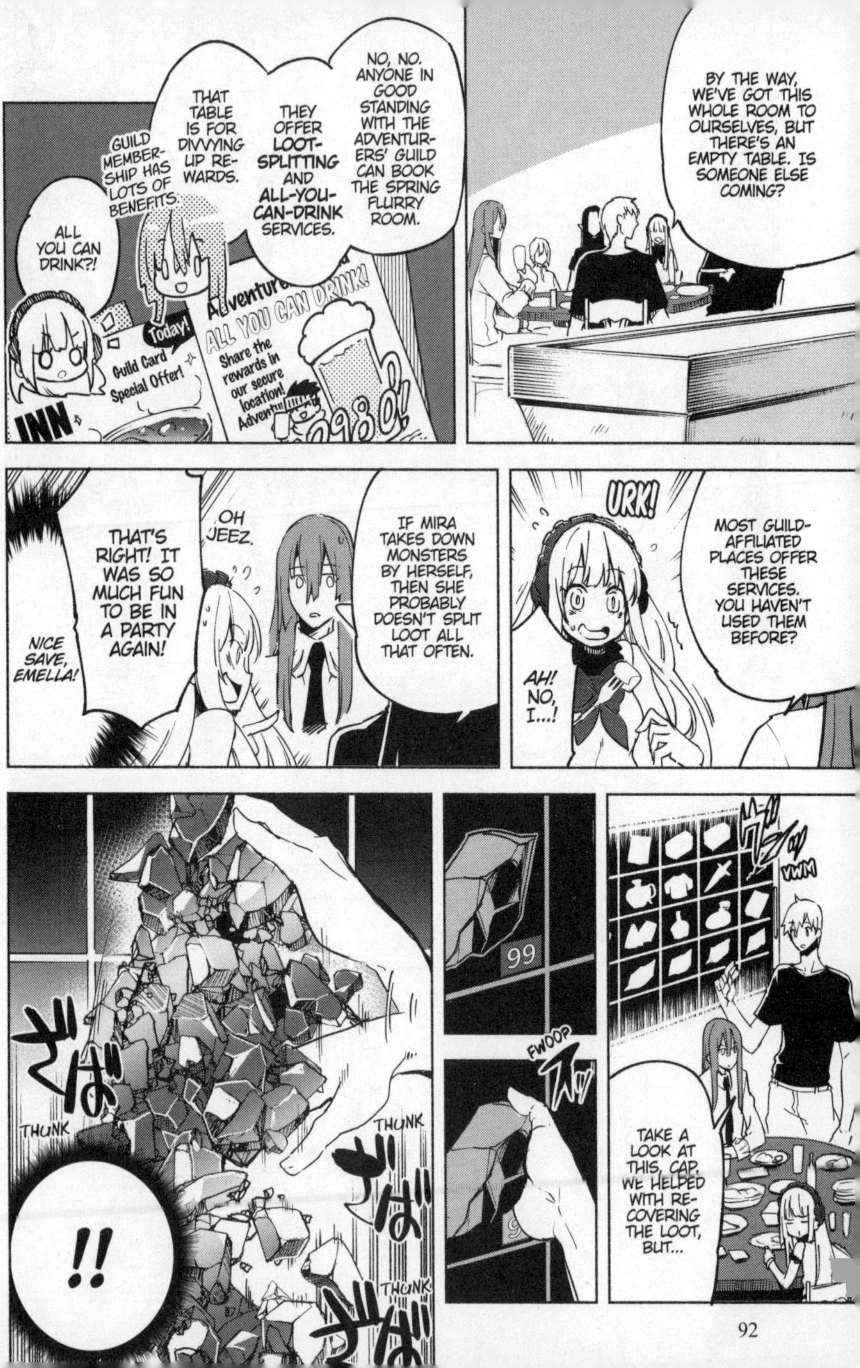

BY THE WAY, WE'VE GOT THIS WHOLE ROOM TO OURSELVES, BUT THERE'S AN EMPTY TABLE. IS SOMEONE ELSE COMING?
NO, NO. ANYONE IN GOOD STANDING WITH THE ADVENTURERS' GUILD CAN BOOK THE SPRING FLURRY ROOM.
THEY OFFER LOOT-SPLITTING AND ALL-YOU-CAN-DRINK SERVICES.
THAT TABLE IS FOR DIVVYING UP REWARDS.
GUILD MEMBERSHIP HAS LOTS OF BENEFITS.
ALL YOU CAN DRINK?!
ALL YOU CAN DRINK!
Today!
Guild Card Special Offer!
Share the rewards in our secure location!
INN
MOST GUILD-AFFILIATED PLACES OFFER THESE SERVICES. YOU HAVEN'T USED THEM BEFORE?
URK!
AH! NO, I...!
IF MIRA TAKES DOWN MONSTERS BY HERSELF, THEN SHE PROBABLY DOESN'T SPLIT LOOT ALL THAT OFTEN.
OH JEEZ.
THAT'S RIGHT! IT WAS SO MUCH FUN TO BE IN A PARTY AGAIN!
NICE SAVE, EMELLA!
VWM
TAKE A LOOK AT THIS, CAP. WE HELPED WITH RECOVERING THE LOOT, BUT...
99
FWOOP
THUNK
THUNK
!!
THUNK

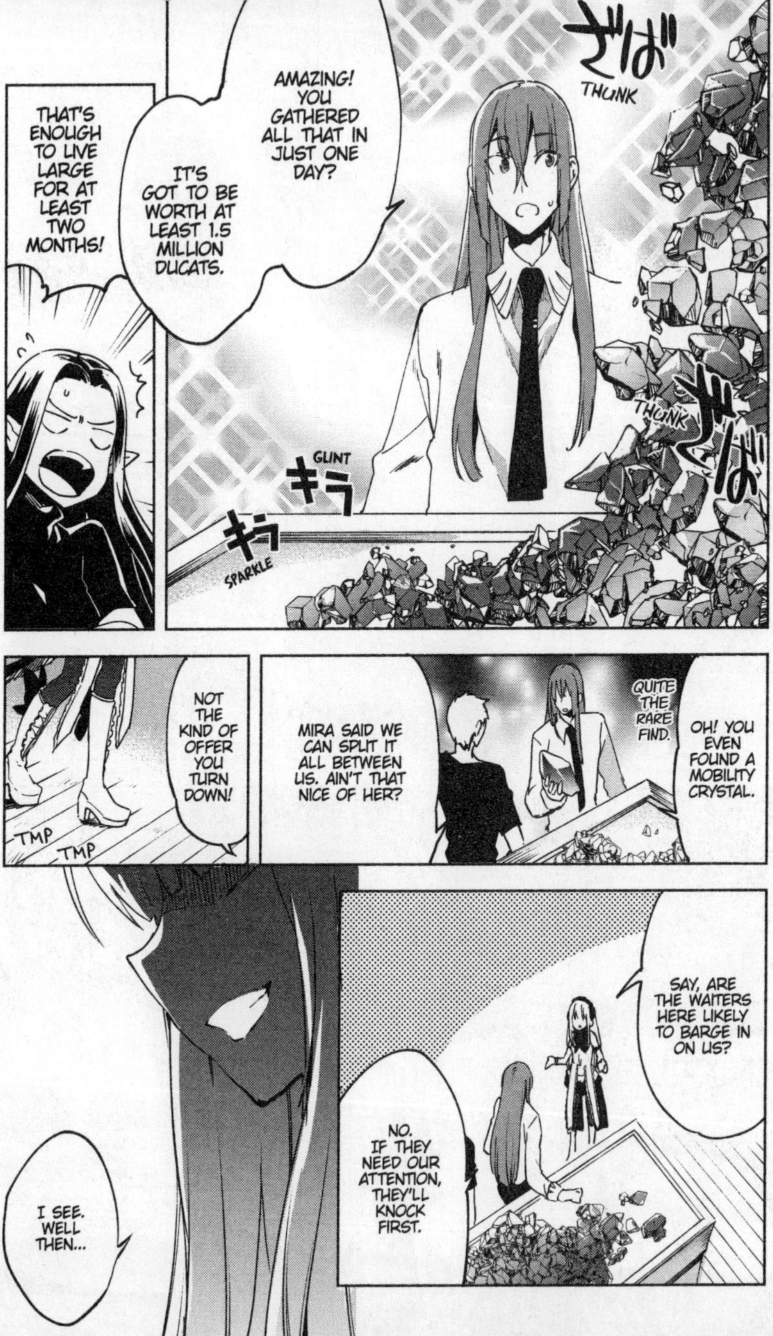
ざば
THUNK
AMAZING! YOU GATHERED ALL THAT IN JUST ONE DAY?
IT'S GOT TO BE WORTH AT LEAST 1.5 MILLION DUCATS.
ざば
THUNK
キラ
GLINT
キラ
SPARKLE
THAT'S ENOUGH TO LIVE LARGE FOR AT LEAST TWO MONTHS!
OH! YOU EVEN FOUND A MOBILITY CRYSTAL.
QUITE THE RARE FIND.
MIRA SAID WE CAN SPLIT IT ALL BETWEEN US. AIN'T THAT NICE OF HER?
NOT THE KIND OF OFFER YOU TURN DOWN!
TMP
TMP
SAY, ARE THE WAITERS HERE LIKELY TO BARGE IN ON US?
NO. IF THEY NEED OUR ATTENTION, THEY'LL KNOCK FIRST.
I SEE. WELL THEN...

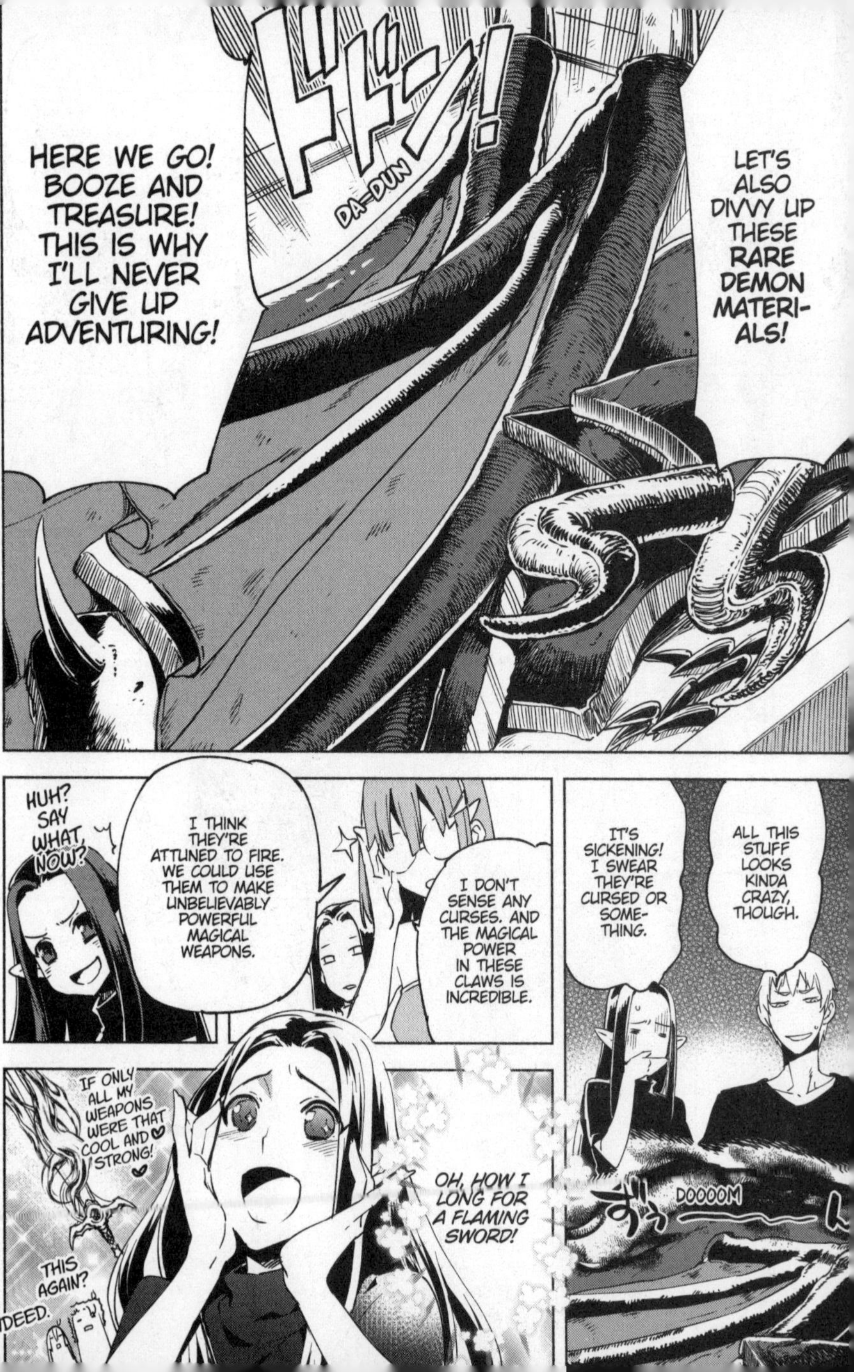
LET'S ALSO DIVVY UP THESE RARE DEMON MATERI-ALS!
DA-DUN
HERE WE GO! BOOZE AND TREASURE! THIS IS WHY I'LL NEVER GIVE UP ADVENTURING!
ALL THIS STUFF LOOKS KINDA CRAZY, THOUGH.
IT'S SICKENING! I SWEAR THEY'RE CURSED OR SOME-THING.
I DON'T SENSE ANY CURSES. AND THE MAGICAL POWER IN THESE CLAWS IS INCREDIBLE.
I THINK THEY'RE ATTUNED TO FIRE. WE COULD USE THEM TO MAKE UNBELIEVABLY POWERFUL MAGICAL WEAPONS.
HUH? SAY WHAT, NOW?
DOOOOM
OH, HOW I LONG FOR A FLAMING SWORD!
IF ONLY ALL MY WEAPONS WERE THAT COOL AND STRONG!
THIS AGAIN?
INDEED.

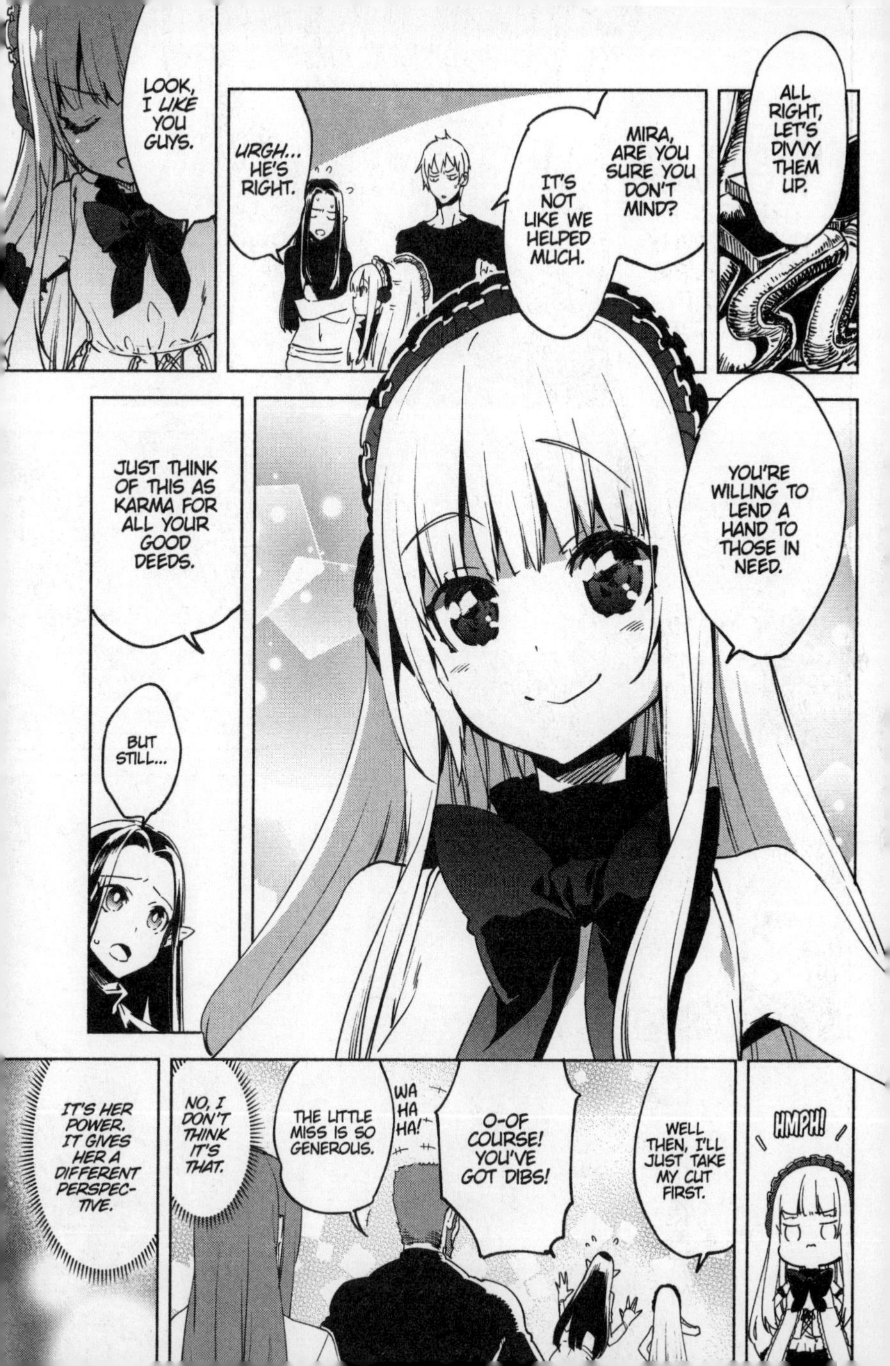

ALL RIGHT, LET'S DIVVY THEM UP.
MIRA, ARE YOU SURE YOU DON'T MIND?
IT'S NOT LIKE WE HELPED MUCH.
URGH... HE'S RIGHT.
LOOK, I LIKE YOU GUYS.
YOU'RE WILLING TO LEND A HAND TO THOSE IN NEED.
JUST THINK OF THIS AS KARMA FOR ALL YOUR GOOD DEEDS.
BUT STILL...
HMPH!
WELL THEN, I'LL JUST TAKE MY CUT FIRST.
O-OF COURSE! YOU'VE GOT DIBS!
WA HA HA!
THE LITTLE MISS IS SO GENEROUS.
NO, I DON'T THINK IT'S THAT.
IT'S HER POWER. IT GIVES HER A DIFFERENT PERSPEC-TIVE.

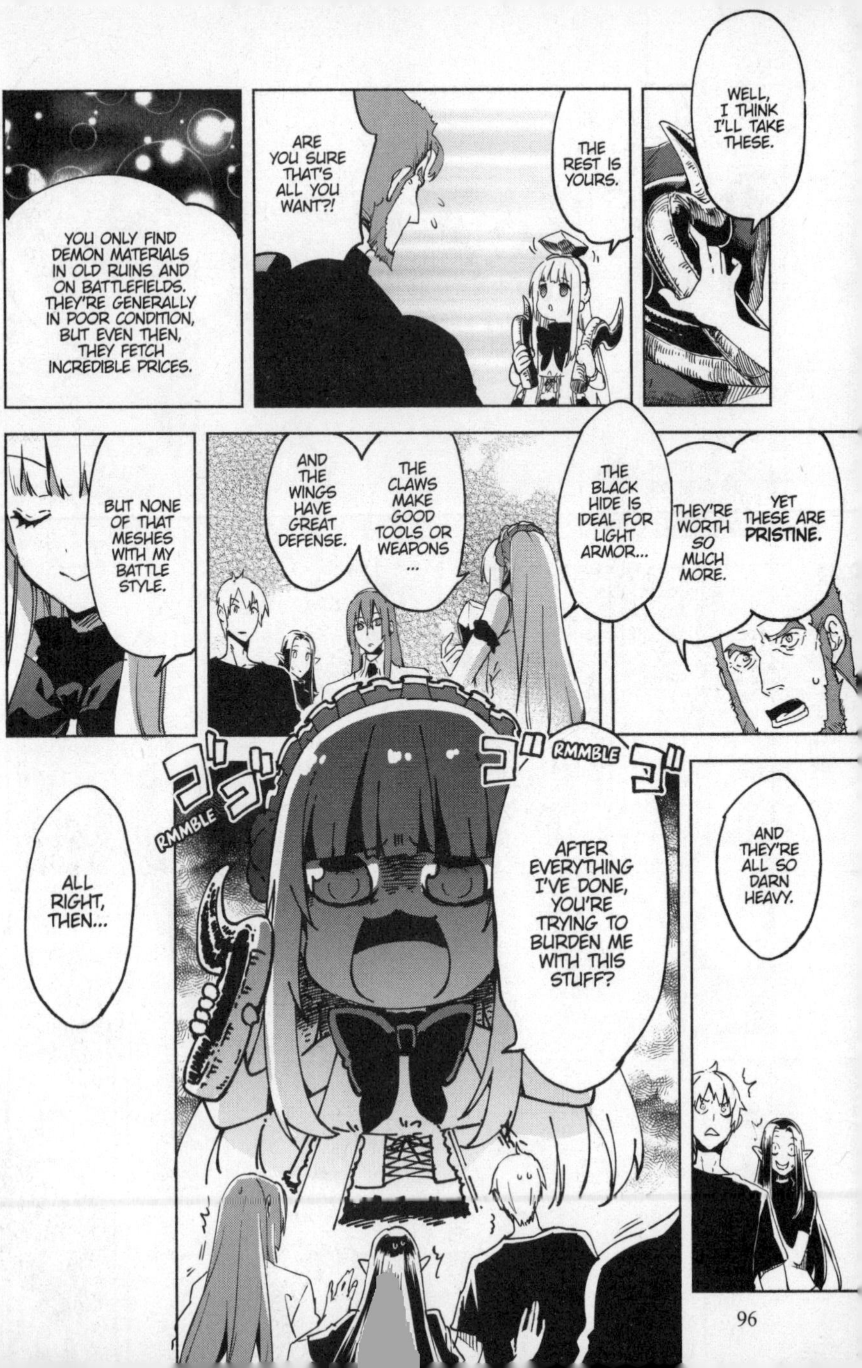
WELL, I THINK I'LL TAKE THESE.
THE REST IS YOURS.
ARE YOU SURE THAT'S ALL YOU WANT?!
YOU ONLY FIND DEMON MATERIALS IN OLD RUINS AND ON BATTLEFIELDS. THEY'RE GENERALLY IN POOR CONDITION, BUT EVEN THEN, THEY FETCH INCREDIBLE PRICES.
YET THESE ARE **PRISTINE.**
THEY'RE WORTH SO MUCH MORE.
THE BLACK HIDE IS IDEAL FOR LIGHT ARMOR...
THE CLAWS MAKE GOOD TOOLS OR WEAPONS...
AND THE WINGS HAVE GREAT DEFENSE.
BUT NONE OF THAT MESHES WITH MY BATTLE STYLE.
AND THEY'RE ALL SO DARN HEAVY.
ゴ RMMBLE ゴ
AFTER EVERYTHING I'VE DONE, YOU'RE TRYING TO BURDEN ME WITH THIS STUFF?
ゴゴ RMMBLE
ALL RIGHT, THEN...

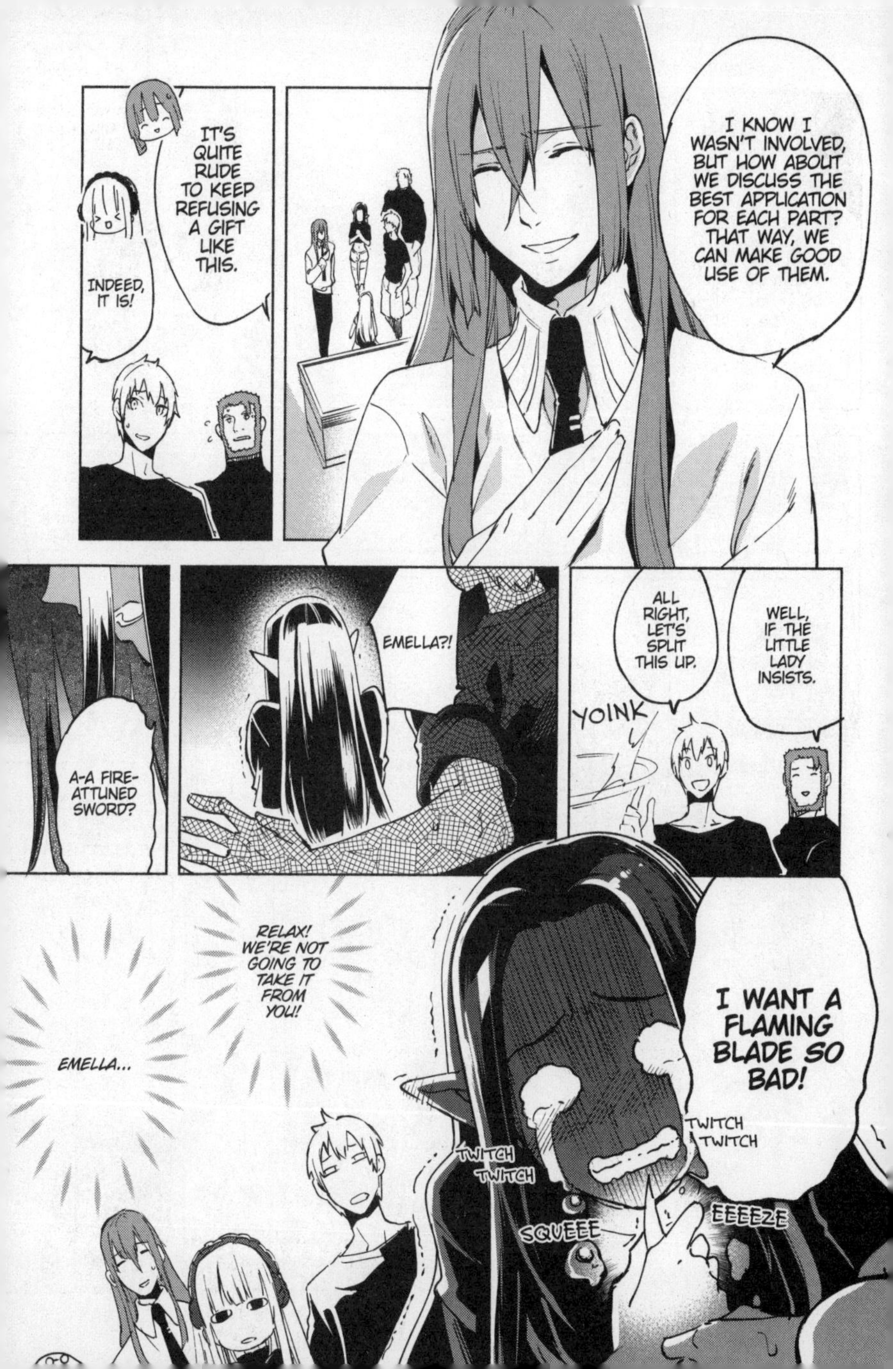
I KNOW I WASN'T INVOLVED, BUT HOW ABOUT WE DISCUSS THE BEST APPLICATION FOR EACH PART? THAT WAY, WE CAN MAKE GOOD USE OF THEM.
IT'S QUITE RUDE TO KEEP REFUSING A GIFT LIKE THIS.
INDEED, IT IS!
WELL, IF THE LITTLE LADY INSISTS.
ALL RIGHT, LET'S SPLIT THIS UP.
YOINK
EMELLA?!
A-A FIRE-ATTUNED SWORD?
I WANT A FLAMING BLADE SO BAD!
TWITCH TWITCH
EEEEZE
SQUEEE
TWITCH TWITCH
RELAX! WE'RE NOT GOING TO TAKE IT FROM YOU!
EMELLA...

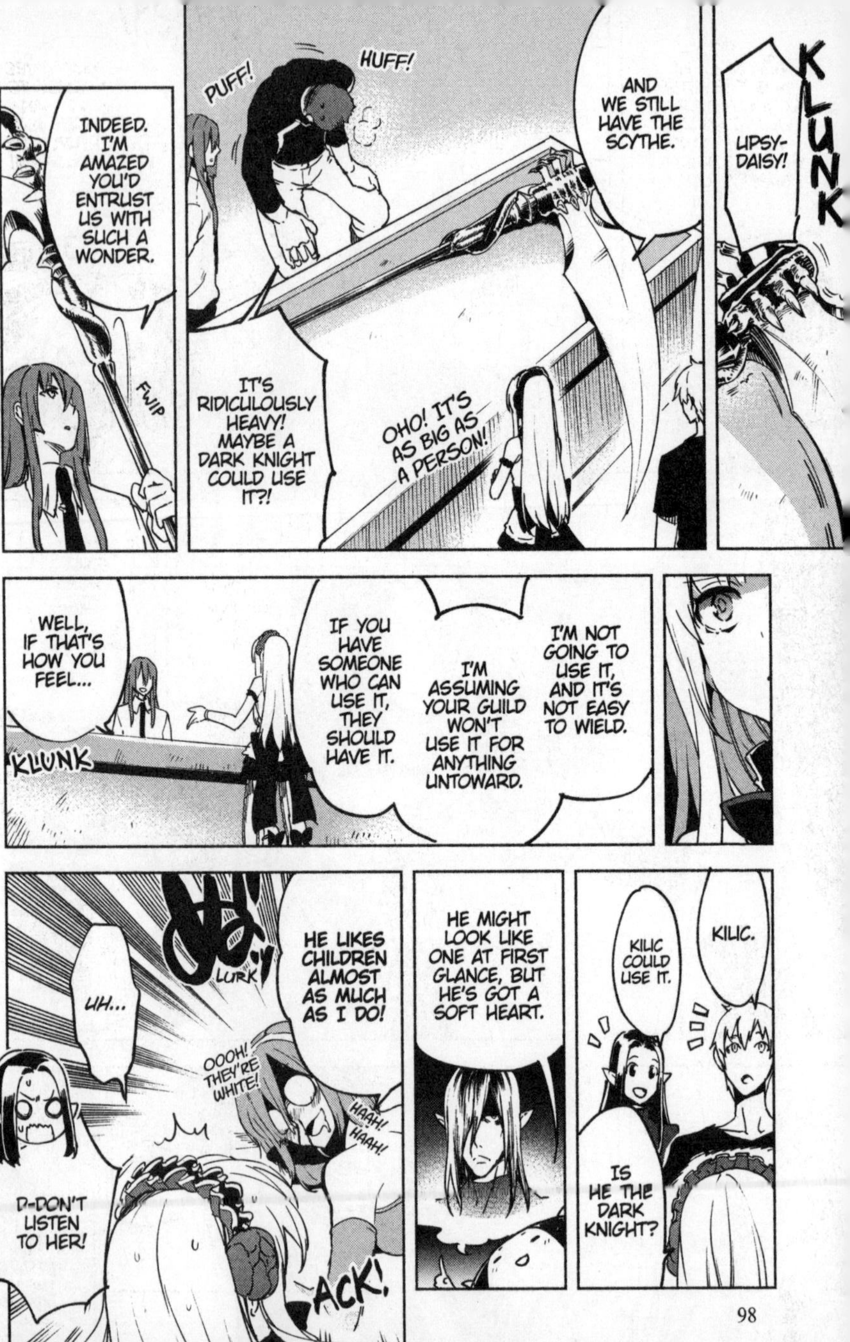
KLUNK
UPSY-DAISY!
AND WE STILL HAVE THE SCYTHE.
OHO! IT'S AS BIG AS A PERSON!
HUFF!
PUFF!
IT'S RIDICULOUSLY HEAVY! MAYBE A DARK KNIGHT COULD USE IT?!
INDEED. I'M AMAZED YOU'D ENTRUST US WITH SUCH A WONDER.
FWIP
I'M NOT GOING TO USE IT, AND IT'S NOT EASY TO WIELD.
I'M ASSUMING YOUR GUILD WON'T USE IT FOR ANYTHING UNTOWARD.
IF YOU HAVE SOMEONE WHO CAN USE IT, THEY SHOULD HAVE IT.
WELL, IF THAT'S HOW YOU FEEL...
KLUNK
KILIC.
KILIC COULD USE IT.
IS HE THE DARK KNIGHT?
HE MIGHT LOOK LIKE ONE AT FIRST GLANCE, BUT HE'S GOT A SOFT HEART.
HE LIKES CHILDREN ALMOST AS MUCH AS I DO!
LURK
OOOH! THEY'RE WHITE!
HAAH! HAAH!
UH...
D-DON'T LISTEN TO HER!
ACK!

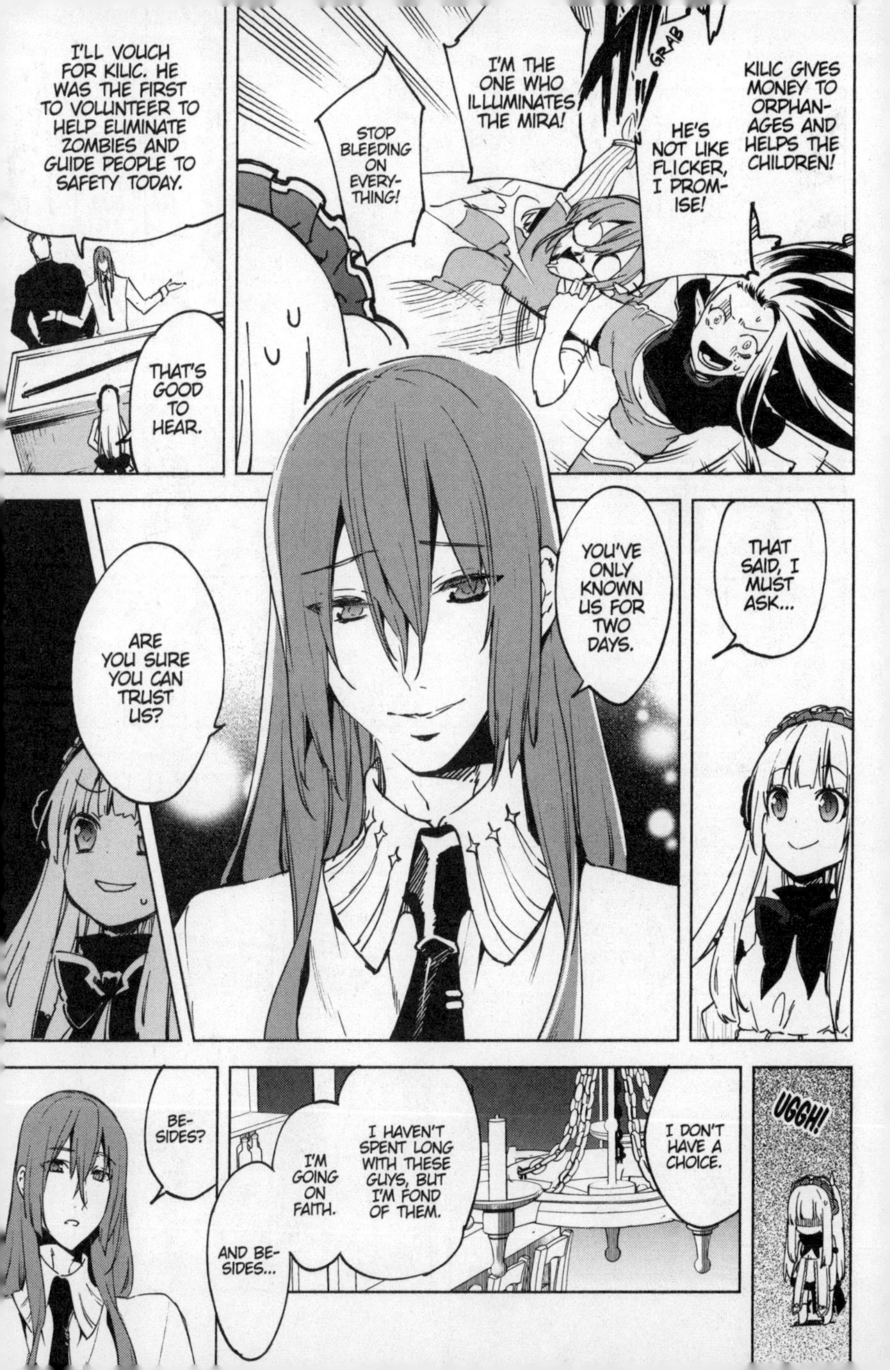

KILIC GIVES MONEY TO ORPHANAGES AND HELPS THE CHILDREN!
HE'S NOT LIKE FLICKER, I PROMISE!
GRAB
I'M THE ONE WHO ILLUMINATES THE MIRA!
STOP BLEEDING ON EVERYTHING!
I'LL VOUCH FOR KILIC. HE WAS THE FIRST TO VOLUNTEER TO HELP ELIMINATE ZOMBIES AND GUIDE PEOPLE TO SAFETY TODAY.
THAT'S GOOD TO HEAR.
THAT SAID, I MUST ASK...
YOU'VE ONLY KNOWN US FOR TWO DAYS.
ARE YOU SURE YOU CAN TRUST US?
UGGH!
I DON'T HAVE A CHOICE.
I HAVEN'T SPENT LONG WITH THESE GUYS, BUT I'M FOND OF THEM.
I'M GOING ON FAITH.
AND BESIDES...
BESIDES?

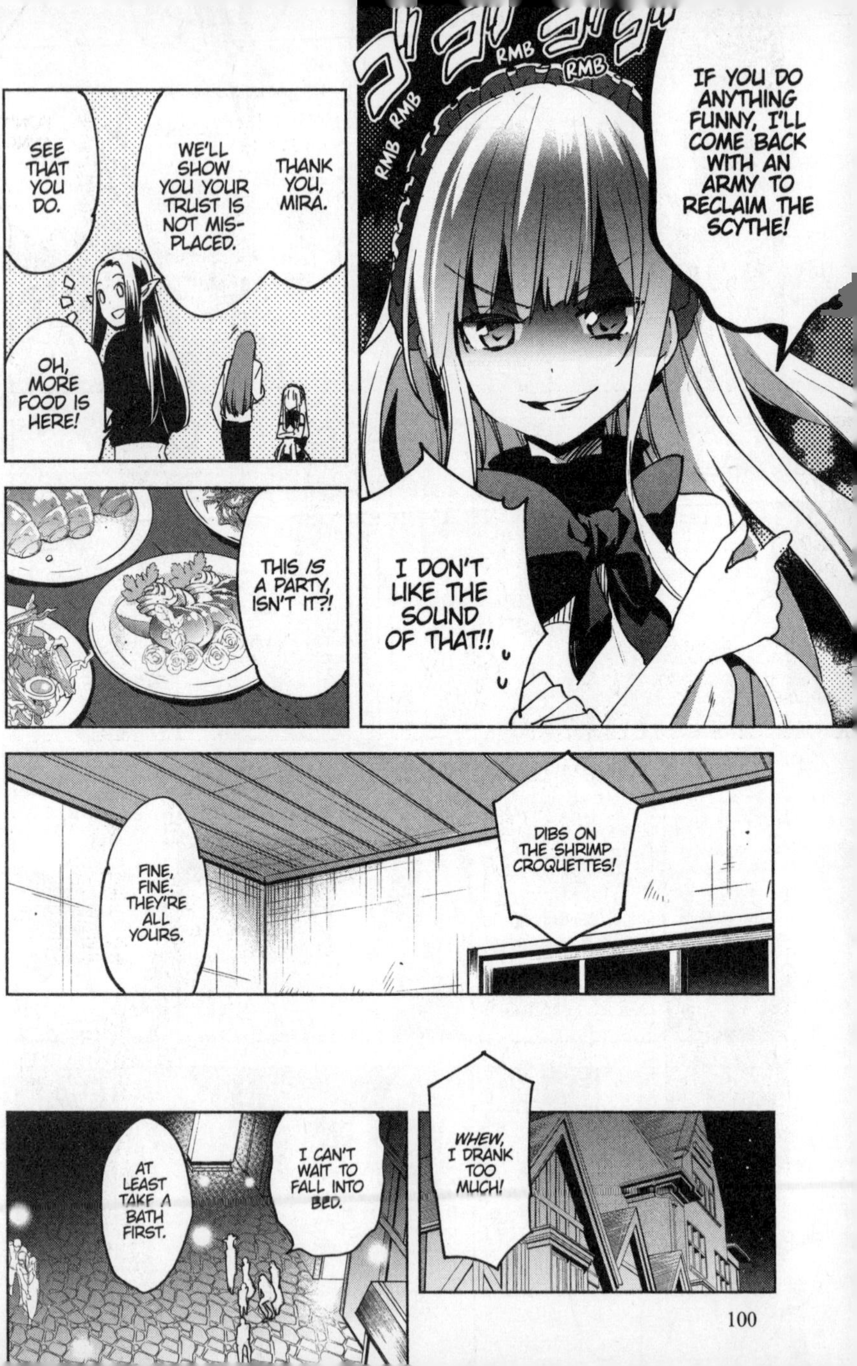
RMB RMB RMB RMB RMB
IF YOU DO ANYTHING FUNNY, I'LL COME BACK WITH AN ARMY TO RECLAIM THE SCYTHE!
I DON'T LIKE THE SOUND OF THAT!!
THANK YOU, MIRA.
WE'LL SHOW YOU YOUR TRUST IS NOT MIS-PLACED.
SEE THAT YOU DO.
OH, MORE FOOD IS HERE!
THIS *IS* A PARTY, ISN'T IT?!
DIBS ON THE SHRIMP CROQUETTES!
FINE, FINE. THEY'RE ALL YOURS.
WHEW, I DRANK TOO MUCH!
I CAN'T WAIT TO FALL INTO BED.
AT LEAST TAKE A BATH FIRST.

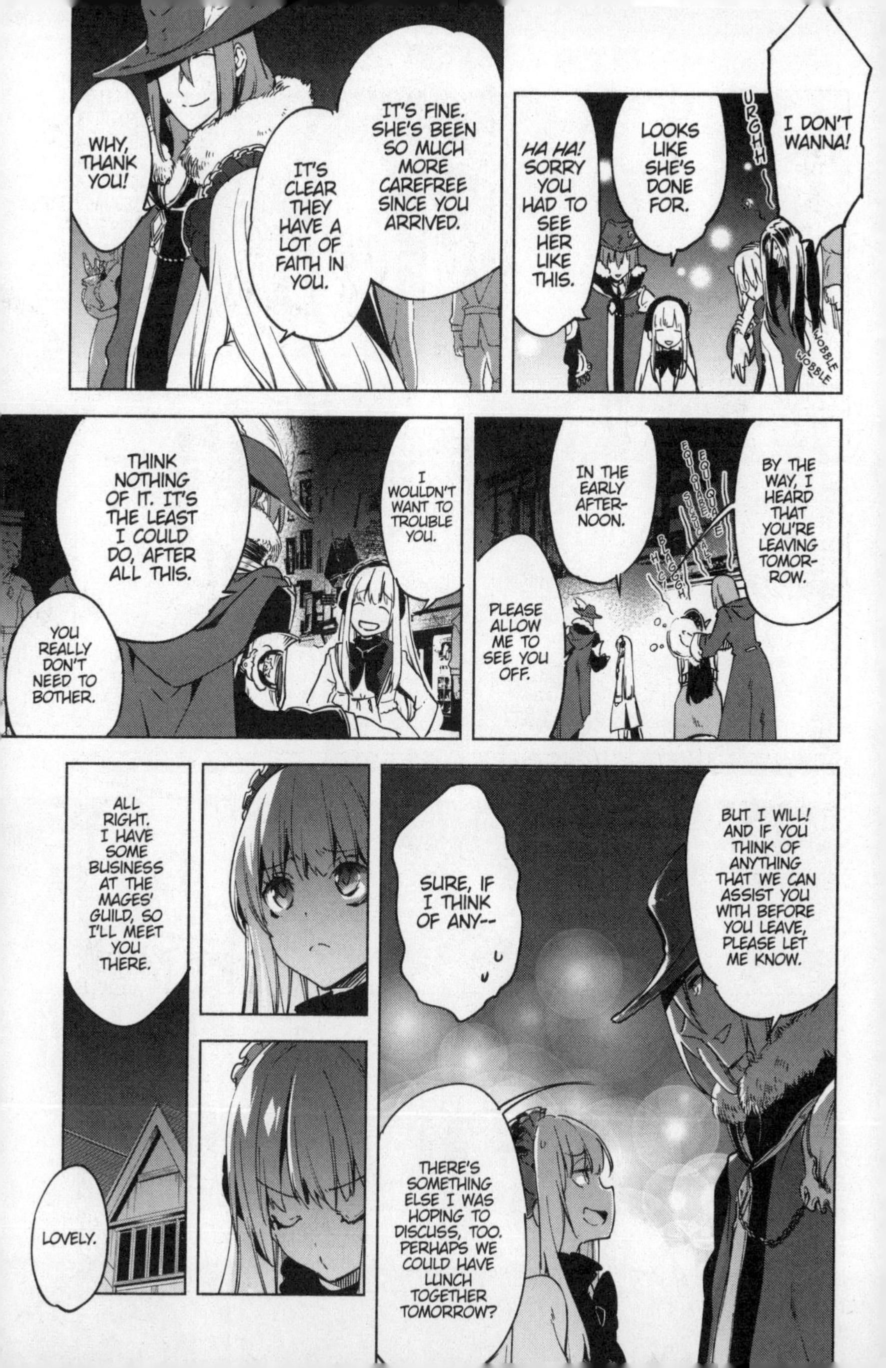
I DON'T WANNA!
URGHH~
LOOKS LIKE SHE'S DONE FOR.
HA HA! SORRY YOU HAD TO SEE HER LIKE THIS.
WOBBLE WOBBLE
IT'S FINE. SHE'S BEEN SO MUCH MORE CAREFREE SINCE YOU ARRIVED.
IT'S CLEAR THEY HAVE A LOT OF FAITH IN YOU.
WHY, THANK YOU!
BY THE WAY, I HEARD THAT YOU'RE LEAVING TOMORROW.
IN THE EARLY AFTER-NOON.
PLEASE ALLOW ME TO SEE YOU OFF.
I WOULDN'T WANT TO TROUBLE YOU.
THINK NOTHING OF IT. IT'S THE LEAST I COULD DO, AFTER ALL THIS.
YOU REALLY DON'T NEED TO BOTHER.
BUT I WILL! AND IF YOU THINK OF ANYTHING THAT WE CAN ASSIST YOU WITH BEFORE YOU LEAVE, PLEASE LET ME KNOW.
SURE, IF I THINK OF ANY--
THERE'S SOMETHING ELSE I WAS HOPING TO DISCUSS, TOO. PERHAPS WE COULD HAVE LUNCH TOGETHER TOMORROW?
ALL RIGHT. I HAVE SOME BUSINESS AT THE MAGES' GUILD, SO I'LL MEET YOU THERE.
LOVELY.

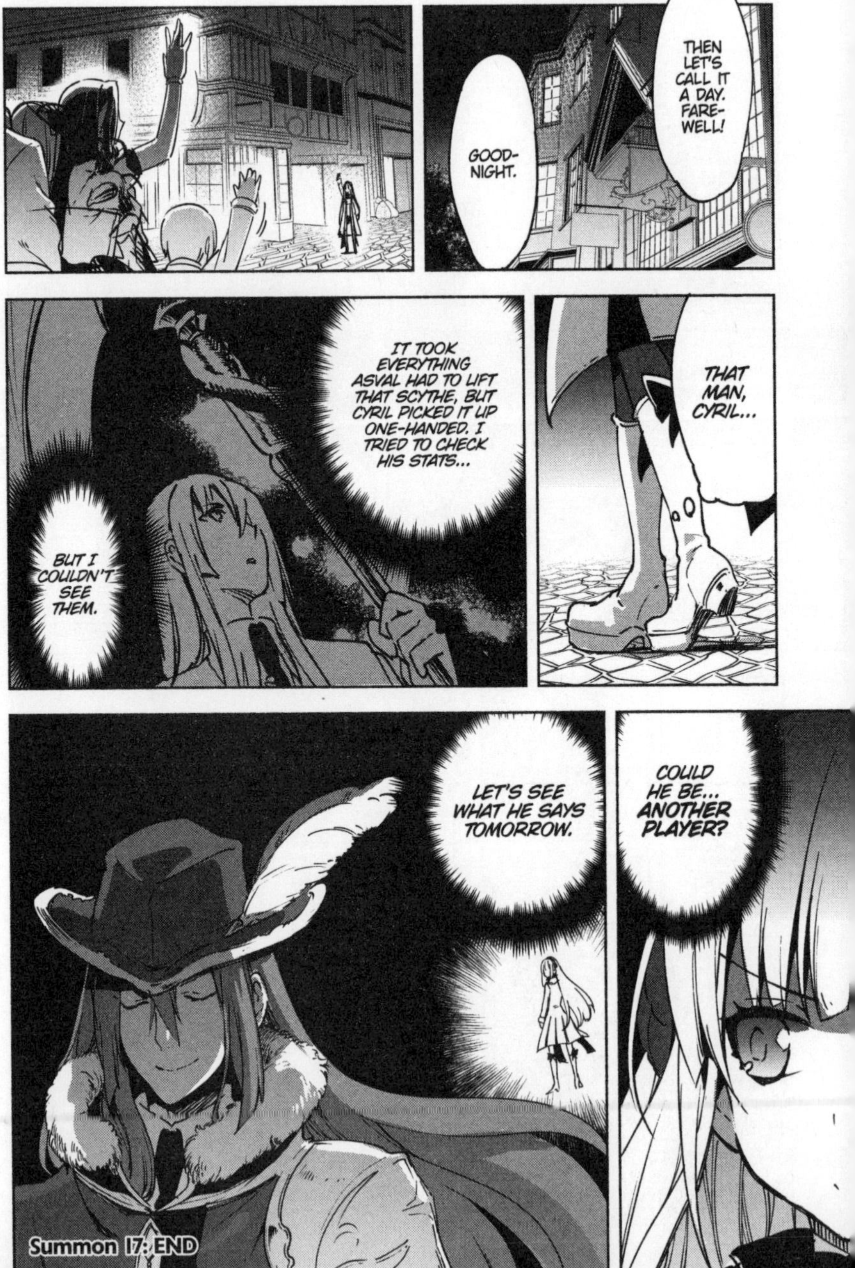
THEN LET'S CALL IT A DAY. FARE-WELL!
GOOD-NIGHT.
THAT MAN, CYRIL...
IT TOOK EVERYTHING ASVAL HAD TO LIFT THAT SCYTHE, BUT CYRIL PICKED IT UP ONE-HANDED. I TRIED TO CHECK HIS STATS...
BUT I COULDN'T SEE THEM.
COULD HE BE... ANOTHER PLAYER?
LET'S SEE WHAT HE SAYS TOMORROW.
Summon 17: END

She
Professed
Herself
Pupil of the
Wise Man

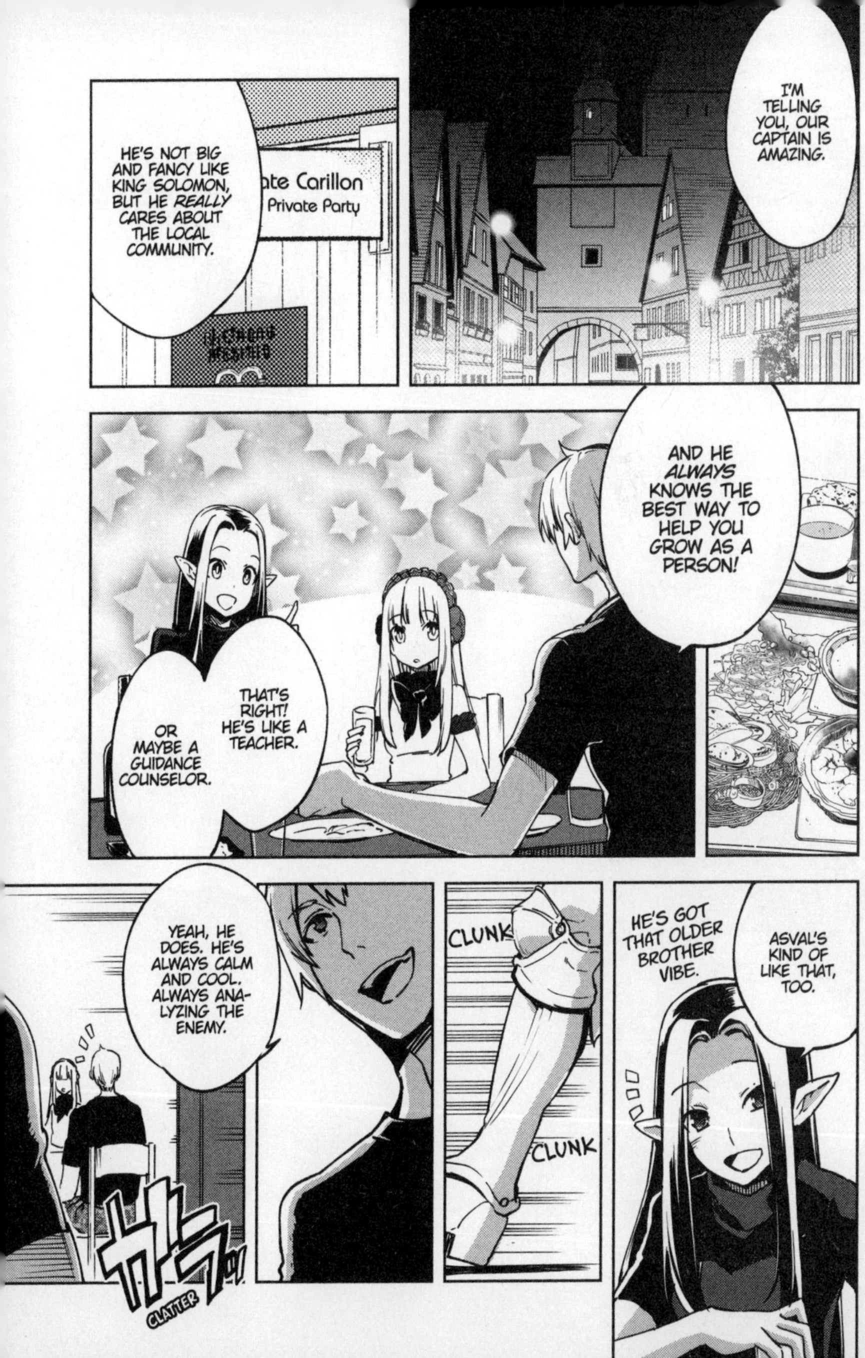
I'M TELLING YOU, OUR CAPTAIN IS AMAZING.
HE'S NOT BIG AND FANCY LIKE KING SOLOMON, BUT HE *REALLY* CARES ABOUT THE LOCAL COMMUNITY.
ate Carillon
Private Party
AND HE *ALWAYS* KNOWS THE BEST WAY TO HELP YOU GROW AS A PERSON!
THAT'S RIGHT! HE'S LIKE A TEACHER.
OR MAYBE A GUIDANCE COUNSELOR.
ASVAL'S KIND OF LIKE THAT, TOO.
HE'S GOT THAT OLDER BROTHER VIBE.
CLUNK
CLUNK
YEAH, HE DOES. HE'S ALWAYS CALM AND COOL. ALWAYS ANALYZING THE ENEMY.
ガラッ
CLATTER

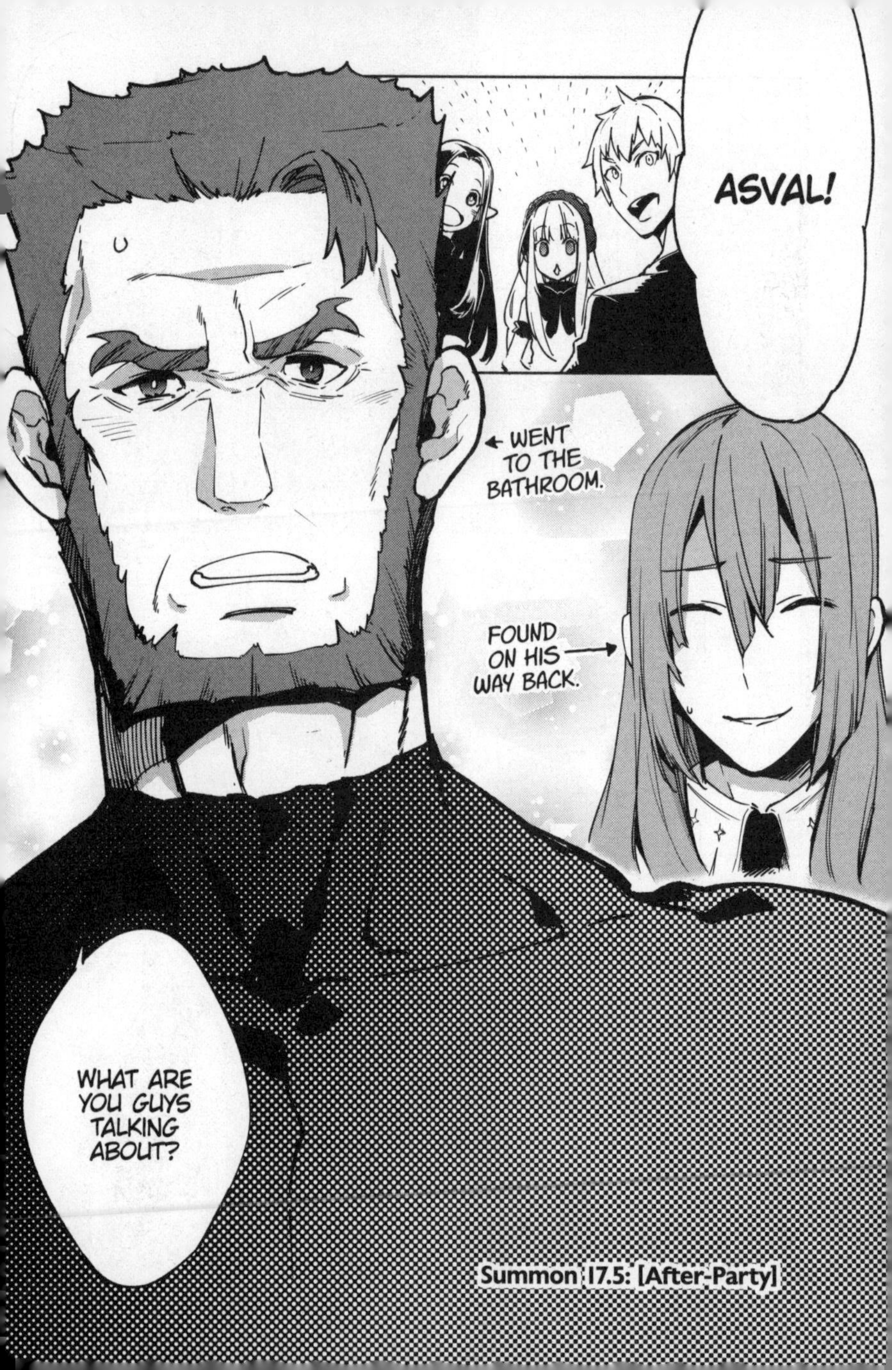
ASVAL!
← WENT TO THE BATHROOM.
FOUND ON HIS WAY BACK. →
WHAT ARE YOU GUYS TALKING ABOUT?

Summon 17.5: [After-Party]

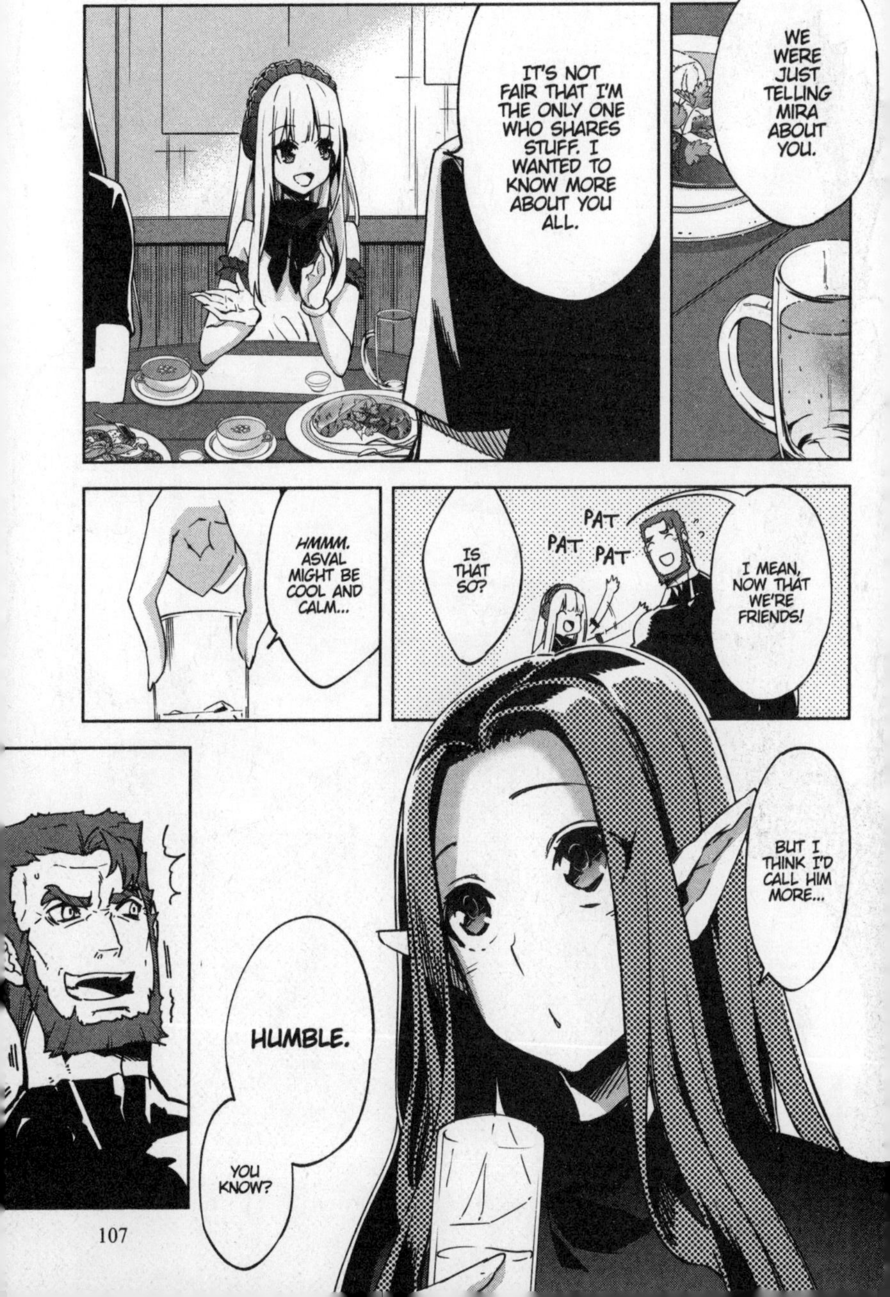
WE WERE JUST TELLING MIRA ABOUT YOU.
IT'S NOT FAIR THAT I'M THE ONLY ONE WHO SHARES STUFF. I WANTED TO KNOW MORE ABOUT YOU ALL.
I MEAN, NOW THAT WE'RE FRIENDS!
PAT PAT PAT
IS THAT SO?
HMMM. ASVAL MIGHT BE COOL AND CALM...
BUT I THINK I'D CALL HIM MORE...
HUMBLE.
YOU KNOW?

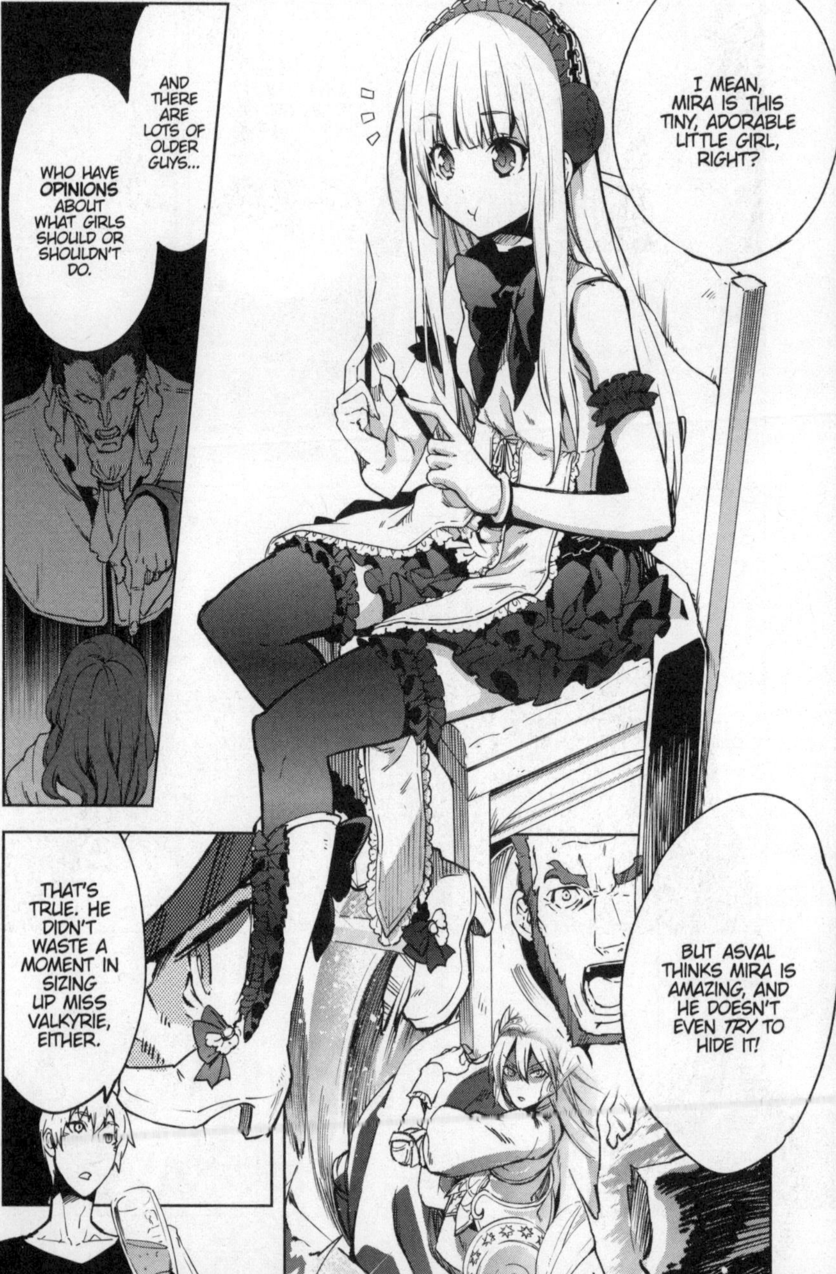
I MEAN, MIRA IS THIS TINY, ADORABLE LITTLE GIRL, RIGHT?
AND THERE ARE LOTS OF OLDER GUYS...
WHO HAVE **OPINIONS** ABOUT WHAT GIRLS SHOULD OR SHOULDN'T DO.
BUT ASVAL THINKS MIRA IS AMAZING, AND HE DOESN'T EVEN *TRY* TO HIDE IT!
THAT'S TRUE. HE DIDN'T WASTE A MOMENT IN SIZING UP MISS VALKYRIE, EITHER.

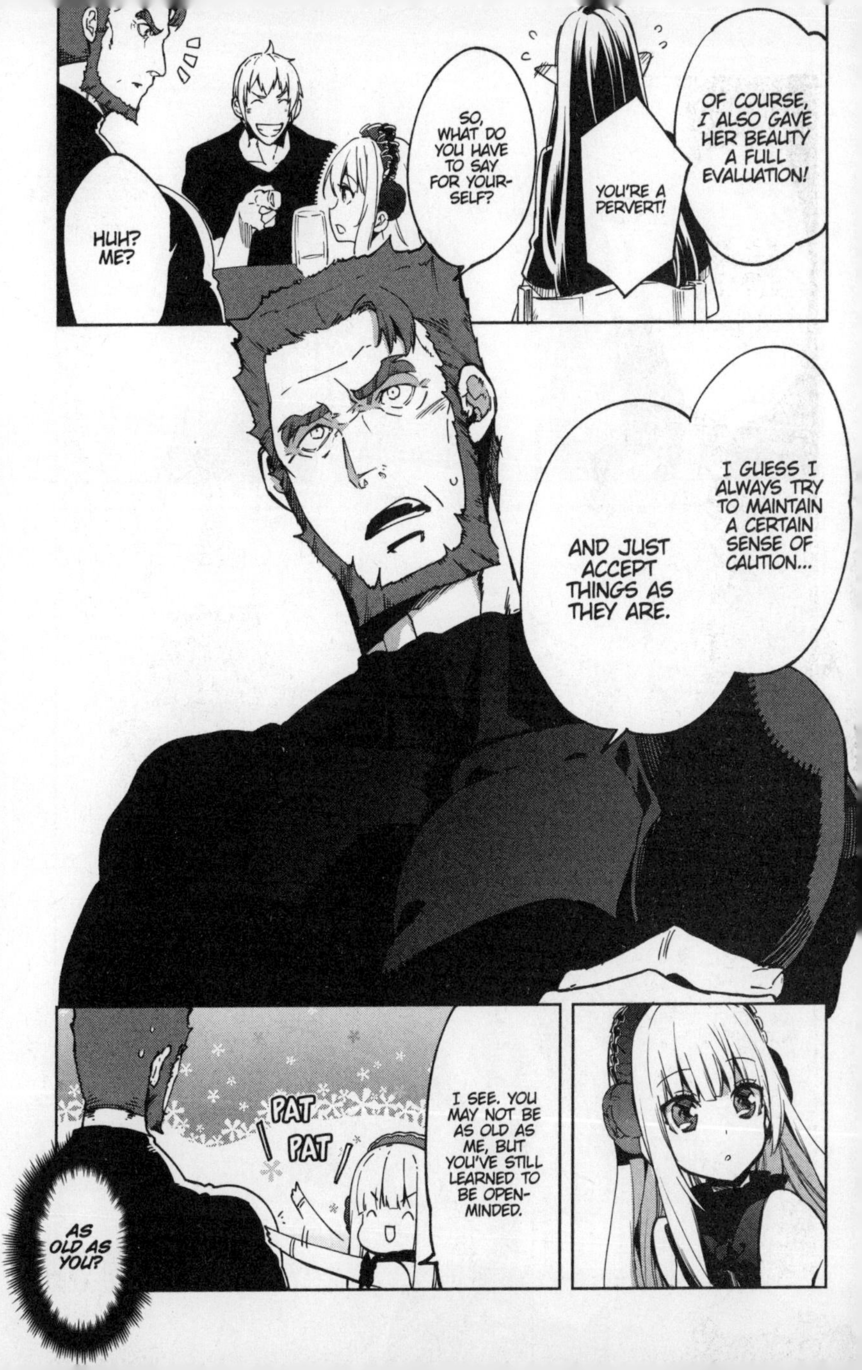
OF COURSE, I ALSO GAVE HER BEAUTY A FULL EVALUATION!
YOU'RE A PERVERT!
SO, WHAT DO YOU HAVE TO SAY FOR YOUR-SELF?
HUH? ME?
I GUESS I ALWAYS TRY TO MAINTAIN A CERTAIN SENSE OF CAUTION...
AND JUST ACCEPT THINGS AS THEY ARE.
I SEE. YOU MAY NOT BE AS OLD AS ME, BUT YOU'VE STILL LEARNED TO BE OPEN-MINDED.
PAT
PAT
AS OLD AS YOU?

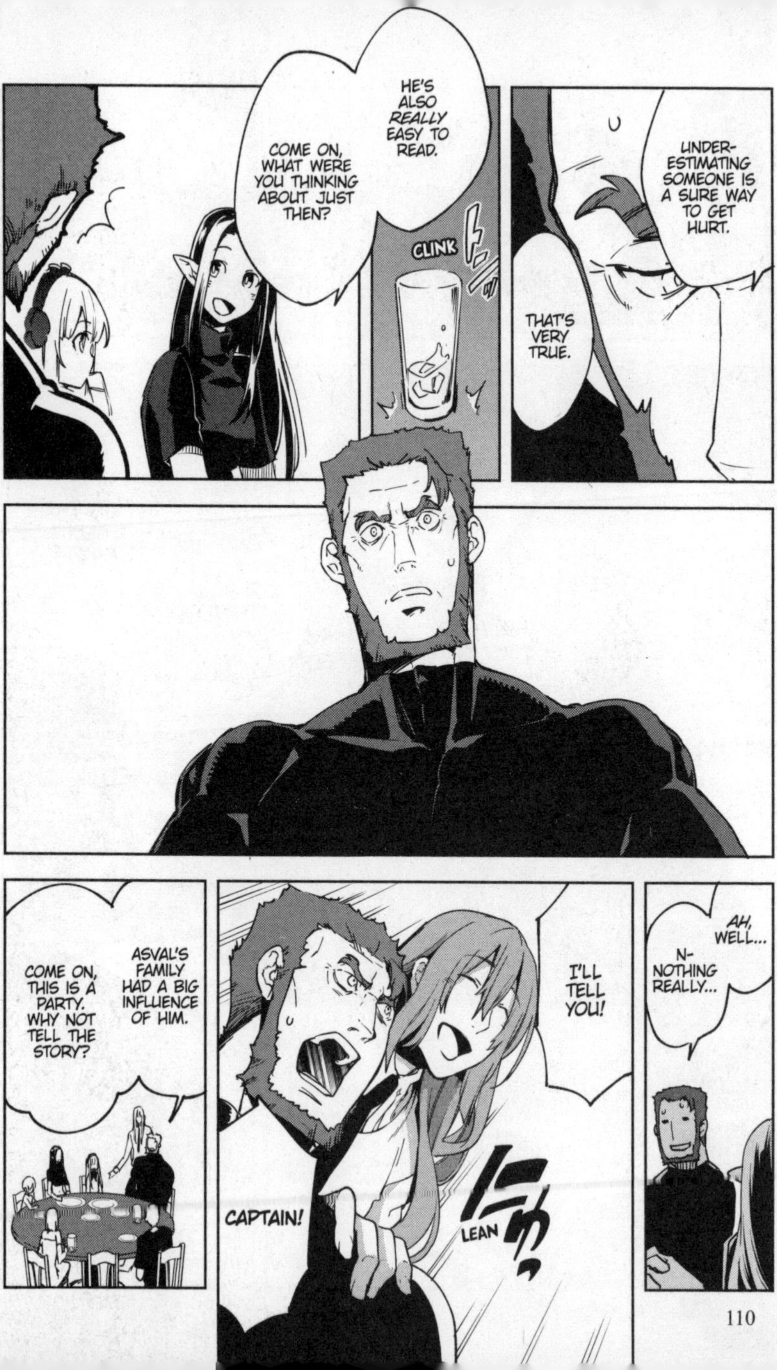
UNDER-ESTIMATING SOMEONE IS A SURE WAY TO GET HURT.
THAT'S VERY TRUE.
HE'S ALSO REALLY EASY TO READ.
COME ON, WHAT WERE YOU THINKING ABOUT JUST THEN?
CLINK
AH, WELL...
N-NOTHING REALLY...
I'LL TELL YOU!
LEAN
CAPTAIN!
ASVAL'S FAMILY HAD A BIG INFLUENCE OF HIM.
COME ON, THIS IS A PARTY. WHY NOT TELL THE STORY?

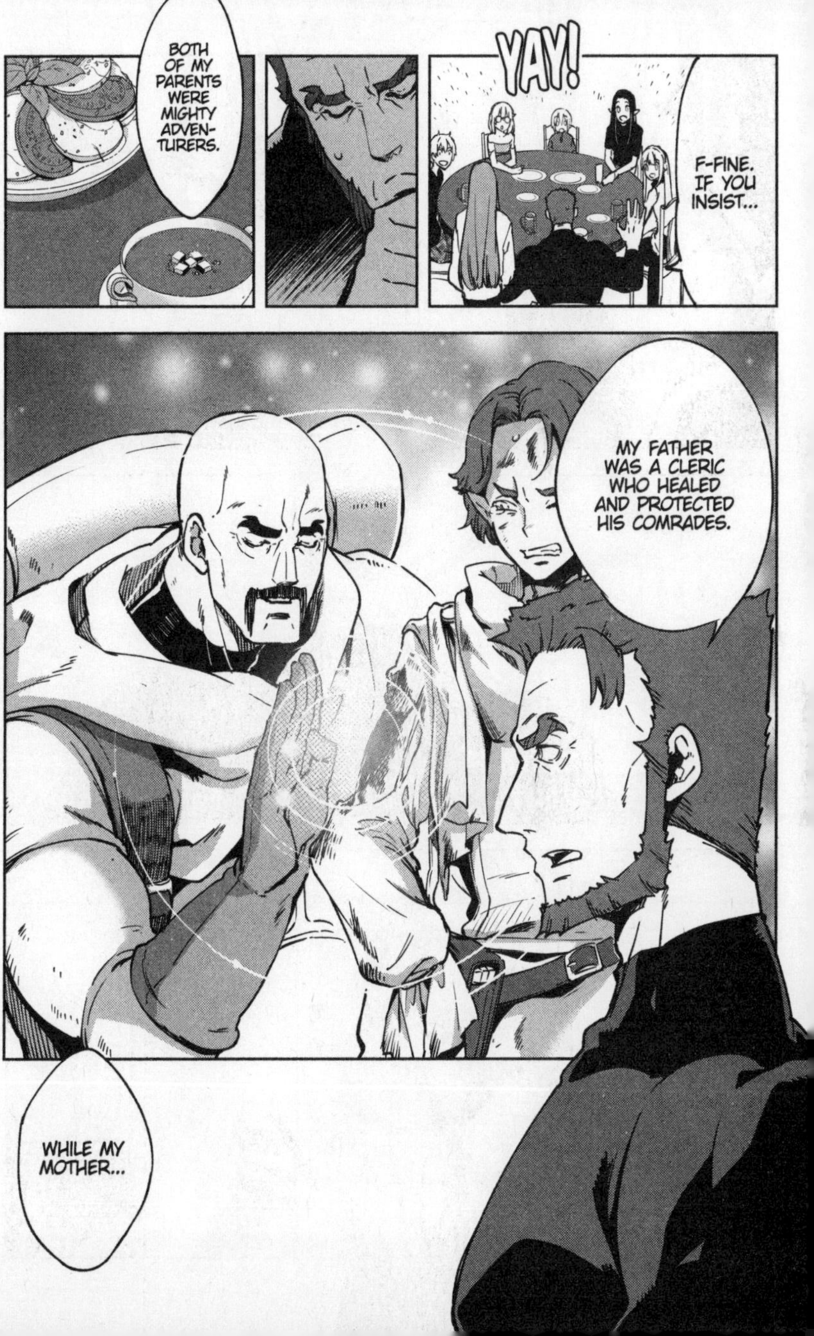
YAY!
F-FINE. IF YOU INSIST...
BOTH OF MY PARENTS WERE MIGHTY ADVEN- TURERS.
MY FATHER WAS A CLERIC WHO HEALED AND PROTECTED HIS COMRADES.
WHILE MY MOTHER...

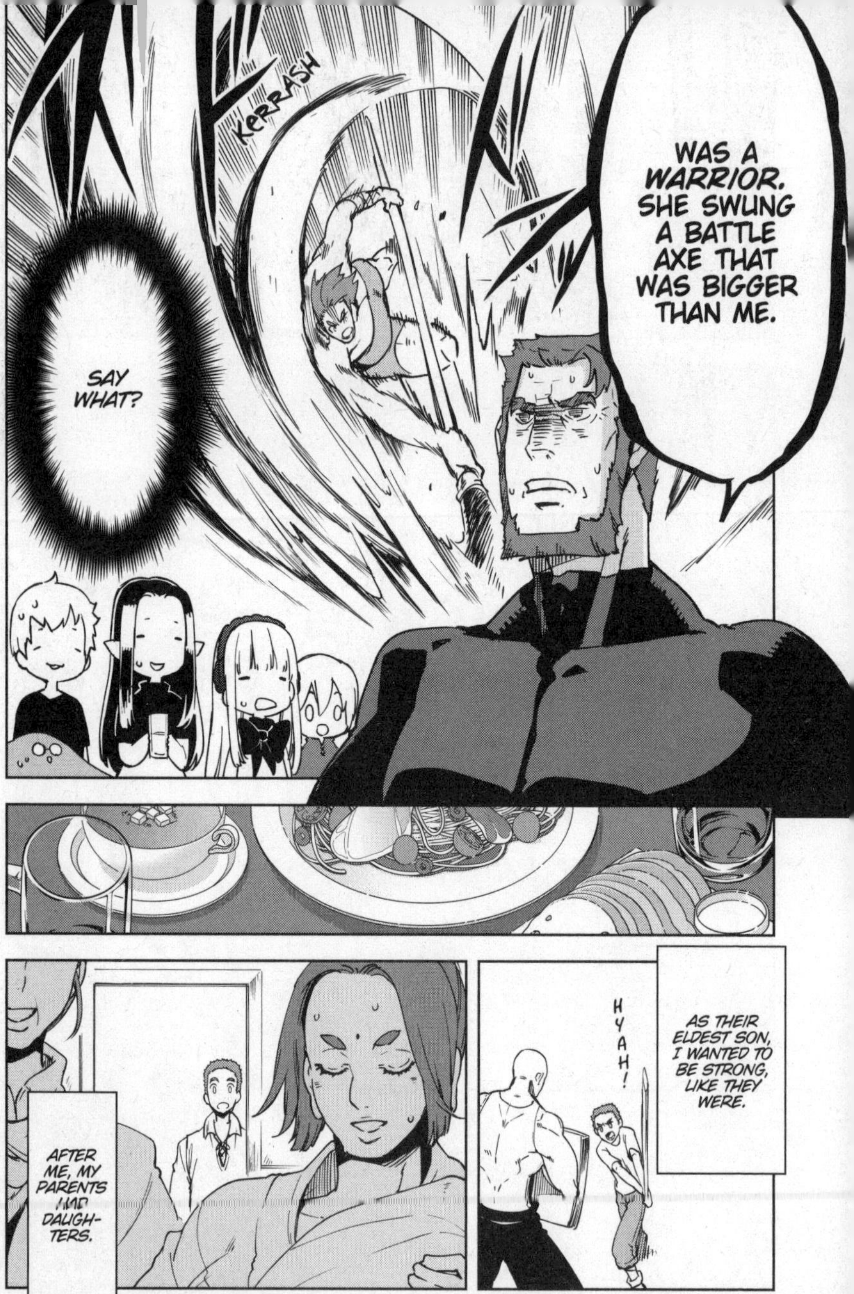
WAS A WARRIOR. SHE SWUNG A BATTLE AXE THAT WAS BIGGER THAN ME.
KERRASH
SAY WHAT?
AS THEIR ELDEST SON, I WANTED TO BE STRONG, LIKE THEY WERE.
HYAH!
AFTER ME, MY PARENTS HAD DAUGHTERS.

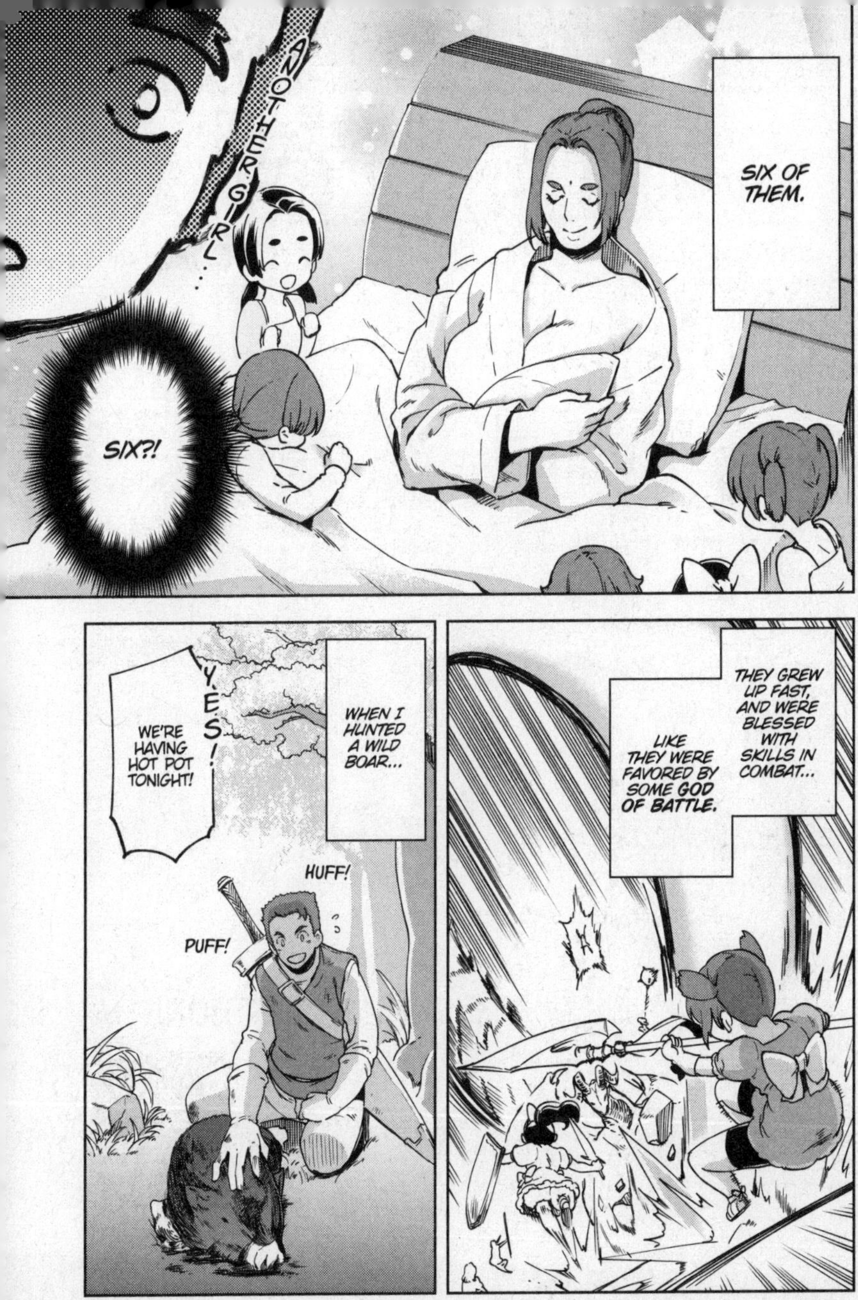
SIX OF THEM.
ANOTHER GIRL...
SIX?!
THEY GREW UP FAST, AND WERE BLESSED WITH SKILLS IN COMBAT...
LIKE THEY WERE FAVORED BY SOME GOD OF BATTLE.
WHEN I HUNTED A WILD BOAR...
YES!
WE'RE HAVING HOT POT TONIGHT!
HUFF!
PUFF!

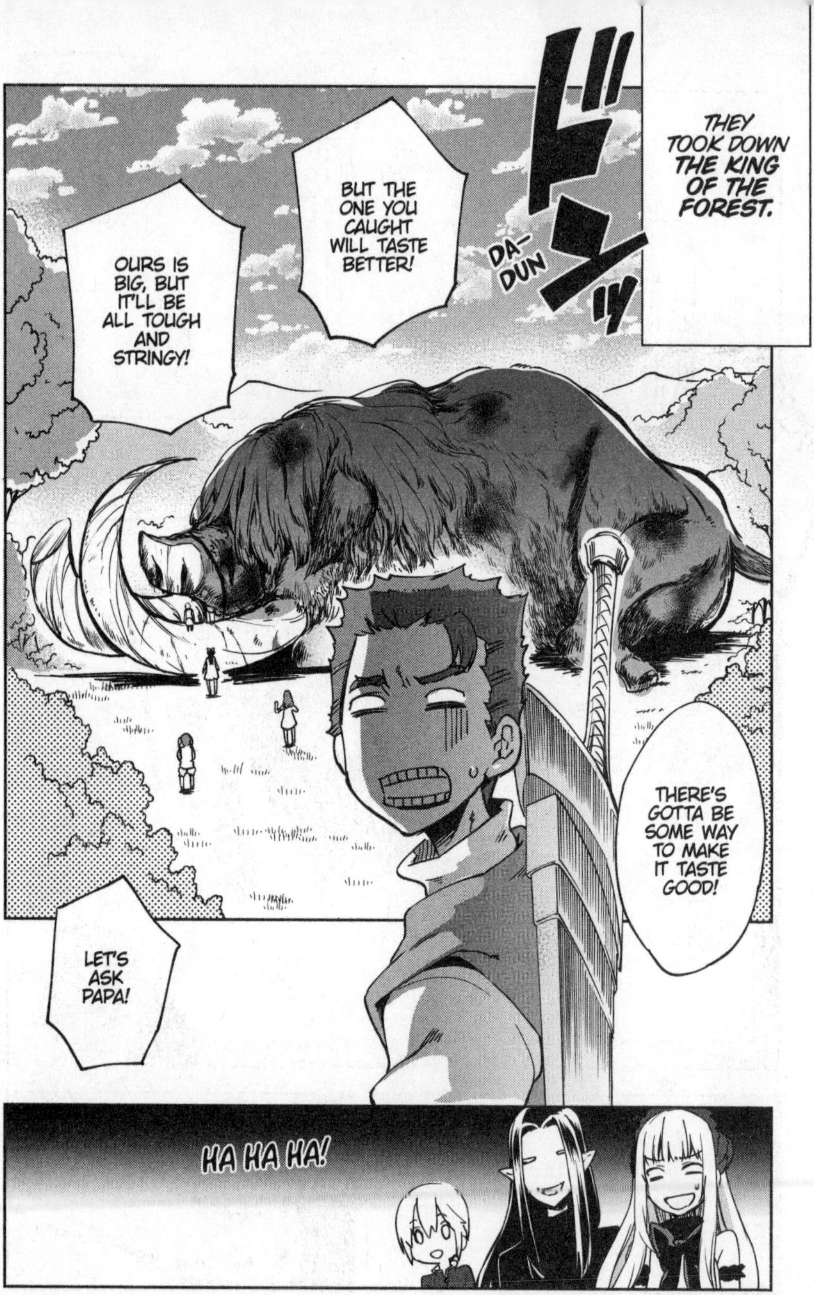
THEY TOOK DOWN THE KING OF THE FOREST.
DA-DUN
BUT THE ONE YOU CAUGHT WILL TASTE BETTER!
OURS IS BIG, BUT IT'LL BE ALL TOUGH AND STRINGY!
THERE'S GOTTA BE SOME WAY TO MAKE IT TASTE GOOD!
LET'S ASK PAPA!
HA HA HA!

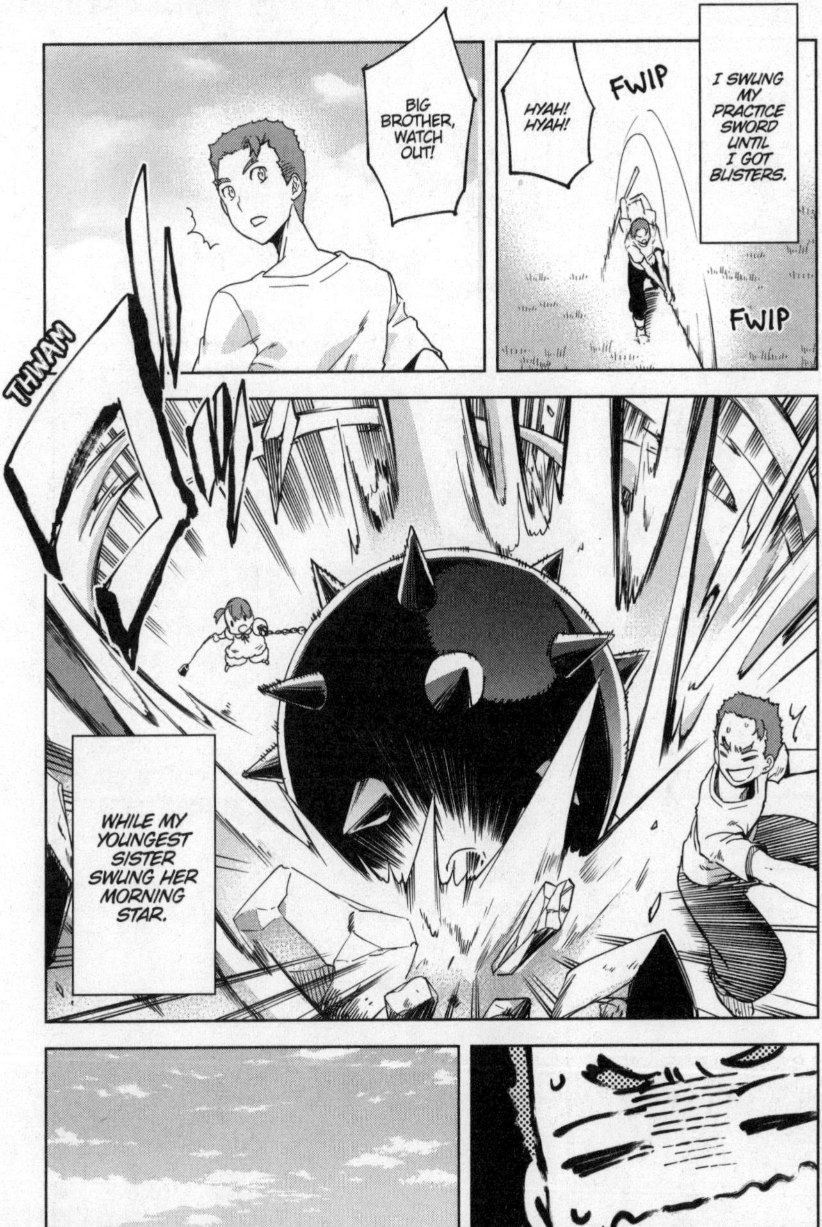
I SWUNG MY PRACTICE SWORD UNTIL I GOT BLISTERS.
FWIP
HYAH! HYAH!
FWIP
BIG BROTHER, WATCH OUT!
THWAM
WHILE MY YOUNGEST SISTER SWUNG HER MORNING STAR.

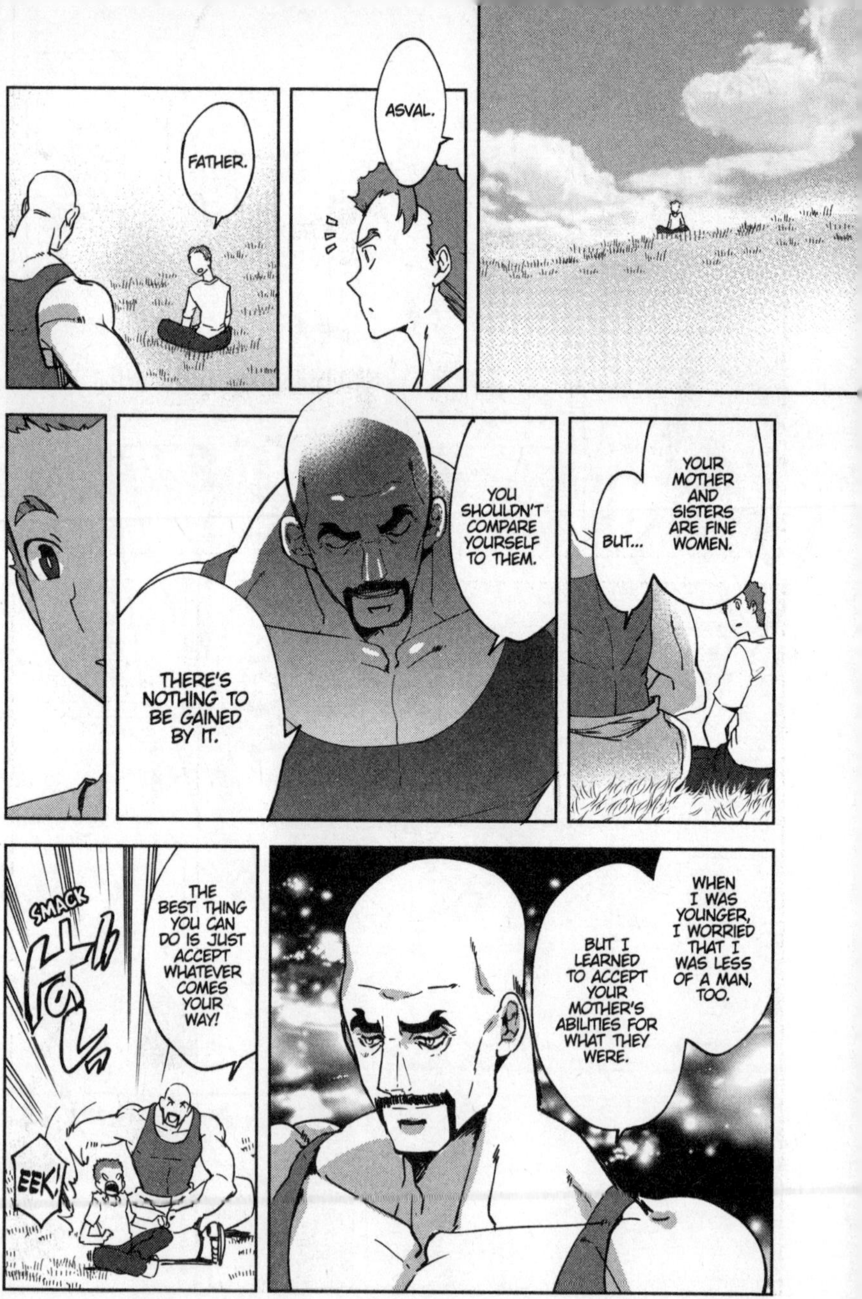

ASVAL.
FATHER.
YOUR MOTHER AND SISTERS ARE FINE WOMEN.
BUT...
YOU SHOULDN'T COMPARE YOURSELF TO THEM.
THERE'S NOTHING TO BE GAINED BY IT.
WHEN I WAS YOUNGER, I WORRIED THAT I WAS LESS OF A MAN, TOO.
BUT I LEARNED TO ACCEPT YOUR MOTHER'S ABILITIES FOR WHAT THEY WERE.
THE BEST THING YOU CAN DO IS JUST ACCEPT WHATEVER COMES YOUR WAY!
SMACK
EEK!

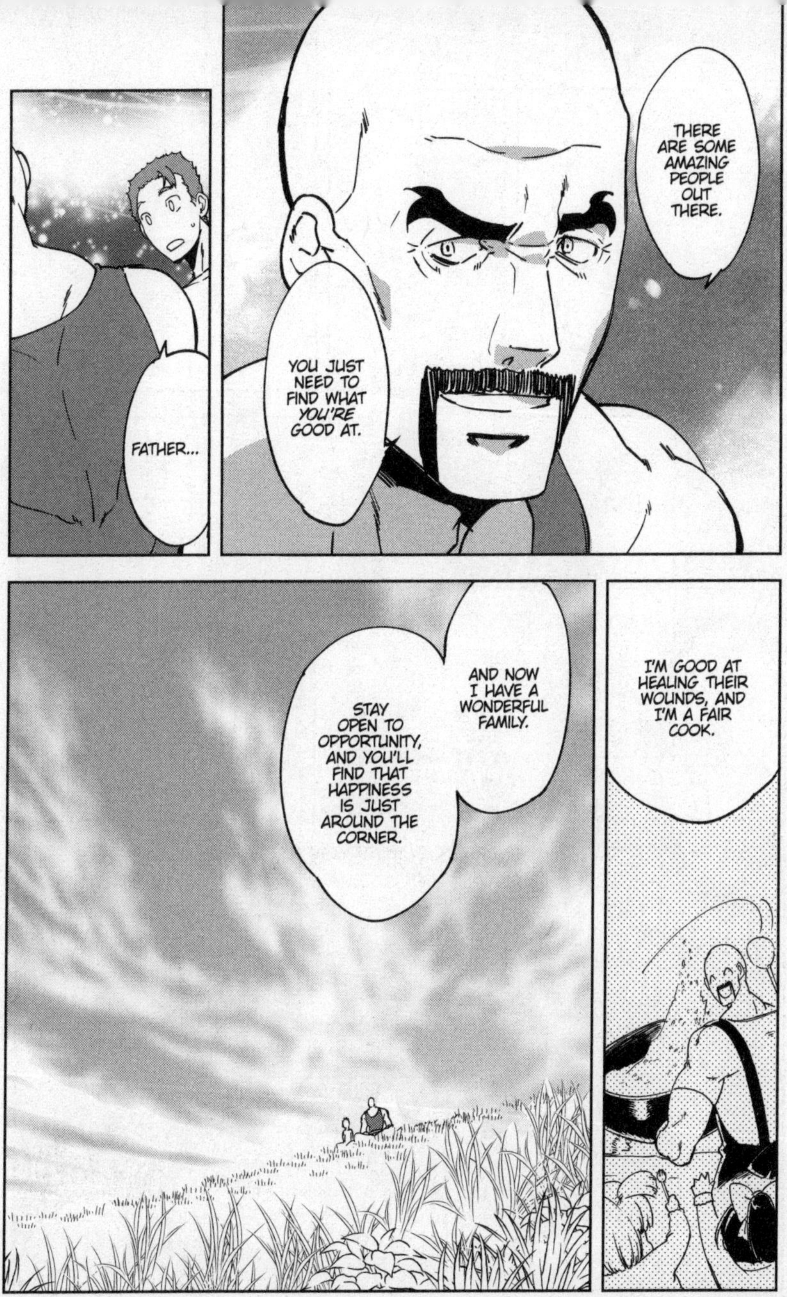
THERE ARE SOME AMAZING PEOPLE OUT THERE.
YOU JUST NEED TO FIND WHAT *YOU'RE* GOOD AT.
FATHER...
I'M GOOD AT HEALING THEIR WOUNDS, AND I'M A FAIR COOK.
AND NOW I HAVE A WONDERFUL FAMILY.
STAY OPEN TO OPPORTUNITY, AND YOU'LL FIND THAT HAPPINESS IS JUST AROUND THE CORNER.

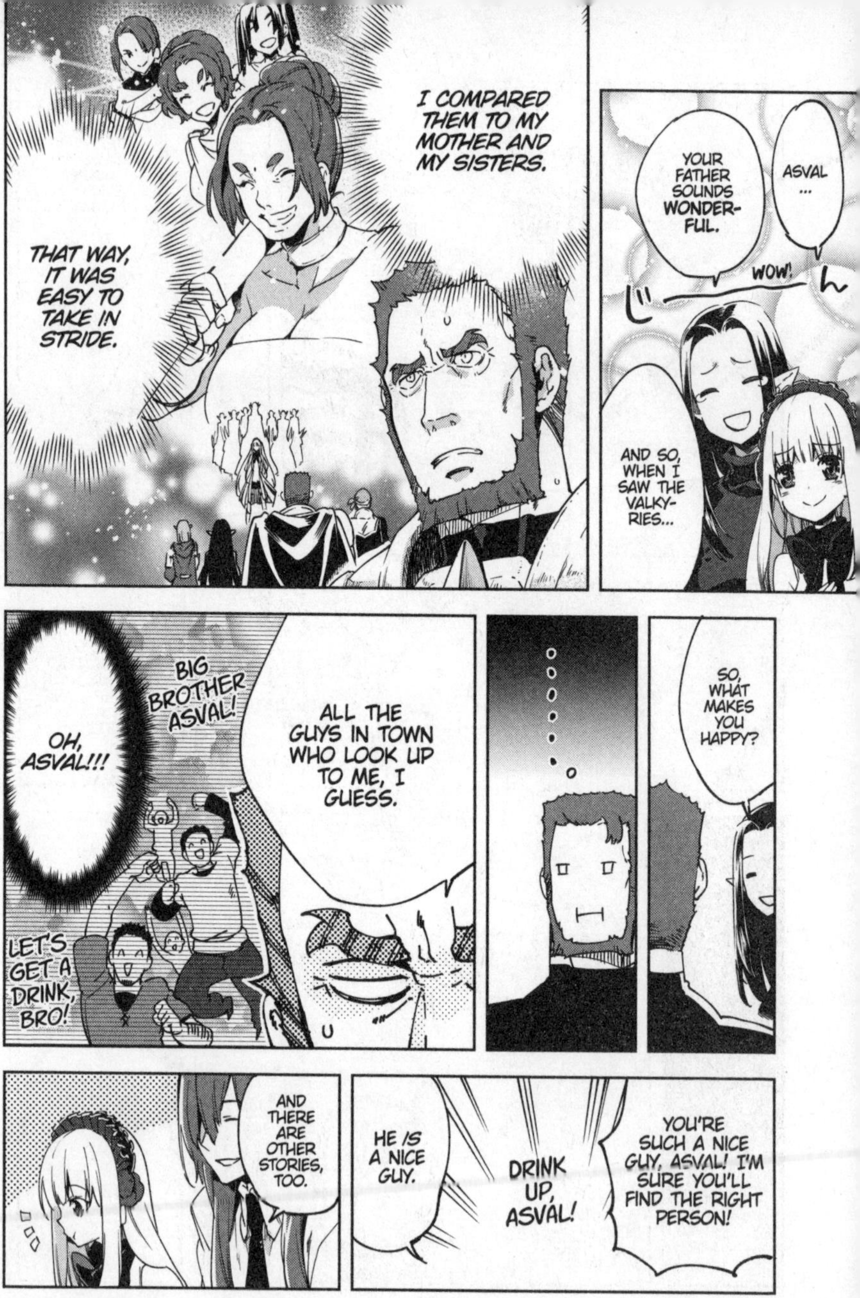
ASVAL ...
YOUR FATHER SOUNDS WONDERFUL.
WOW!
AND SO, WHEN I SAW THE VALKYRIES...
I COMPARED THEM TO MY MOTHER AND MY SISTERS.
THAT WAY, IT WAS EASY TO TAKE IN STRIDE.
SO, WHAT MAKES YOU HAPPY?
......
ALL THE GUYS IN TOWN WHO LOOK UP TO ME, I GUESS.
BIG BROTHER ASVAL!
OH, ASVAL!!!
LET'S GET A DRINK, BRO!
YOU'RE SUCH A NICE GUY, ASVAL! I'M SURE YOU'LL FIND THE RIGHT PERSON!
DRINK UP, ASVAL!
HE IS A NICE GUY.
AND THERE ARE OTHER STORIES, TOO.

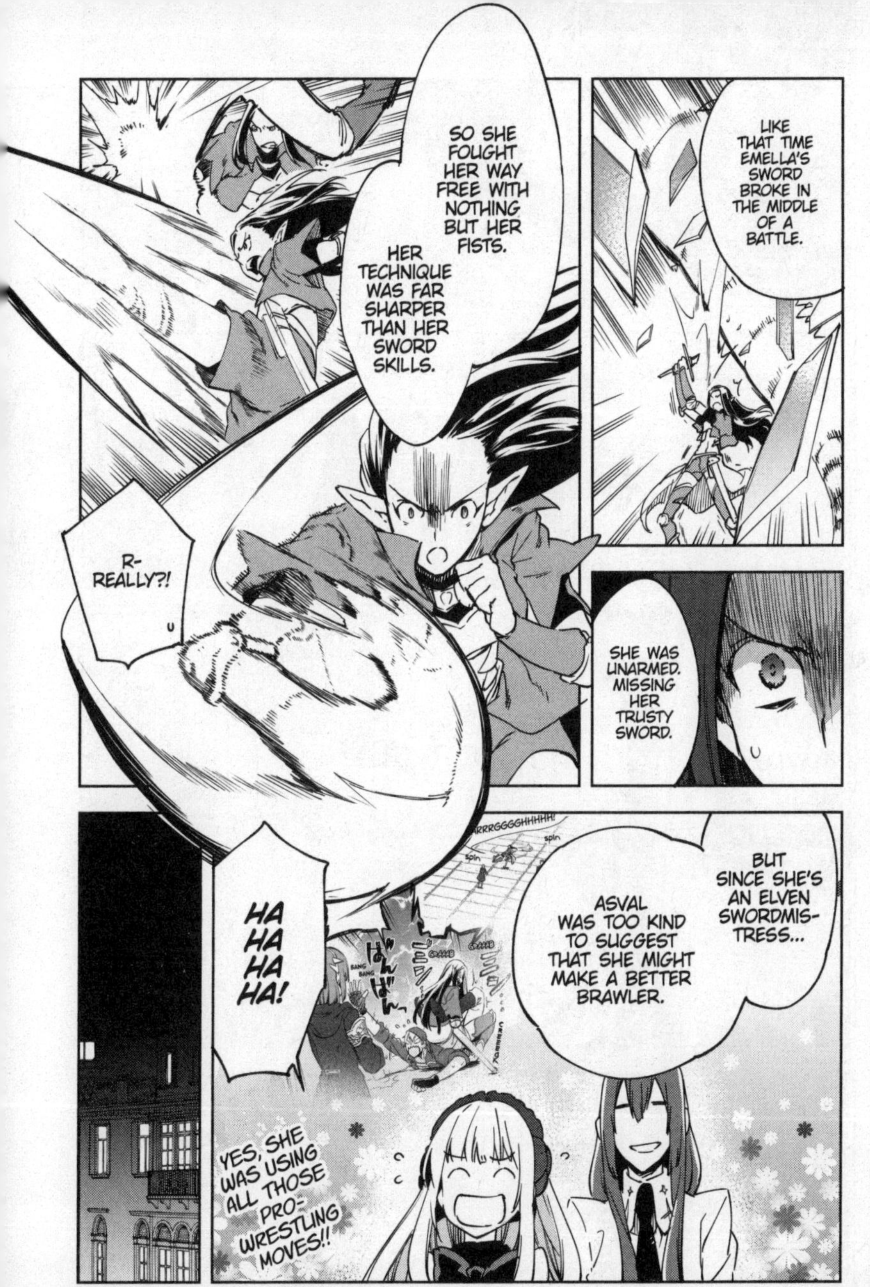
LIKE THAT TIME EMELLA'S SWORD BROKE IN THE MIDDLE OF A BATTLE.
SO SHE FOUGHT HER WAY FREE WITH NOTHING BUT HER FISTS.
HER TECHNIQUE WAS FAR SHARPER THAN HER SWORD SKILLS.
SHE WAS UNARMED. MISSING HER TRUSTY SWORD.
R-REALLY?!
BUT SINCE SHE'S AN ELVEN SWORDMIS-TRESS...
ASVAL WAS TOO KIND TO SUGGEST THAT SHE MIGHT MAKE A BETTER BRAWLER.
spin
spin
HA HA HA HA!
YES, SHE WAS USING ALL THOSE PRO-WRESTLING MOVES!!

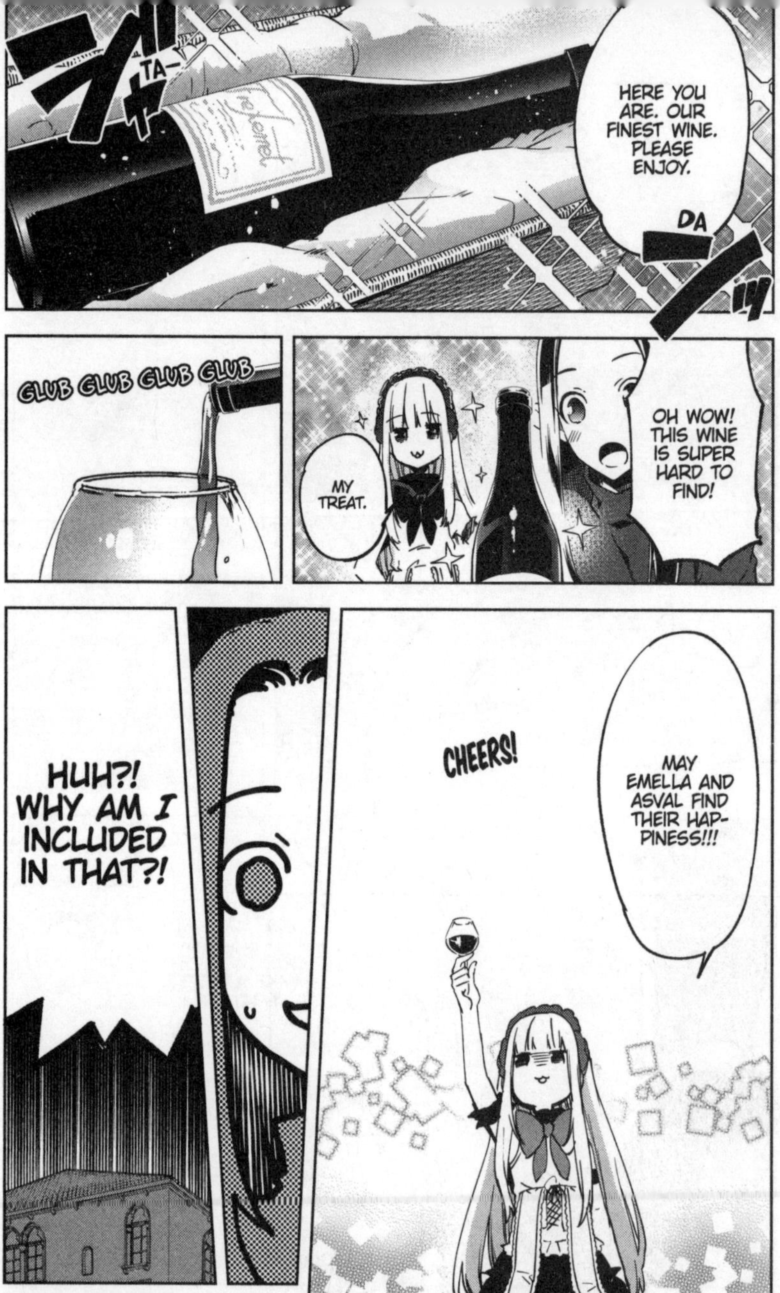
HERE YOU ARE. OUR FINEST WINE. PLEASE ENJOY.
TA—
DA—
OH WOW! THIS WINE IS SUPER HARD TO FIND!
MY TREAT.
GLUB GLUB GLUB GLUB
MAY EMELLA AND ASVAL FIND THEIR HAP-PINESS!!!
CHEERS!
HUH?! WHY AM I INCLUDED IN THAT?!

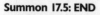

Summon 17.5: END

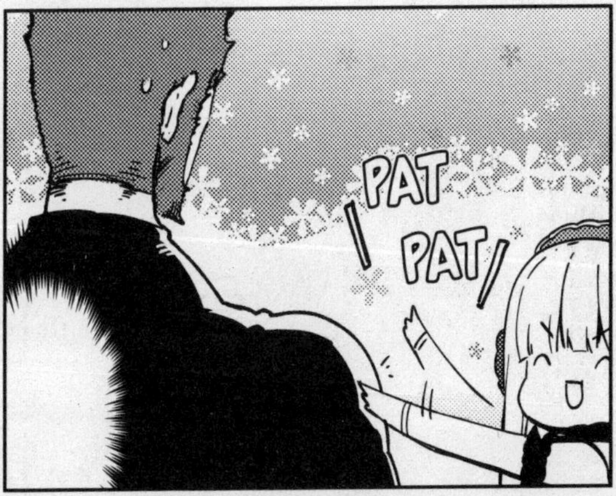
PAT
PAT

She
Professed
Herself
Pupil of
the
Wise Man

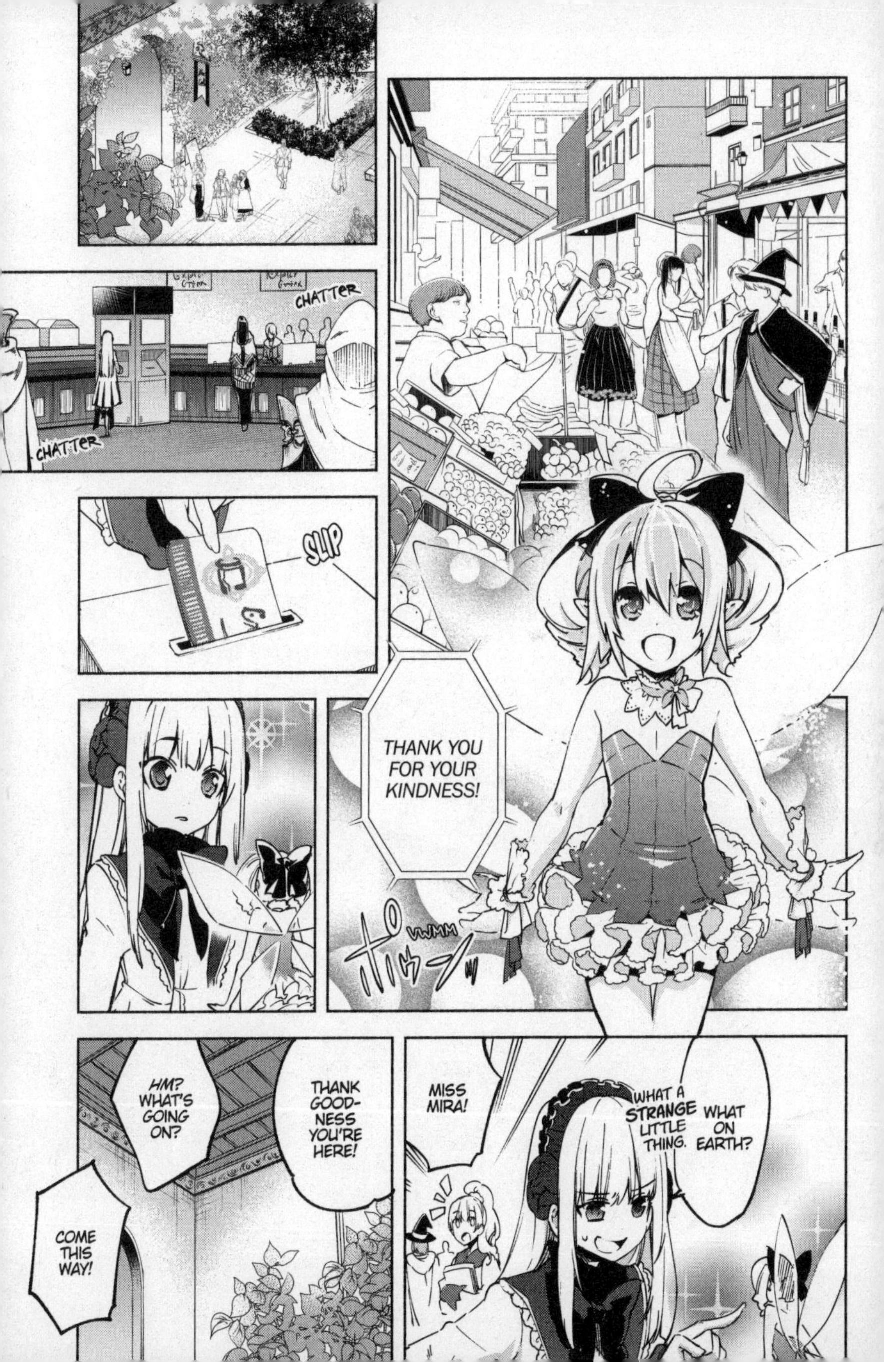
CHATTER
CHATTER
SLIP
THANK YOU FOR YOUR KINDNESS!
VWMM
WHAT ON EARTH?
WHAT A STRANGE LITTLE THING.
MISS MIRA!
THANK GOODNESS YOU'RE HERE!
HM? WHAT'S GOING ON?
COME THIS WAY!

Summon 18: [Life in the New World]

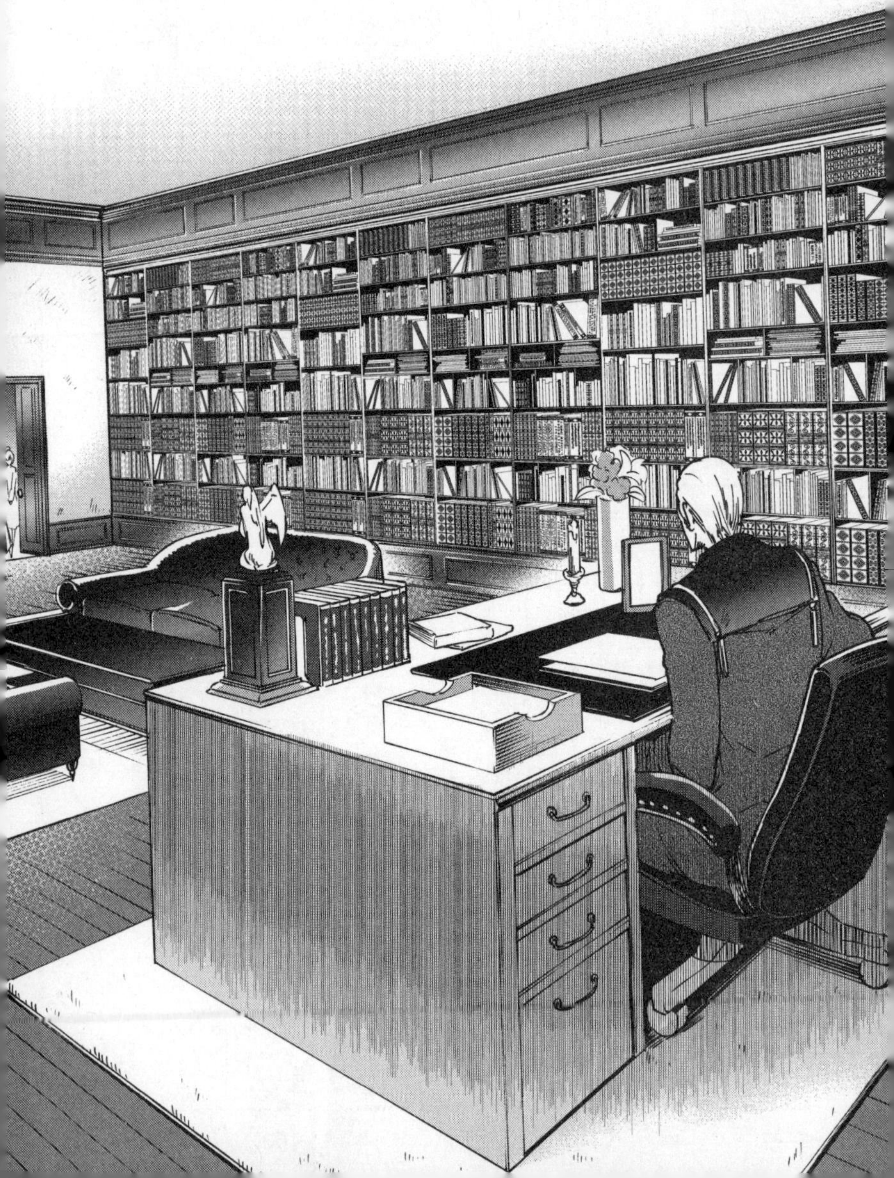

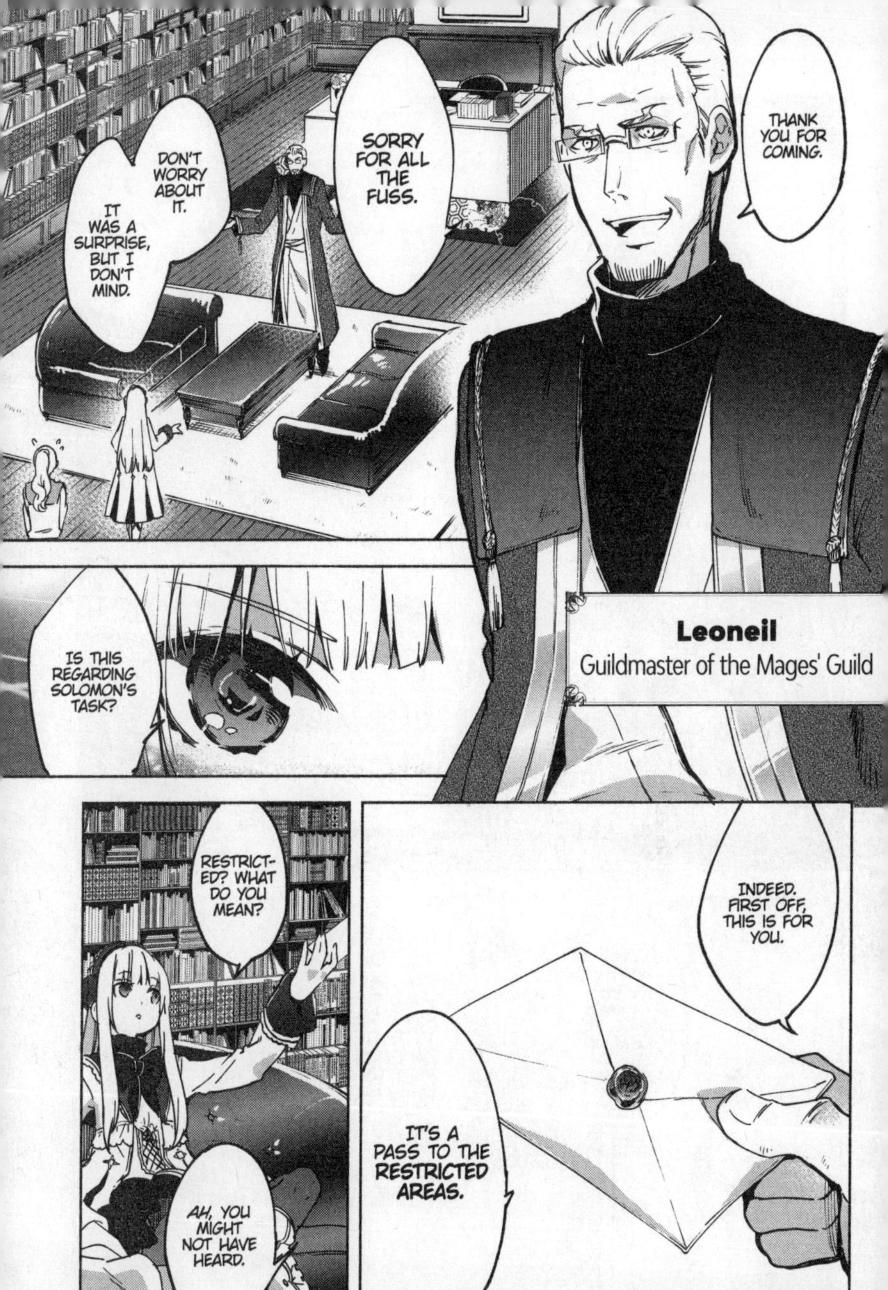
THANK YOU FOR COMING.
Leoneil
Guildmaster of the Mages' Guild
SORRY FOR ALL THE FUSS.
DON'T WORRY ABOUT IT.
IT WAS A SURPRISE, BUT I DON'T MIND.
IS THIS REGARDING SOLOMON'S TASK?
INDEED. FIRST OFF, THIS IS FOR YOU.
IT'S A PASS TO THE RESTRICTED AREAS.
RESTRICTED? WHAT DO YOU MEAN?
AH, YOU MIGHT NOT HAVE HEARD.

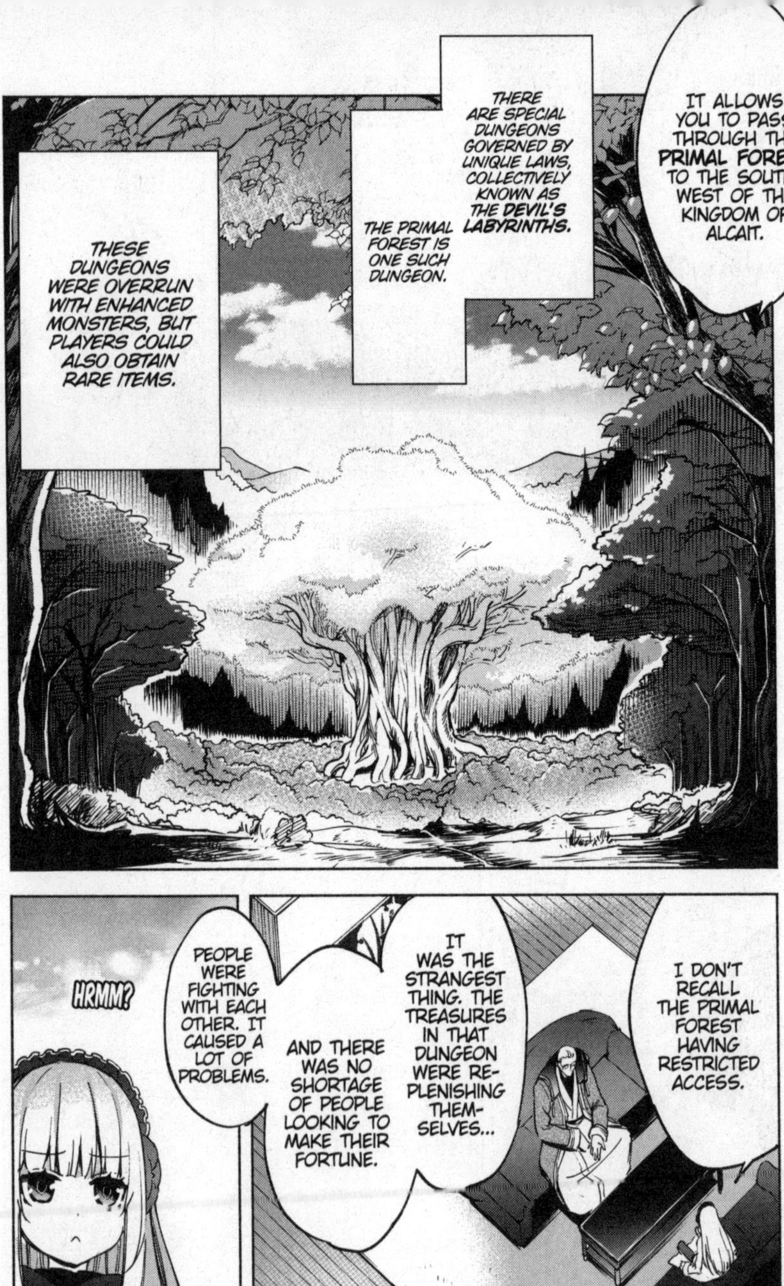
IT ALLOWS YOU TO PASS THROUGH THE **PRIMAL FOREST** TO THE SOUTH-WEST OF THE KINGDOM OF ALCAIT.
THERE ARE SPECIAL DUNGEONS GOVERNED BY UNIQUE LAWS, COLLECTIVELY KNOWN AS THE **DEVIL'S LABYRINTHS.**
THE PRIMAL FOREST IS ONE SUCH DUNGEON.
THESE DUNGEONS WERE OVERRUN WITH ENHANCED MONSTERS, BUT PLAYERS COULD ALSO OBTAIN RARE ITEMS.
I DON'T RECALL THE PRIMAL FOREST HAVING RESTRICTED ACCESS.
IT WAS THE STRANGEST THING. THE TREASURES IN THAT DUNGEON WERE RE-PLENISHING THEM-SELVES...
AND THERE WAS NO SHORTAGE OF PEOPLE LOOKING TO MAKE THEIR FORTUNE.
PEOPLE WERE FIGHTING WITH EACH OTHER. IT CAUSED A LOT OF PROBLEMS.
HRMM?

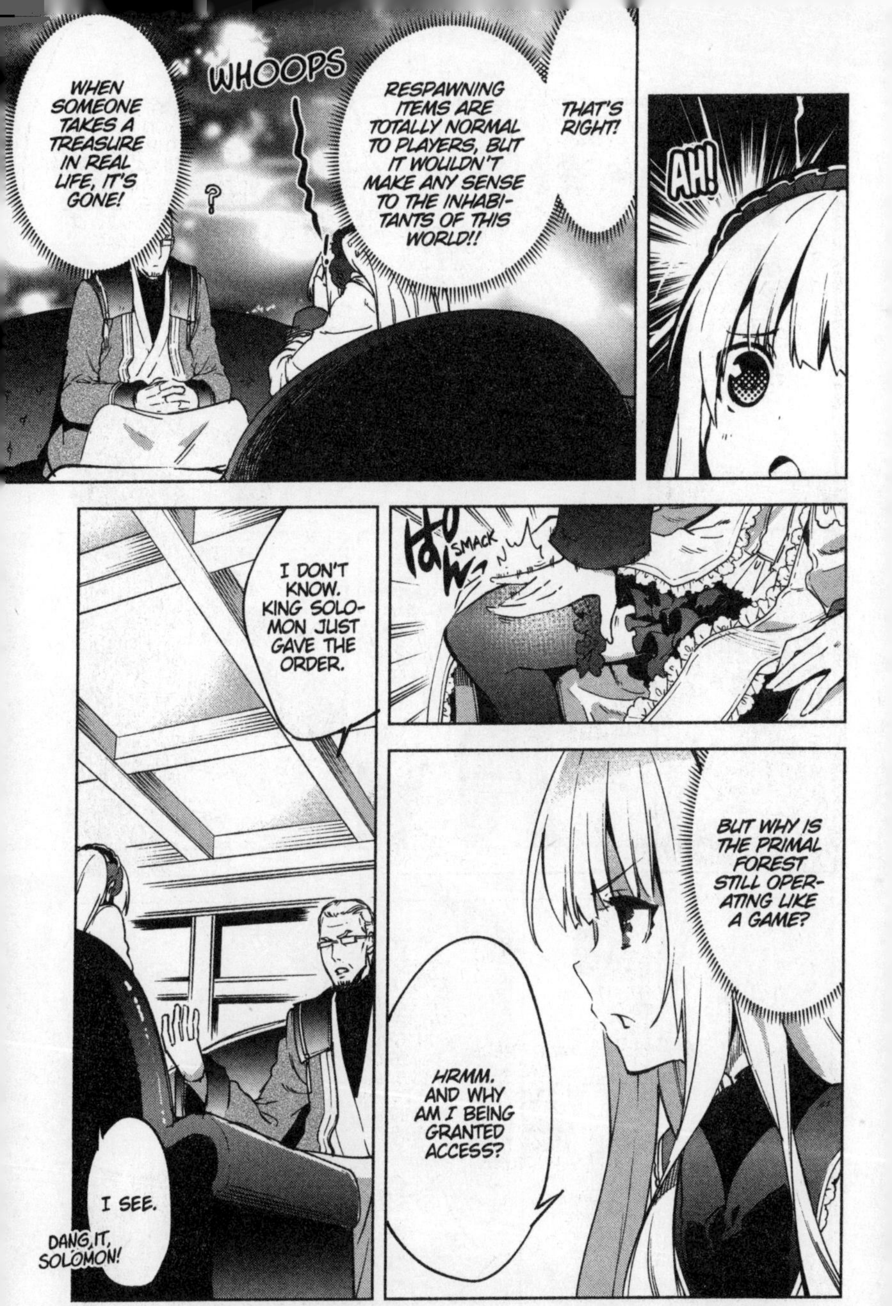
AH!
THAT'S RIGHT!
RESPAWNING ITEMS ARE TOTALLY NORMAL TO PLAYERS, BUT IT WOULDN'T MAKE ANY SENSE TO THE INHABITANTS OF THIS WORLD!!
WHOOPS
WHEN SOMEONE TAKES A TREASURE IN REAL LIFE, IT'S GONE!
?
SMACK
BUT WHY IS THE PRIMAL FOREST STILL OPERATING LIKE A GAME?
HRMM. AND WHY AM I BEING GRANTED ACCESS?
I DON'T KNOW. KING SOLOMON JUST GAVE THE ORDER.
I SEE.
DANG IT, SOLOMON!

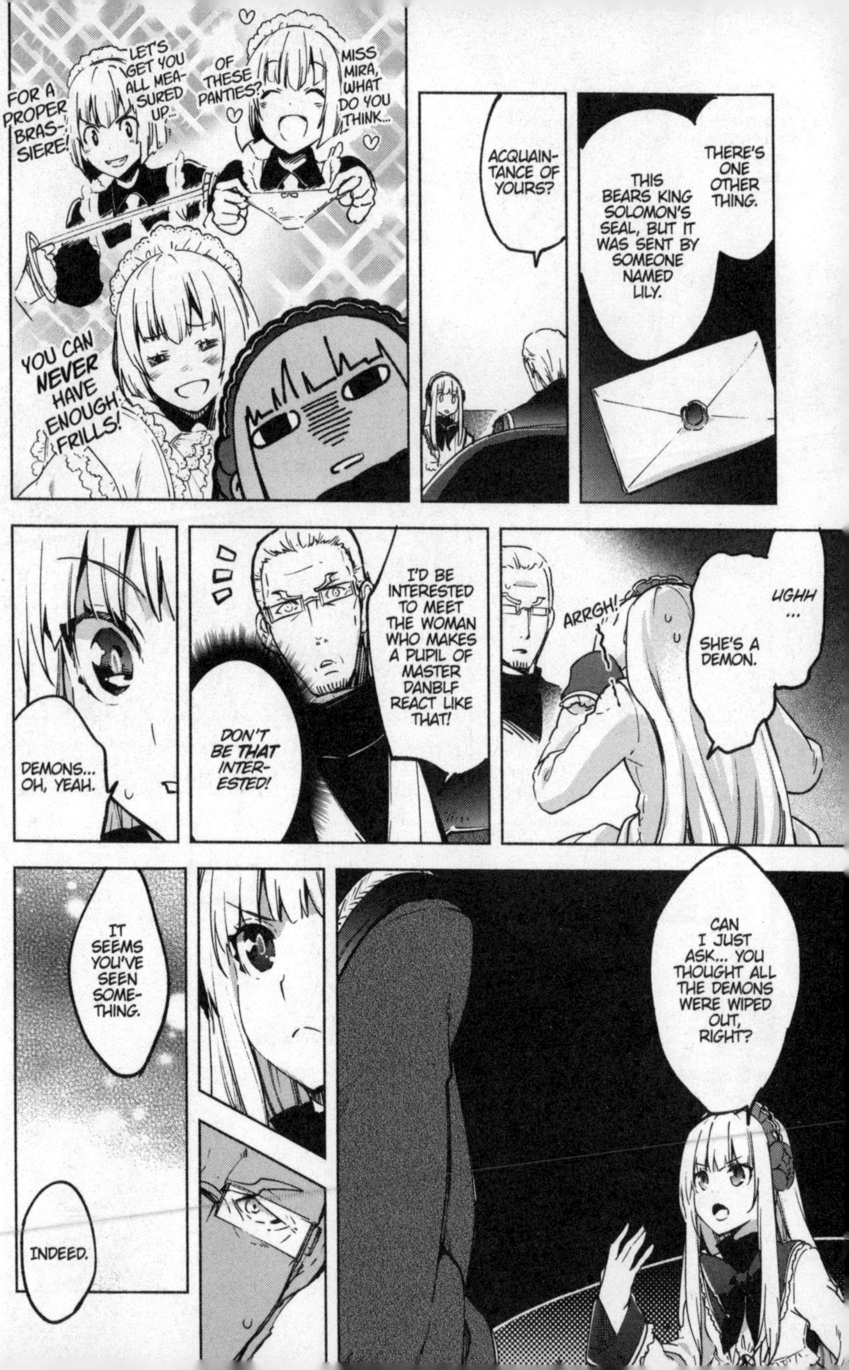
THERE'S ONE OTHER THING.
THIS BEARS KING SOLOMON'S SEAL, BUT IT WAS SENT BY SOMEONE NAMED LILY.
ACQUAINTANCE OF YOURS?
MISS MIRA, WHAT DO YOU THINK...
OF THESE PANTIES?
LET'S GET YOU ALL MEA-SURED UP...
FOR A PROPER BRAS-SIERE!
YOU CAN NEVER HAVE ENOUGH FRILLS!
UGHH...
SHE'S A DEMON.
ARRGH!
I'D BE INTERESTED TO MEET THE WOMAN WHO MAKES A PUPIL OF MASTER DANBLF REACT LIKE THAT!
DON'T BE THAT INTER-ESTED!
DEMONS... OH, YEAH.
CAN I JUST ASK... YOU THOUGHT ALL THE DEMONS WERE WIPED OUT, RIGHT?
IT SEEMS YOU'VE SEEN SOME-THING.
INDEED.

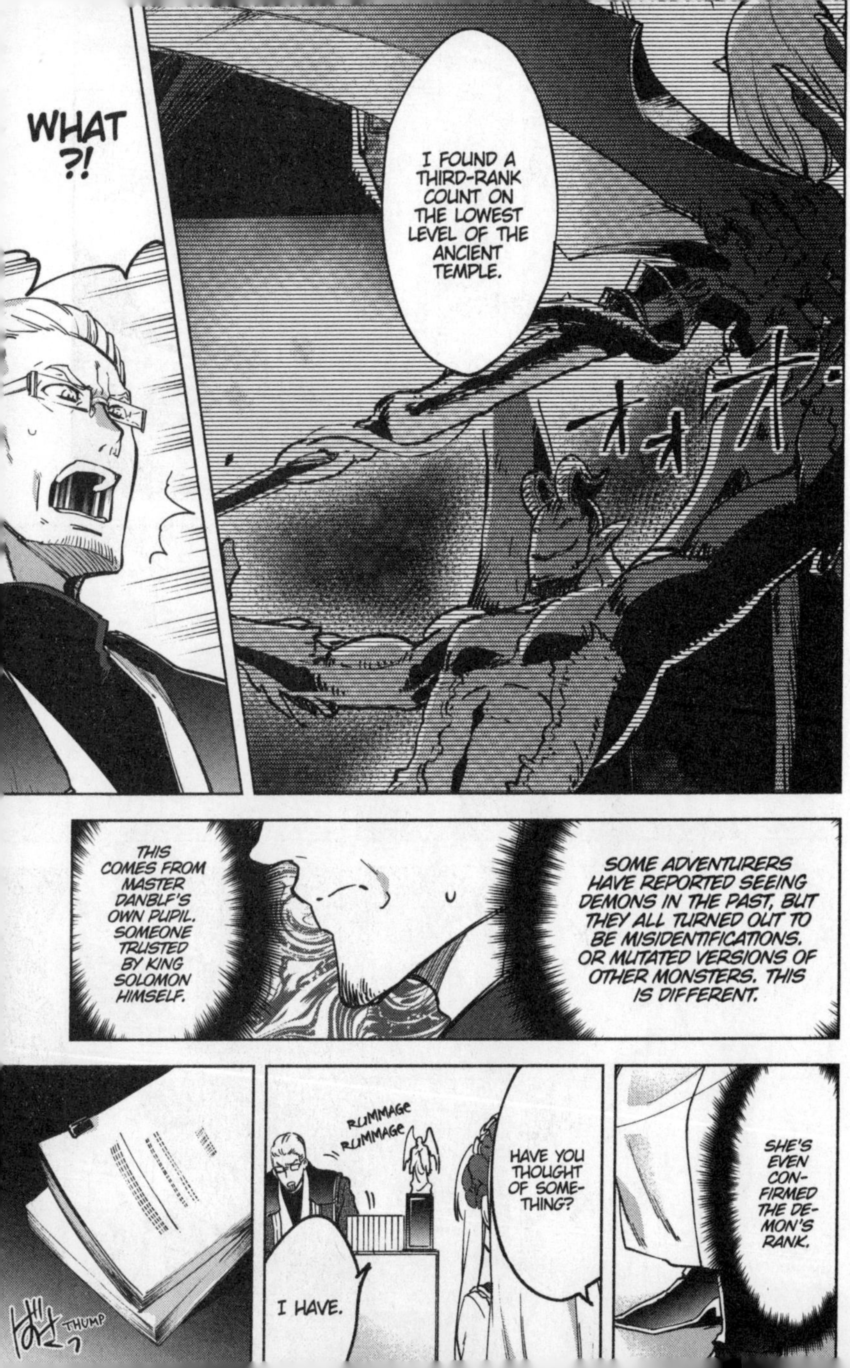
I FOUND A THIRD-RANK COUNT ON THE LOWEST LEVEL OF THE ANCIENT TEMPLE.
WHAT ?!
SOME ADVENTURERS HAVE REPORTED SEEING DEMONS IN THE PAST, BUT THEY ALL TURNED OUT TO BE MISIDENTIFICATIONS. OR MUTATED VERSIONS OF OTHER MONSTERS. THIS IS DIFFERENT.
THIS COMES FROM MASTER DANBLF'S OWN PUPIL. SOMEONE TRUSTED BY KING SOLOMON HIMSELF.
SHE'S EVEN CON-FIRMED THE DE-MON'S RANK.
HAVE YOU THOUGHT OF SOME-THING?
RUMMAGE RUMMAGE
I HAVE.
THUMP

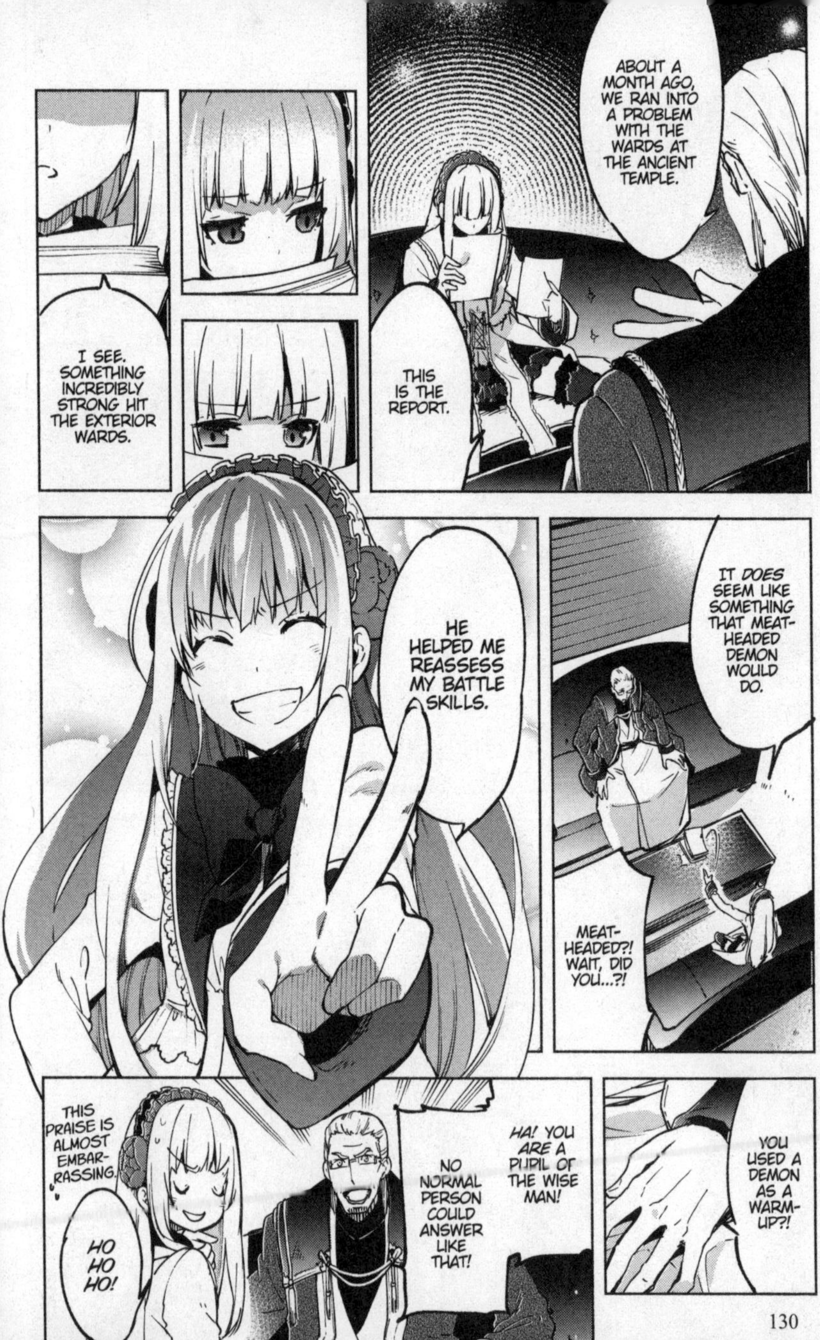
ABOUT A MONTH AGO, WE RAN INTO A PROBLEM WITH THE WARDS AT THE ANCIENT TEMPLE.
THIS IS THE REPORT.
I SEE. SOMETHING INCREDIBLY STRONG HIT THE EXTERIOR WARDS.
IT *DOES* SEEM LIKE SOMETHING THAT MEAT-HEADED DEMON WOULD DO.
MEAT-HEADED?! WAIT, DID YOU...?!
HE HELPED ME REASSESS MY BATTLE SKILLS.
YOU USED A DEMON AS A WARM-UP?!
HA! YOU *ARE* A PUPIL OF THE WISE MAN!
NO NORMAL PERSON COULD ANSWER LIKE THAT!
THIS PRAISE IS ALMOST EMBARRASSING.
HO HO HO!

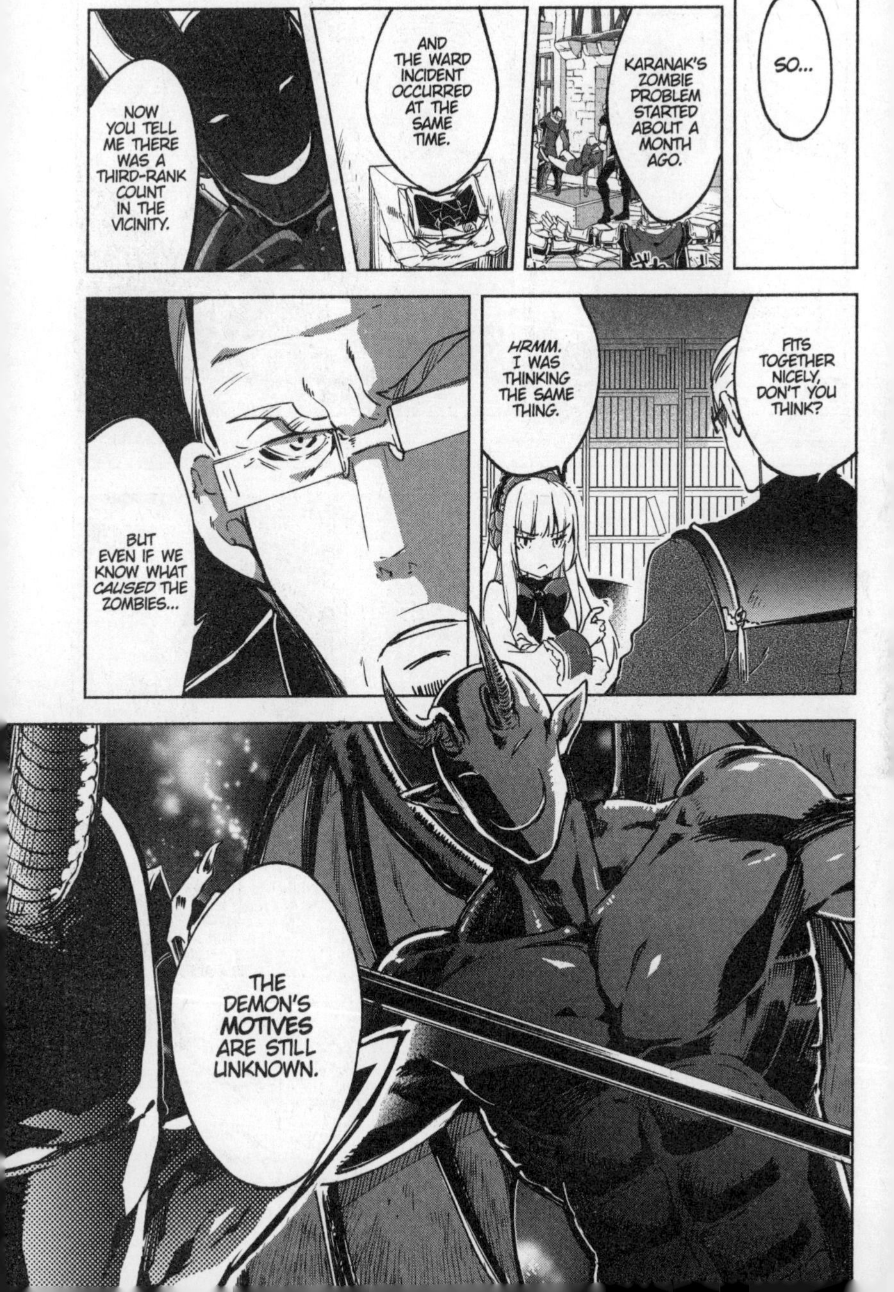
SO...
KARANAK'S ZOMBIE PROBLEM STARTED ABOUT A MONTH AGO.
AND THE WARD INCIDENT OCCURRED AT THE SAME TIME.
NOW YOU TELL ME THERE WAS A THIRD-RANK COUNT IN THE VICINITY.
FITS TOGETHER NICELY, DON'T YOU THINK?
HRMM. I WAS THINKING THE SAME THING.
BUT EVEN IF WE KNOW WHAT *CAUSED* THE ZOMBIES...
THE DEMON'S MOTIVES ARE STILL UNKNOWN.

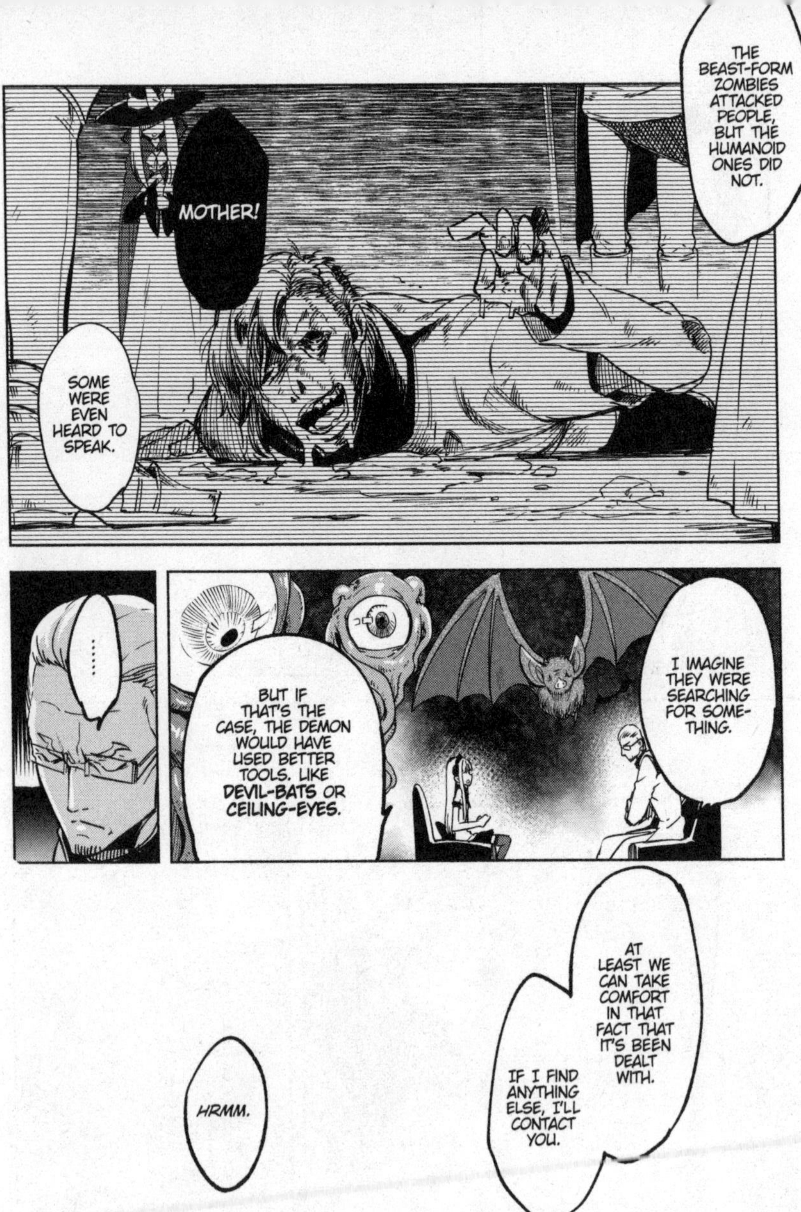
THE BEAST-FORM ZOMBIES ATTACKED PEOPLE, BUT THE HUMANOID ONES DID NOT.
MOTHER!
SOME WERE EVEN HEARD TO SPEAK.
I IMAGINE THEY WERE SEARCHING FOR SOME-THING.
BUT IF THAT'S THE CASE, THE DEMON WOULD HAVE USED BETTER TOOLS. LIKE DEVIL-BATS OR CEILING-EYES.
......
AT LEAST WE CAN TAKE COMFORT IN THAT FACT THAT IT'S BEEN DEALT WITH.
IF I FIND ANYTHING ELSE, I'LL CONTACT YOU.
HRMM.

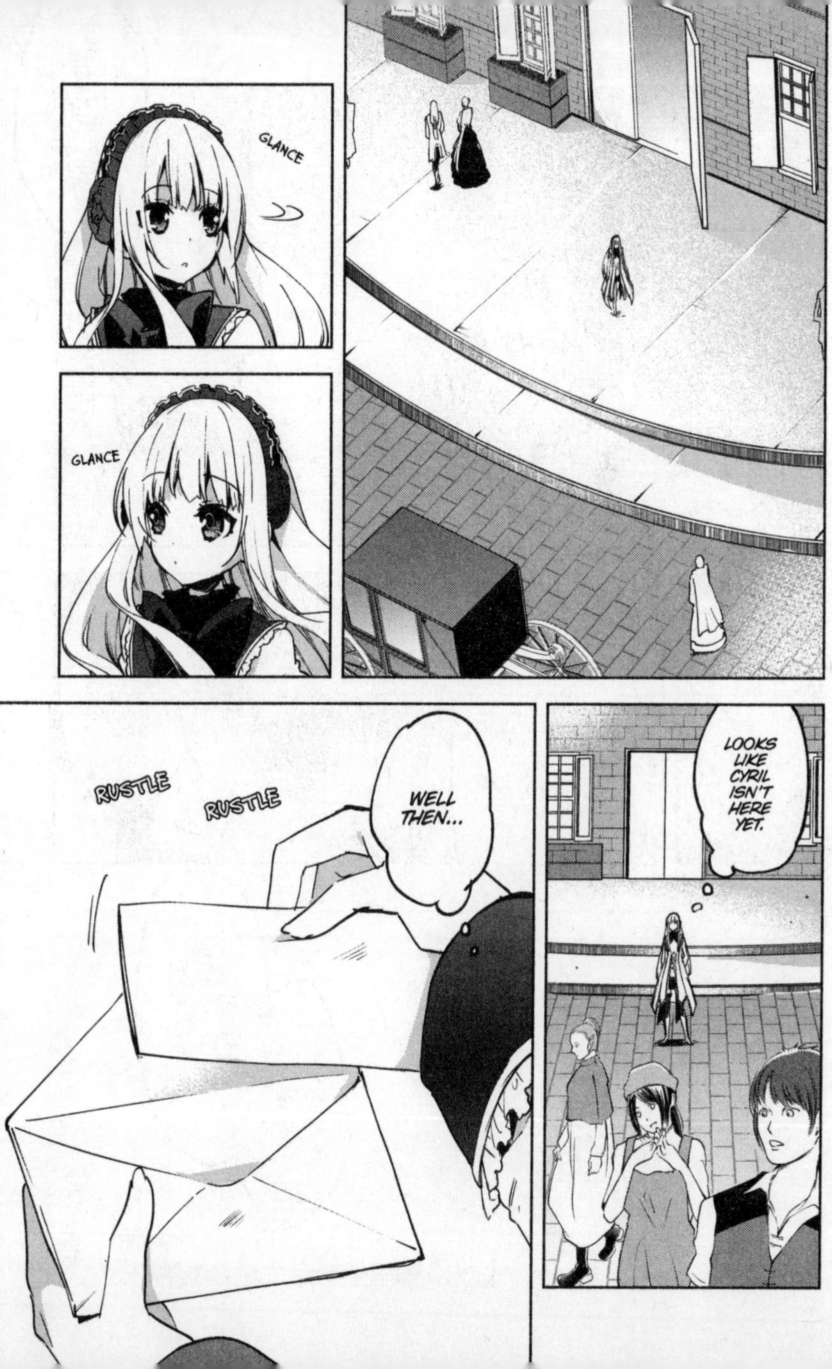
GLANCE
GLANCE
LOOKS LIKE CYRIL ISN'T HERE YET.
WELL THEN...
RUSTLE
RUSTLE

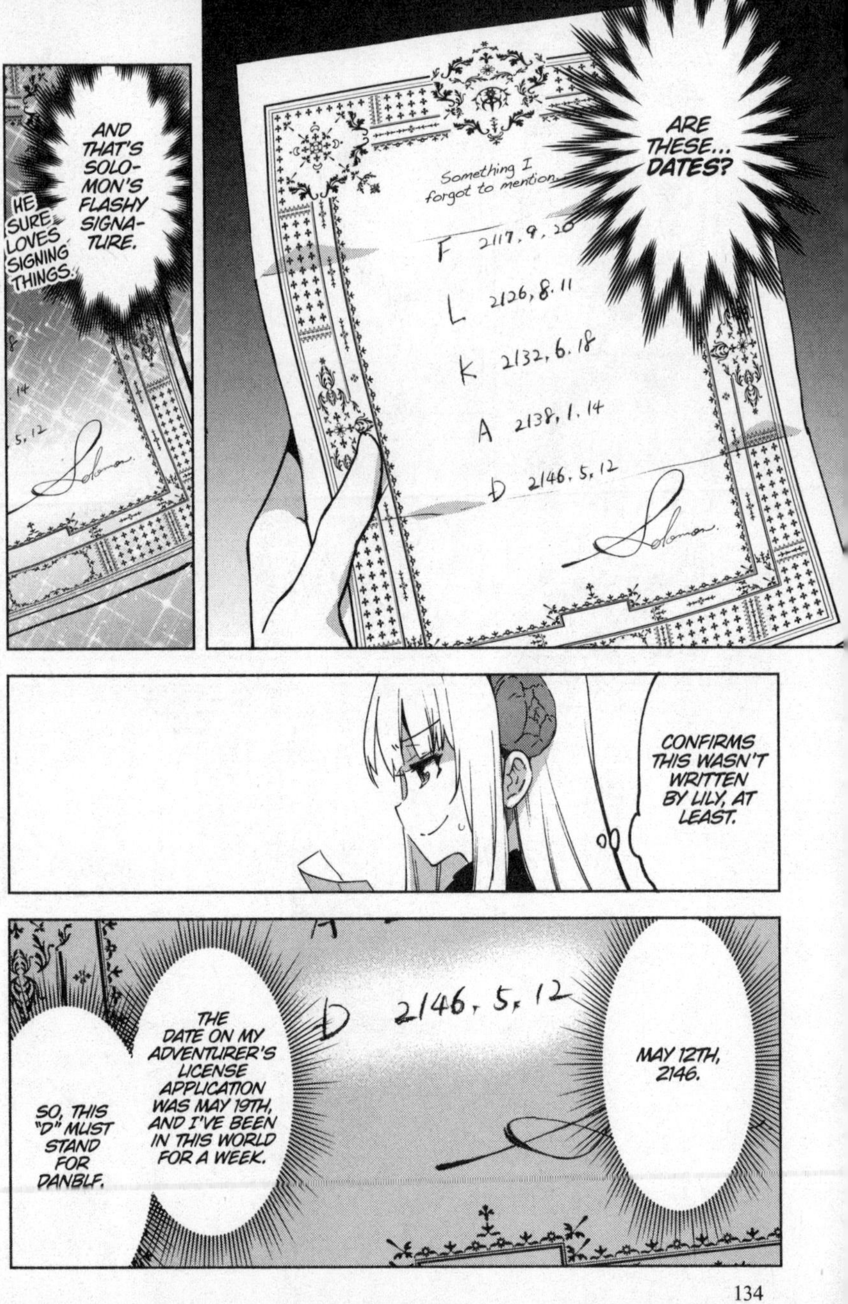
Something I forgot to mention
F 2117, 9, 20
L 2126, 8.11
K 2132, 6.18
A 2138, 1.14
D 2146, 5, 12
Solomon
ARE THESE... DATES?
AND THAT'S SOLOMON'S FLASHY SIGNATURE.
HE SURE LOVES SIGNING THINGS.
CONFIRMS THIS WASN'T WRITTEN BY LILY, AT LEAST.
MAY 12TH, 2146.
D 2146, 5, 12
THE DATE ON MY ADVENTURER'S LICENSE APPLICATION WAS MAY 19TH, AND I'VE BEEN IN THIS WORLD FOR A WEEK.
SO, THIS "D" MUST STAND FOR DANBLF.

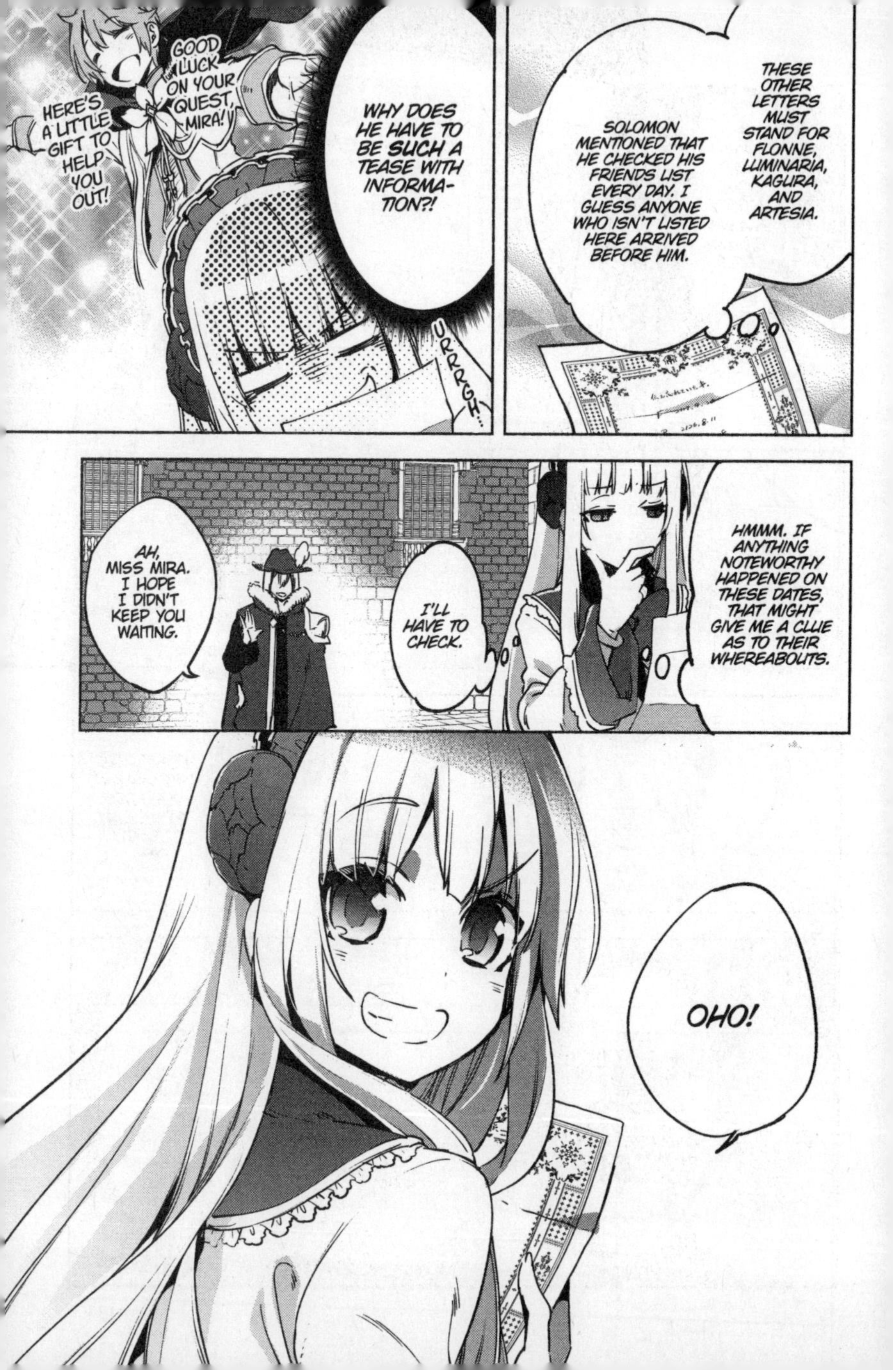
THESE OTHER LETTERS MUST STAND FOR FLONNE, LUMINARIA, KAGURA, AND ARTESIA.
SOLOMON MENTIONED THAT HE CHECKED HIS FRIENDS LIST EVERY DAY. I GUESS ANYONE WHO ISN'T LISTED HERE ARRIVED BEFORE HIM.
WHY DOES HE HAVE TO BE SUCH A TEASE WITH INFORMATION?!
GOOD LUCK ON YOUR QUEST, MIRA!
HERE'S A LITTLE GIFT TO HELP YOU OUT!
URRRGH...
HMMM. IF ANYTHING NOTEWORTHY HAPPENED ON THESE DATES, THAT MIGHT GIVE ME A CLUE AS TO THEIR WHEREABOUTS.
I'LL HAVE TO CHECK.
AH, MISS MIRA. I HOPE I DIDN'T KEEP YOU WAITING.
OHO!

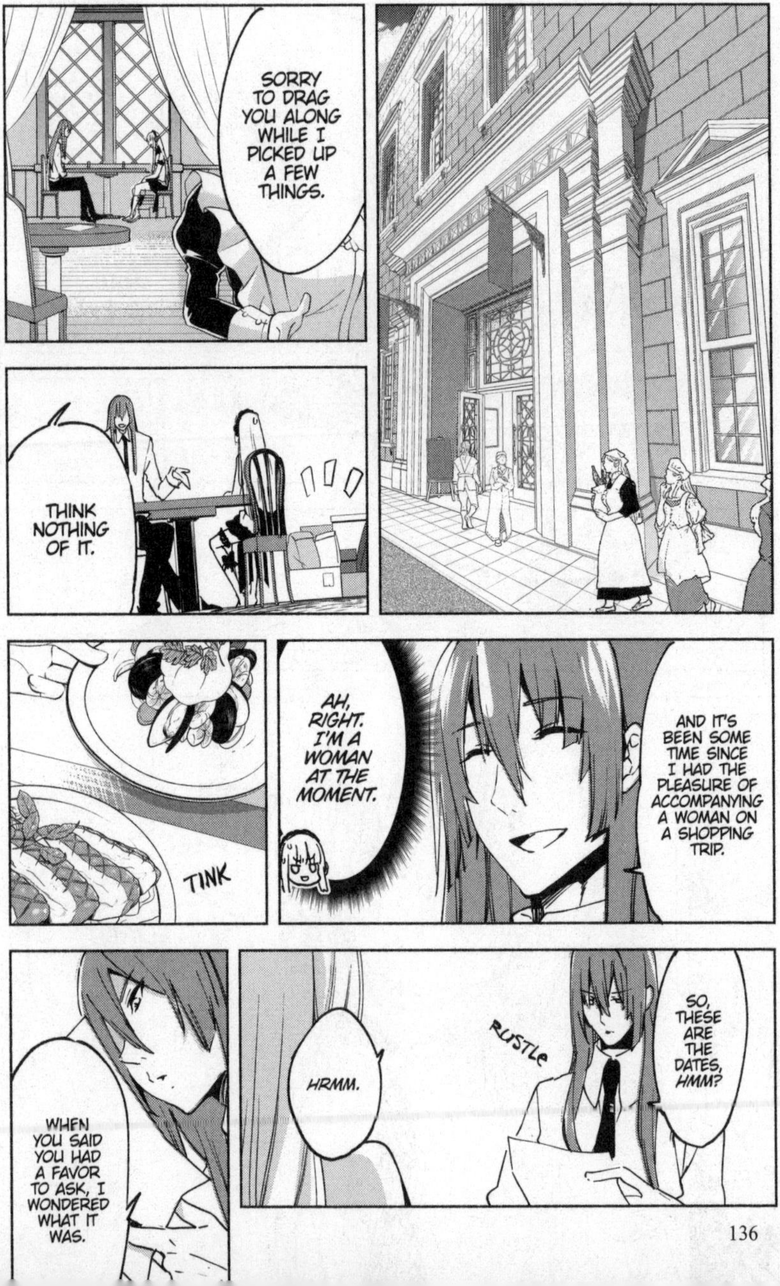
SORRY TO DRAG YOU ALONG WHILE I PICKED UP A FEW THINGS.
THINK NOTHING OF IT.
AND IT'S BEEN SOME TIME SINCE I HAD THE PLEASURE OF ACCOMPANYING A WOMAN ON A SHOPPING TRIP.
AH, RIGHT. I'M A WOMAN AT THE MOMENT.
TINK
SO, THESE ARE THE DATES, HMM?
RUSTLE
HRMM.
WHEN YOU SAID YOU HAD A FAVOR TO ASK, I WONDERED WHAT IT WAS.

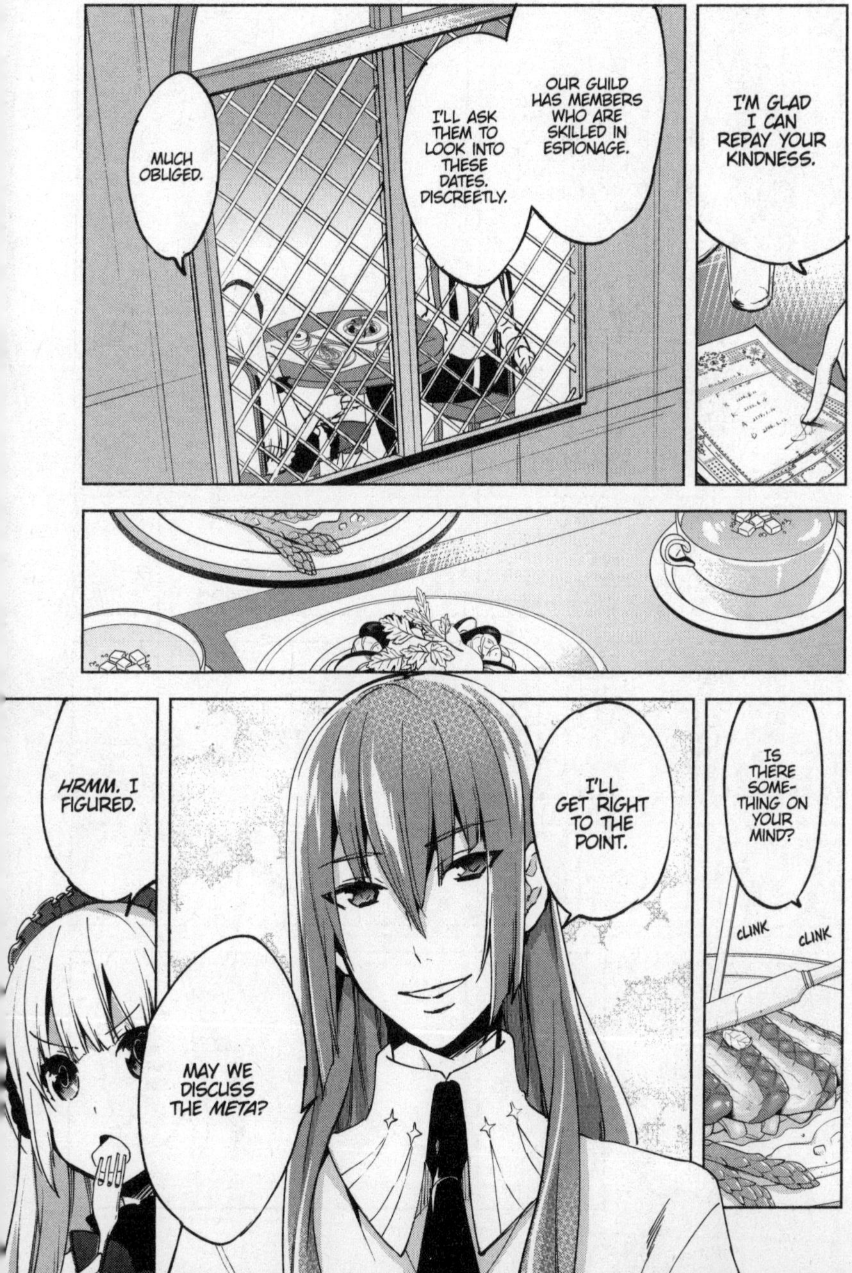
I'M GLAD I CAN REPAY YOUR KINDNESS.
OUR GUILD HAS MEMBERS WHO ARE SKILLED IN ESPIONAGE.
I'LL ASK THEM TO LOOK INTO THESE DATES. DISCREETLY.
MUCH OBLIGED.
IS THERE SOME-THING ON YOUR MIND?
CLINK
CLINK
I'LL GET RIGHT TO THE POINT.
MAY WE DISCUSS THE *META*?
HRMM. I FIGURED.

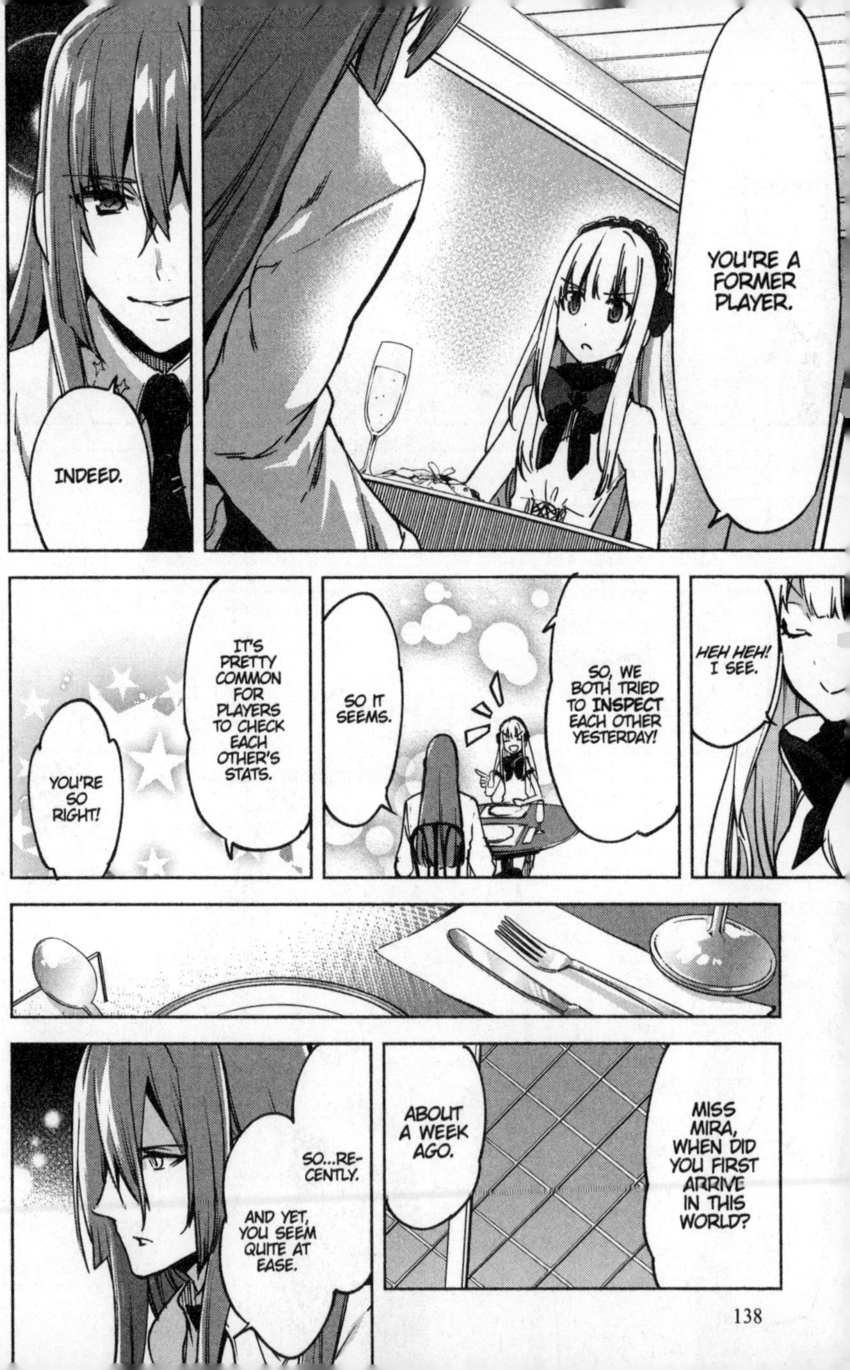
YOU'RE A FORMER PLAYER.
INDEED.
HEH HEH! I SEE.
SO, WE BOTH TRIED TO INSPECT EACH OTHER YESTERDAY!
SO IT SEEMS.
IT'S PRETTY COMMON FOR PLAYERS TO CHECK EACH OTHER'S STATS.
YOU'RE SO RIGHT!
MISS MIRA, WHEN DID YOU FIRST ARRIVE IN THIS WORLD?
ABOUT A WEEK AGO.
SO...RE-CENTLY.
AND YET, YOU SEEM QUITE AT EASE.

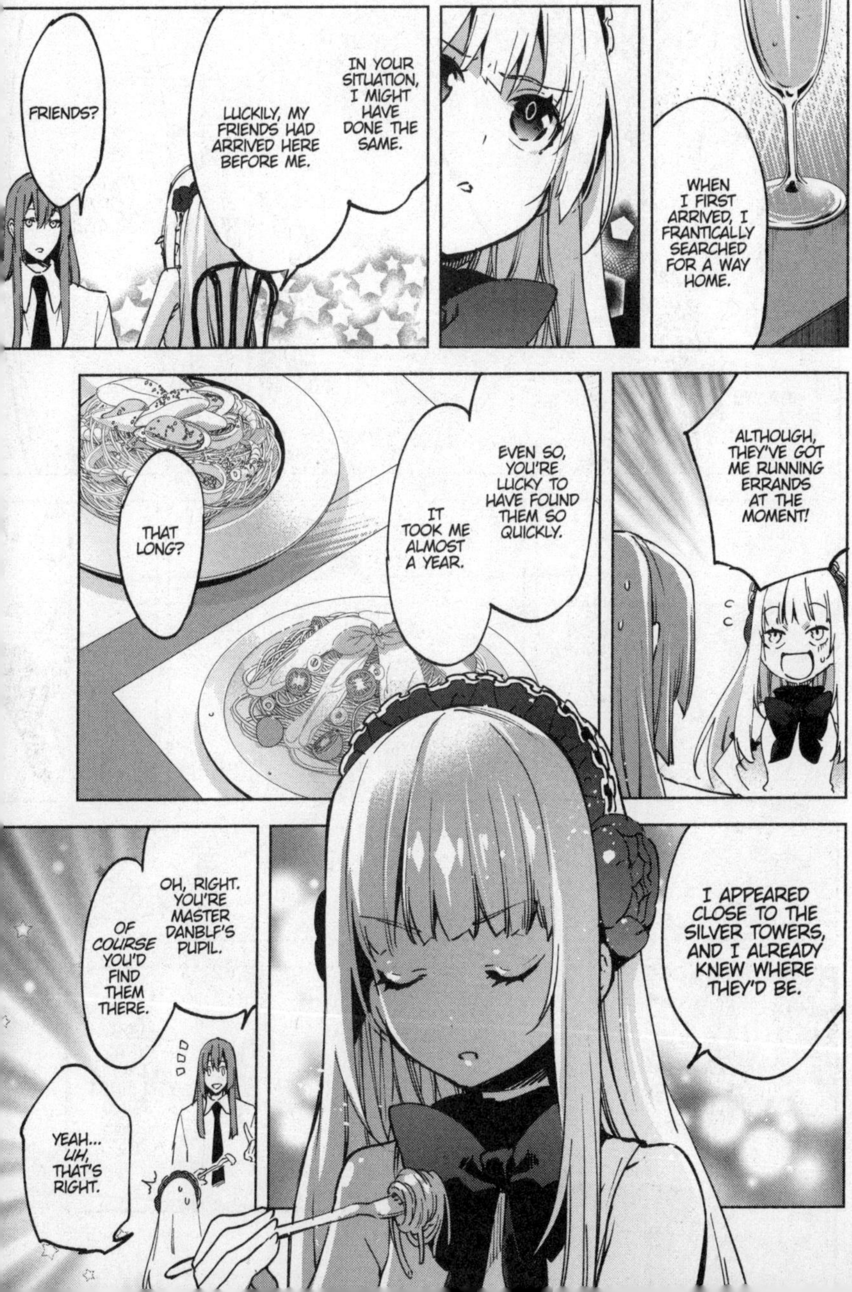
WHEN I FIRST ARRIVED, I FRANTICALLY SEARCHED FOR A WAY HOME.
IN YOUR SITUATION, I MIGHT HAVE DONE THE SAME.
LUCKILY, MY FRIENDS HAD ARRIVED HERE BEFORE ME.
FRIENDS?
ALTHOUGH, THEY'VE GOT ME RUNNING ERRANDS AT THE MOMENT!
EVEN SO, YOU'RE LUCKY TO HAVE FOUND THEM SO QUICKLY.
IT TOOK ME ALMOST A YEAR.
THAT LONG?
I APPEARED CLOSE TO THE SILVER TOWERS, AND I ALREADY KNEW WHERE THEY'D BE.
OH, RIGHT. YOU'RE MASTER DANBLF'S PUPIL.
OF COURSE YOU'D FIND THEM THERE.
YEAH... UH, THAT'S RIGHT.

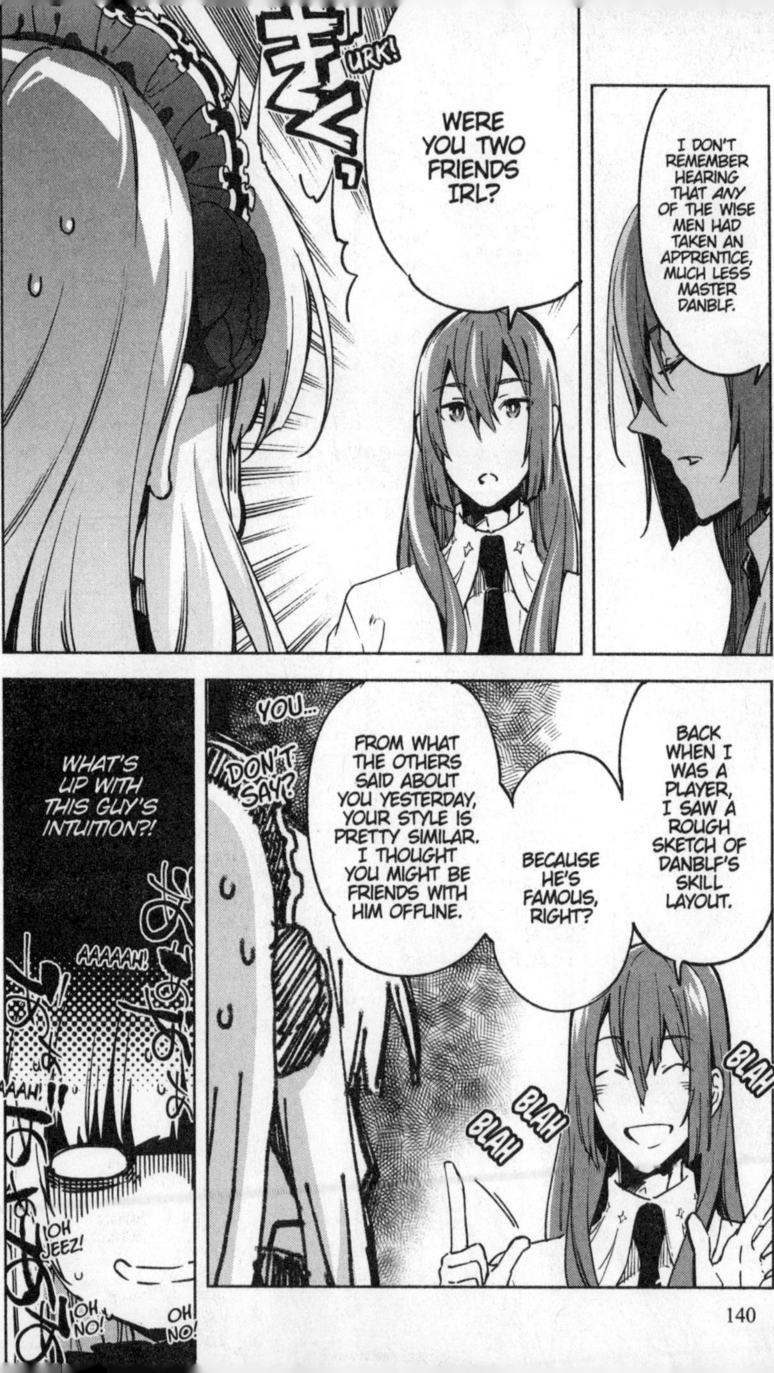
I DON'T REMEMBER HEARING THAT ANY OF THE WISE MEN HAD TAKEN AN APPRENTICE, MUCH LESS MASTER DANBLF.
WERE YOU TWO FRIENDS IRL?
URK!
BACK WHEN I WAS A PLAYER, I SAW A ROUGH SKETCH OF DANBLF'S SKILL LAYOUT.
BECAUSE HE'S FAMOUS, RIGHT?
FROM WHAT THE OTHERS SAID ABOUT YOU YESTERDAY, YOUR STYLE IS PRETTY SIMILAR. I THOUGHT YOU MIGHT BE FRIENDS WITH HIM OFFLINE.
YOU... DON'T SAY?
BLAH
BLAH
BLAH
WHAT'S UP WITH THIS GUY'S INTUITION?!
AAAAAH!
AAAAAH!
OH JEEZ!
OH NO!
OH NO!

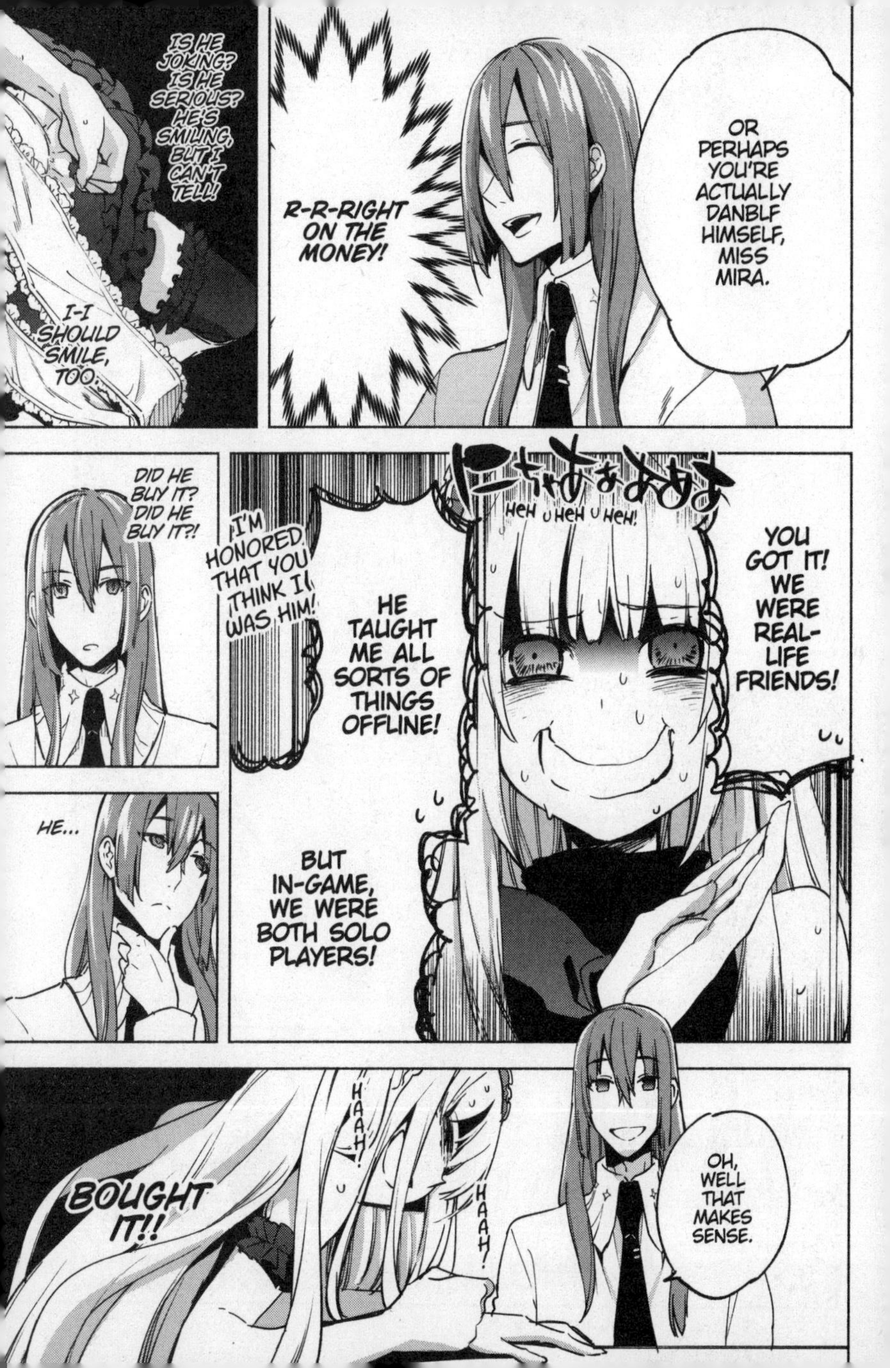
OR PERHAPS YOU'RE ACTUALLY DANBLF HIMSELF, MISS MIRA.
R-R-RIGHT ON THE MONEY!
IS HE JOKING? IS HE SERIOUS? HE'S SMILING, BUT I CAN'T TELL!
I-I SHOULD SMILE, TOO.
HEH HEH HEH!
YOU GOT IT! WE WERE REAL-LIFE FRIENDS!
HE TAUGHT ME ALL SORTS OF THINGS OFFLINE!
BUT IN-GAME, WE WERE BOTH SOLO PLAYERS!
I'M HONORED THAT YOU THINK I WAS HIM!
DID HE BUY IT? DID HE BUY IT?!
HE...
OH, WELL THAT MAKES SENSE.
HAAAH!
HAAAH!
BOUGHT IT!!

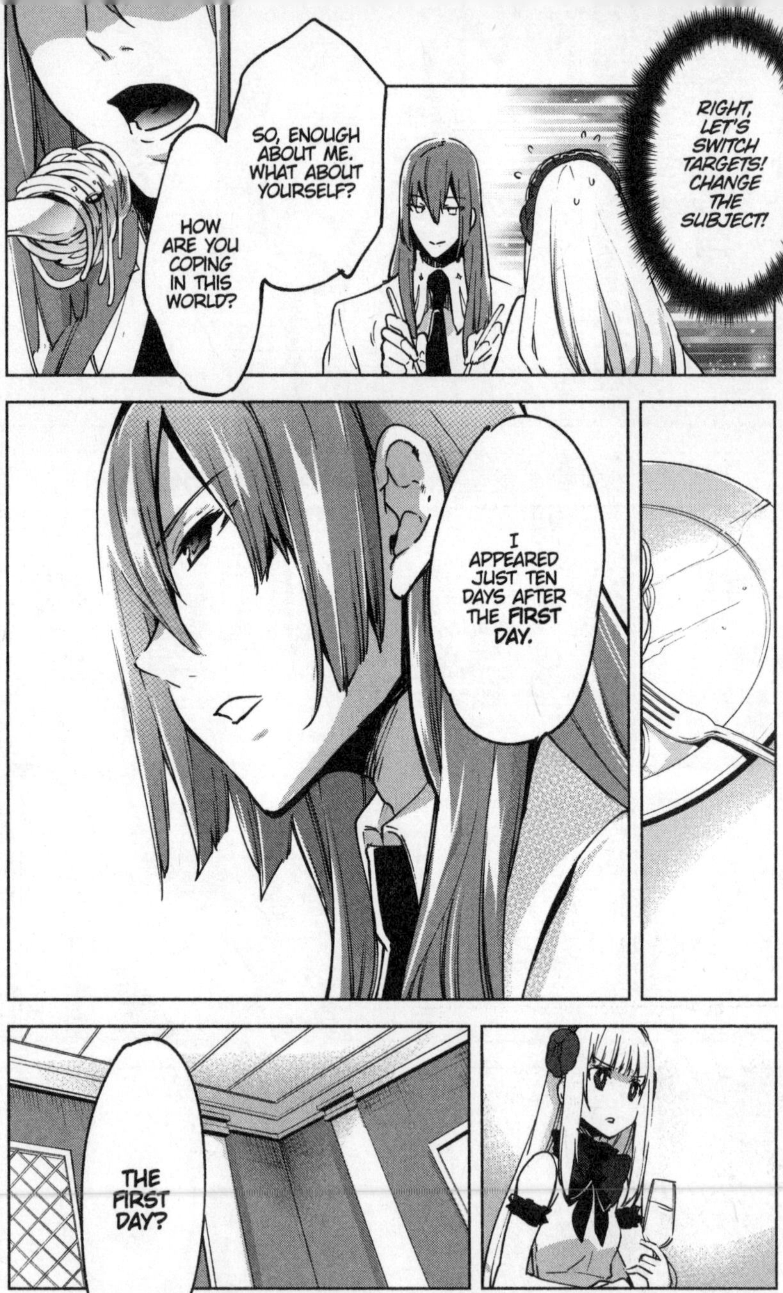
RIGHT, LET'S SWITCH TARGETS! CHANGE THE SUBJECT!
SO, ENOUGH ABOUT ME. WHAT ABOUT YOURSELF?
HOW ARE YOU COPING IN THIS WORLD?
I APPEARED JUST TEN DAYS AFTER THE FIRST DAY.
THE FIRST DAY?

Summon 18: END

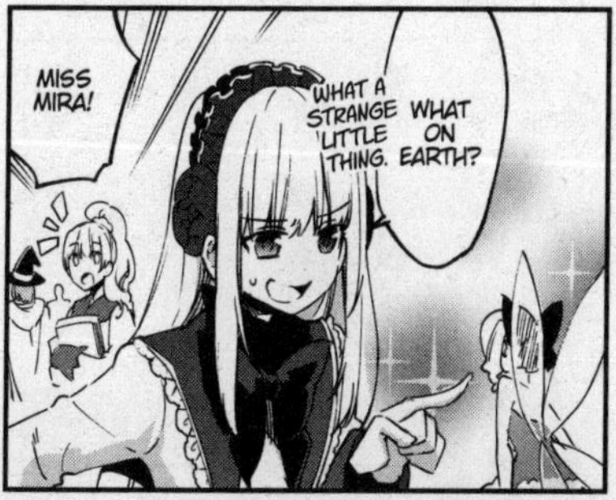
WHAT ON EARTH?
WHAT A STRANGE LITTLE THING.
MISS MIRA!

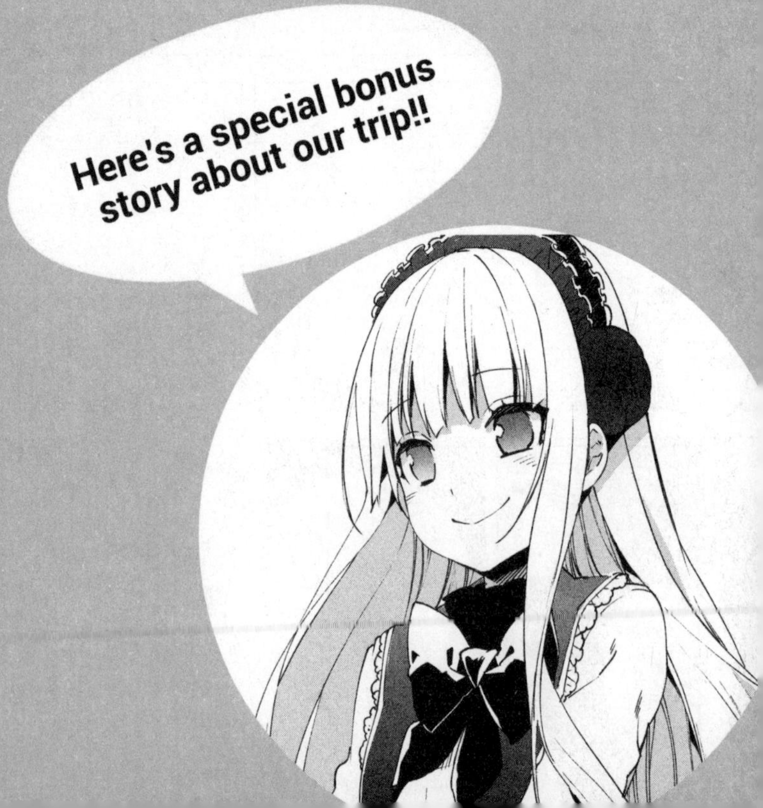
Here's a special bonus story about our trip!!

Bonus Summon: [A Breather]

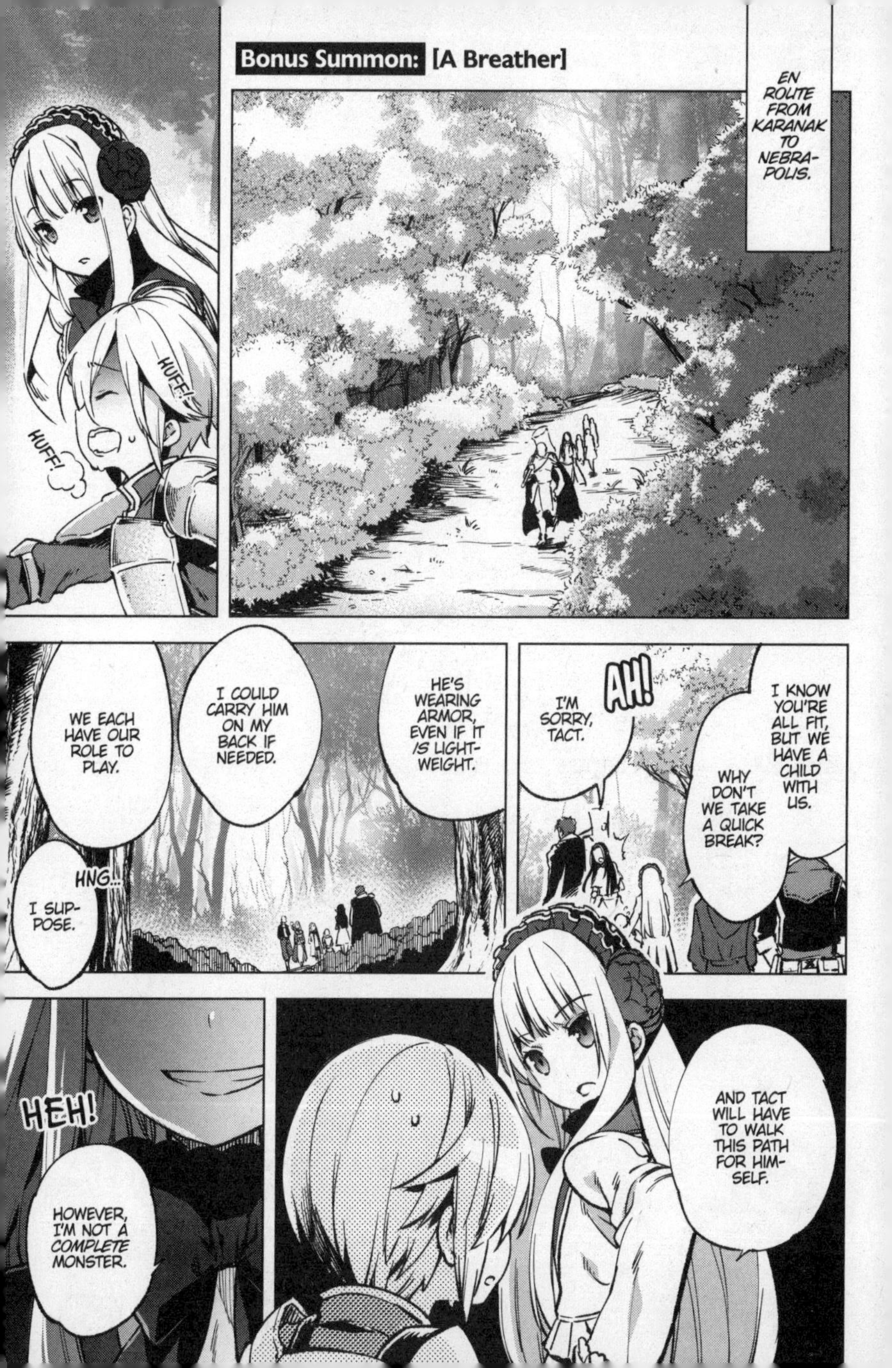
EN ROUTE FROM KARANAK TO NEBRAPOLIS.
HUFF!
HUFF!
I KNOW YOU'RE ALL FIT, BUT WE HAVE A CHILD WITH US.
WHY DON'T WE TAKE A QUICK BREAK?
AH!
I'M SORRY, TACT.
HE'S WEARING ARMOR, EVEN IF IT IS LIGHT-WEIGHT.
I COULD CARRY HIM ON MY BACK IF NEEDED.
WE EACH HAVE OUR ROLE TO PLAY.
HNG...
I SUP-POSE.
AND TACT WILL HAVE TO WALK THIS PATH FOR HIM-SELF.
HEH!
HOWEVER, I'M NOT A COMPLETE MONSTER.

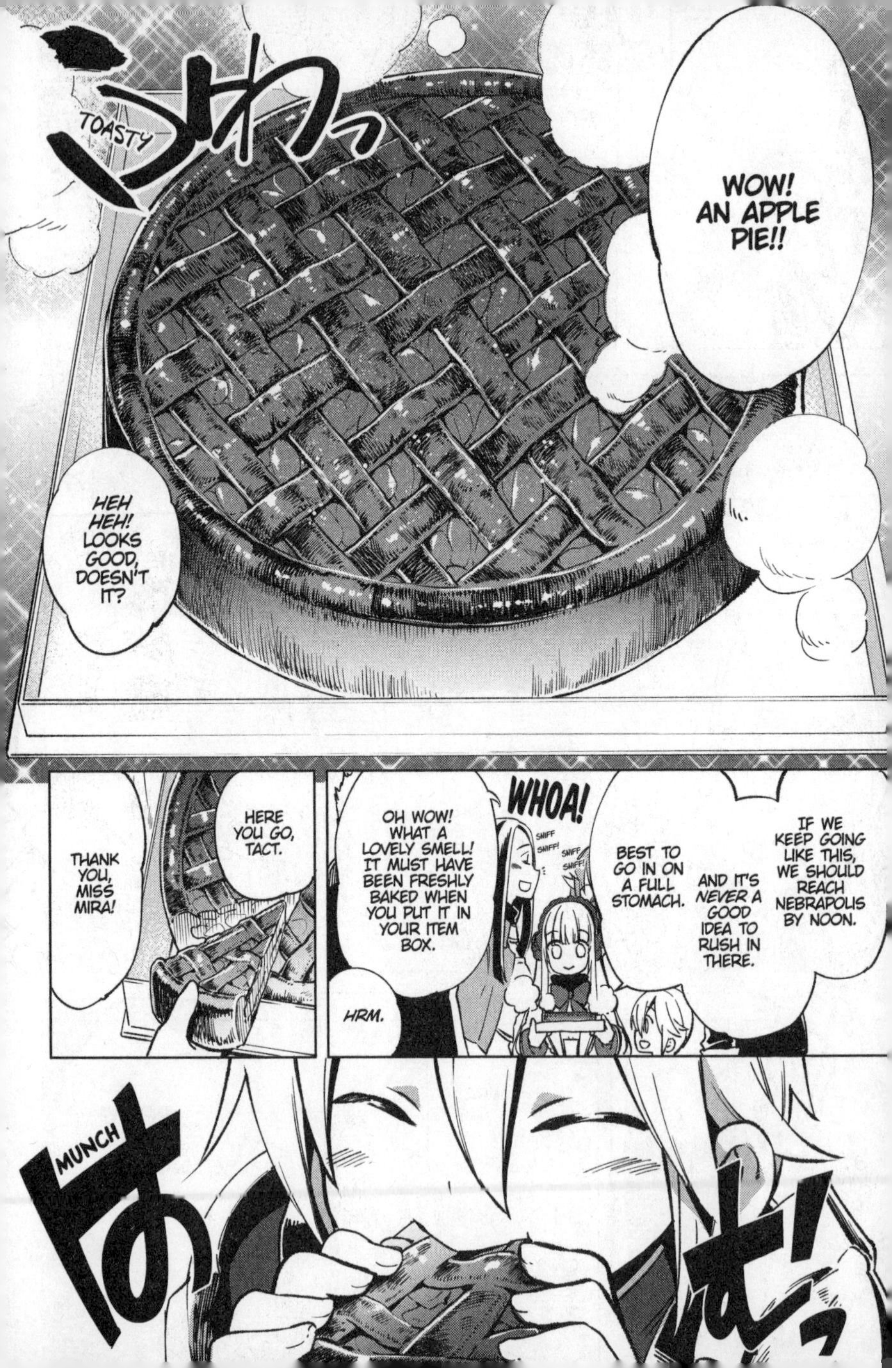

WOW! AN APPLE PIE!!
TOASTY
HEH HEH! LOOKS GOOD, DOESN'T IT?
IF WE KEEP GOING LIKE THIS, WE SHOULD REACH NEBRAPOLIS BY NOON.
AND IT'S *NEVER* A GOOD IDEA TO RUSH IN THERE.
BEST TO GO IN ON A FULL STOMACH.
WHOA!
SNIFF SNIFF!
SNIFF SNIFF!
OH WOW! WHAT A LOVELY SMELL! IT MUST HAVE BEEN FRESHLY BAKED WHEN YOU PUT IT IN YOUR ITEM BOX.
HRM.
HERE YOU GO, TACT.
THANK YOU, MISS MIRA!
MUNCH

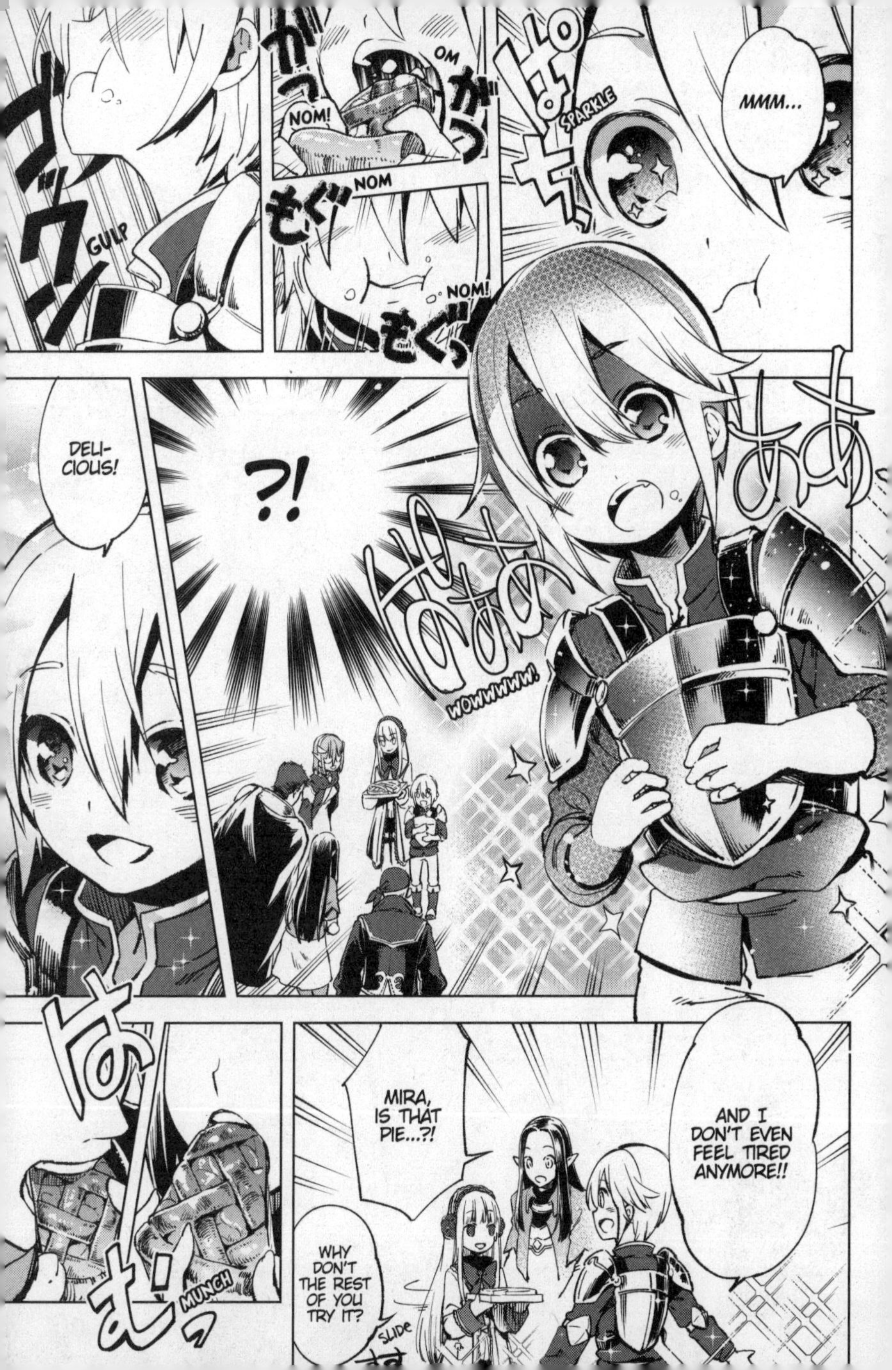
MMM...
SPARKLE
OM
NOM!
NOM
NOM!
GULP
WOWWWWW!
?!
DELI-CIOUS!
AND I DON'T EVEN FEEL TIRED ANYMORE!!
MIRA, IS THAT PIE...?!
WHY DON'T THE REST OF YOU TRY IT?
SLIDE
MUNCH

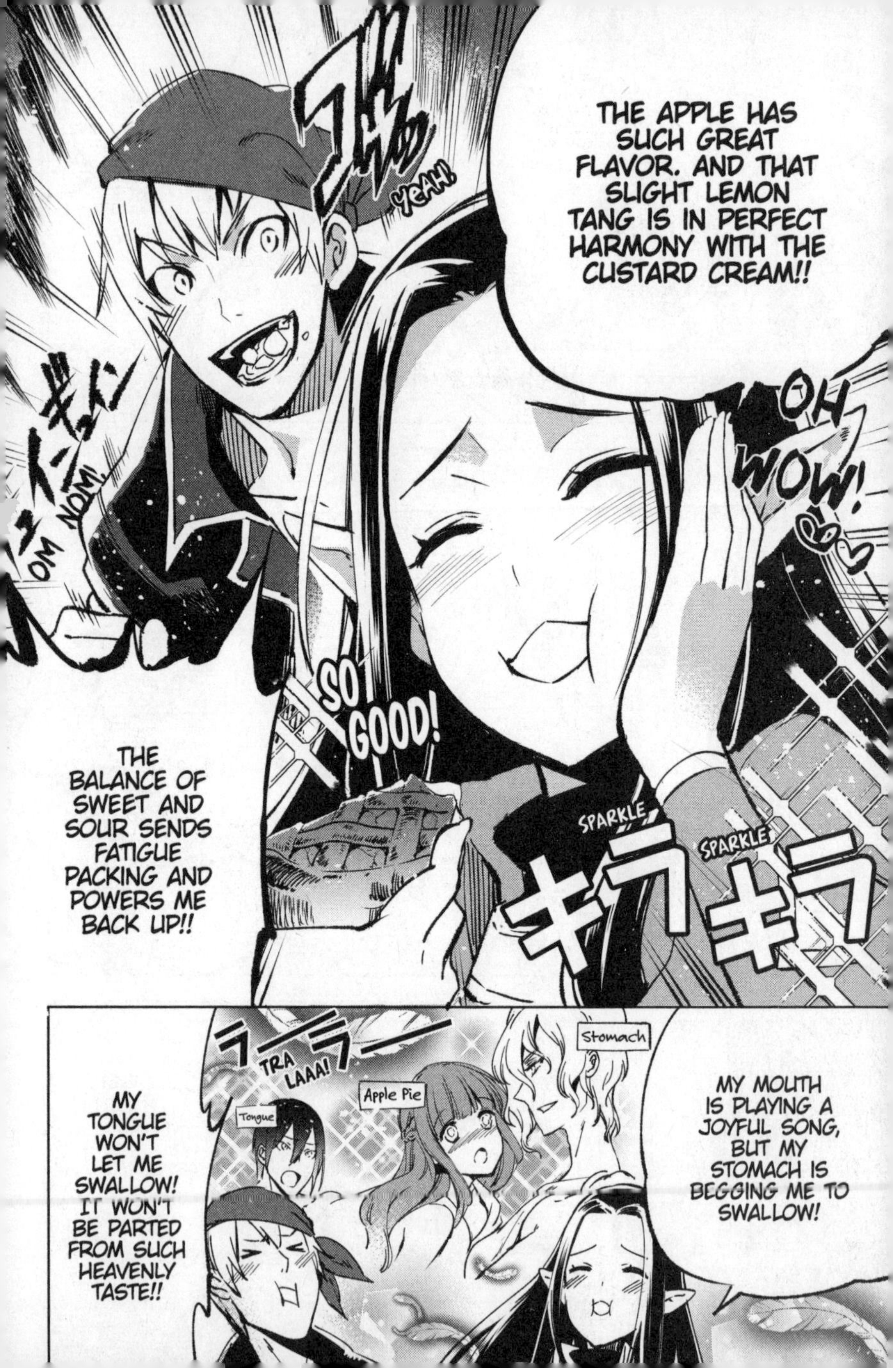
THE APPLE HAS SUCH GREAT FLAVOR. AND THAT SLIGHT LEMON TANG IS IN PERFECT HARMONY WITH THE CUSTARD CREAM!!
OH WOW!
YEAH!
OM NOM!
SO GOOD!
SPARKLE
SPARKLE
キラキラ
THE BALANCE OF SWEET AND SOUR SENDS FATIGUE PACKING AND POWERS ME BACK UP!!
MY MOUTH IS PLAYING A JOYFUL SONG, BUT MY STOMACH IS BEGGING ME TO SWALLOW!
Stomach
Apple Pie
ラーラー
TRA LAAA!
Tongue
MY TONGUE WON'T LET ME SWALLOW! IT WON'T BE PARTED FROM SUCH HEAVENLY TASTE!!

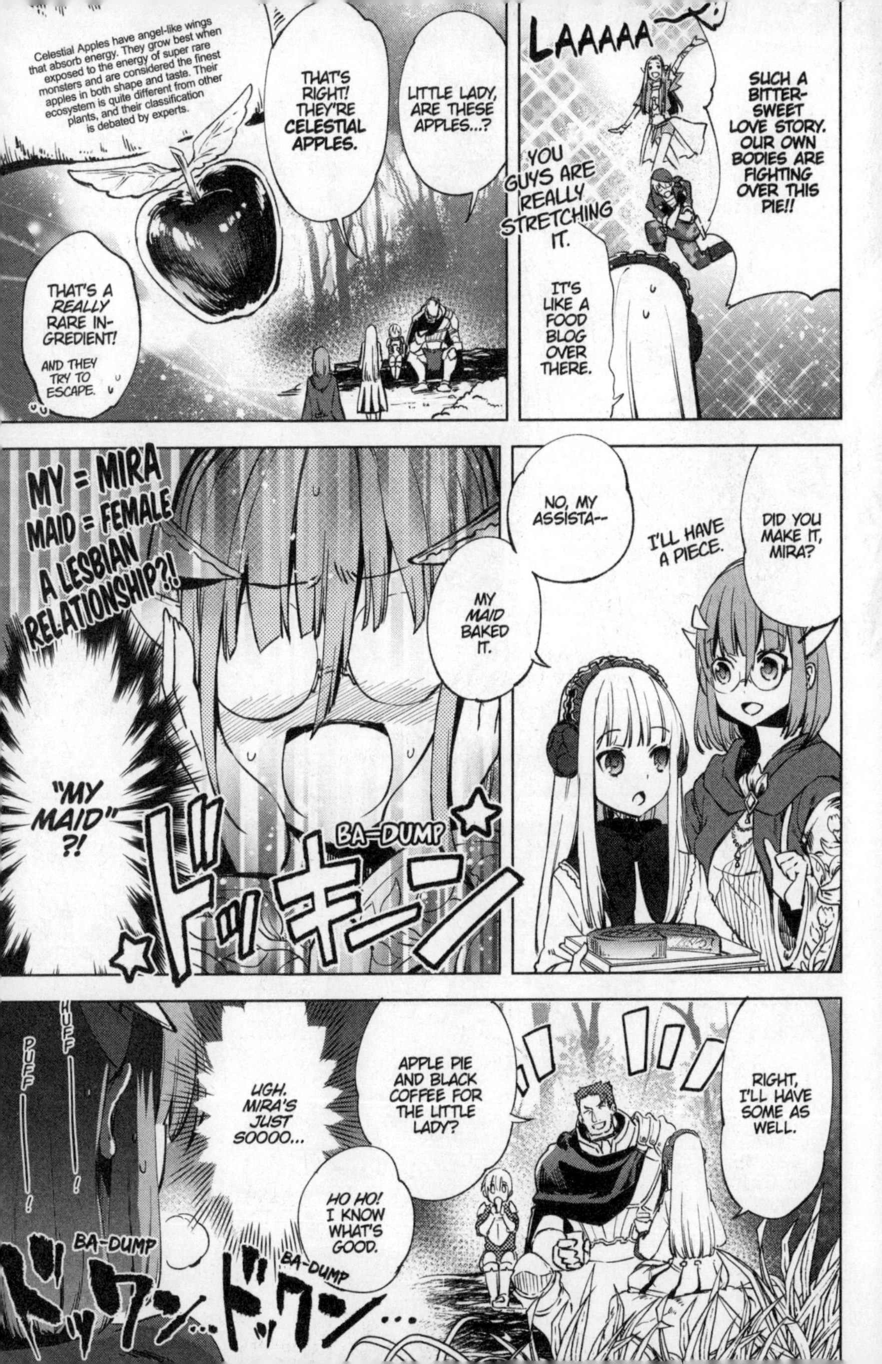
LAAAAA
SUCH A BITTER-SWEET LOVE STORY. OUR OWN BODIES ARE FIGHTING OVER THIS PIE!!
YOU GUYS ARE REALLY STRETCHING IT.
IT'S LIKE A FOOD BLOG OVER THERE.
LITTLE LADY, ARE THESE APPLES...?
THAT'S RIGHT! THEY'RE CELESTIAL APPLES.
Celestial Apples have angel-like wings that absorb energy. They grow best when exposed to the energy of super rare monsters and are considered the finest apples in both shape and taste. Their ecosystem is quite different from other plants, and their classification is debated by experts.
THAT'S A REALLY RARE INGREDIENT!
AND THEY TRY TO ESCAPE.
DID YOU MAKE IT, MIRA?
I'LL HAVE A PIECE.
NO, MY ASSISTA--
MY MAID BAKED IT.
MY = MIRA
MAID = FEMALE
A LESBIAN RELATIONSHIP?!
"MY MAID"?!
BA-DUMP
ドッキーン
RIGHT, I'LL HAVE SOME AS WELL.
APPLE PIE AND BLACK COFFEE FOR THE LITTLE LADY?
HO HO! I KNOW WHAT'S GOOD.
UGH. MIRA'S JUST SOOOO...
HUFF
PUFF
BA-DUMP
BA-DUMP
ドックン…ドクン…

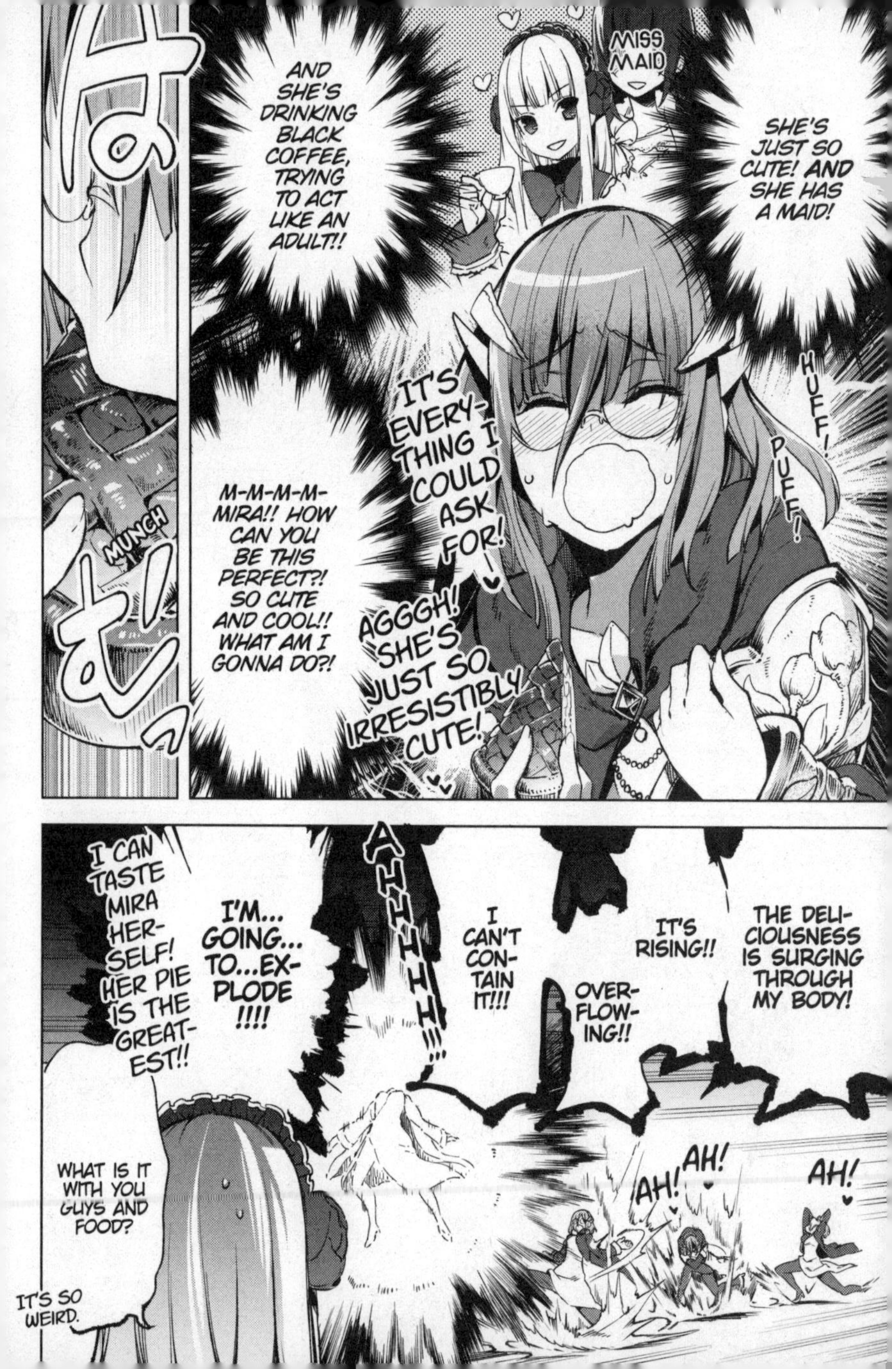
MISS MAID
SHE'S JUST SO CUTE! AND SHE HAS A MAID!
AND SHE'S DRINKING BLACK COFFEE, TRYING TO ACT LIKE AN ADULT!!
HUFF! PUFF!
IT'S EVERYTHING I COULD ASK FOR!
AGGGH! SHE'S JUST SO IRRESISTIBLY CUTE!
M-M-M-M-MIRA!! HOW CAN YOU BE THIS PERFECT?! SO CUTE AND COOL!! WHAT AM I GONNA DO?!
はむっ
MUNCH
THE DELICIOUSNESS IS SURGING THROUGH MY BODY!
IT'S RISING!!
OVERFLOWING!!
I CAN'T CONTAIN IT!!!
AHHHHHH!!!
I'M... GOING... TO...EXPLODE!!!!
I CAN TASTE MIRA HERSELF! HER PIE IS THE GREATEST!!
AH!
AH!
AH!
WHAT IS IT WITH YOU GUYS AND FOOD?
IT'S SO WEIRD.

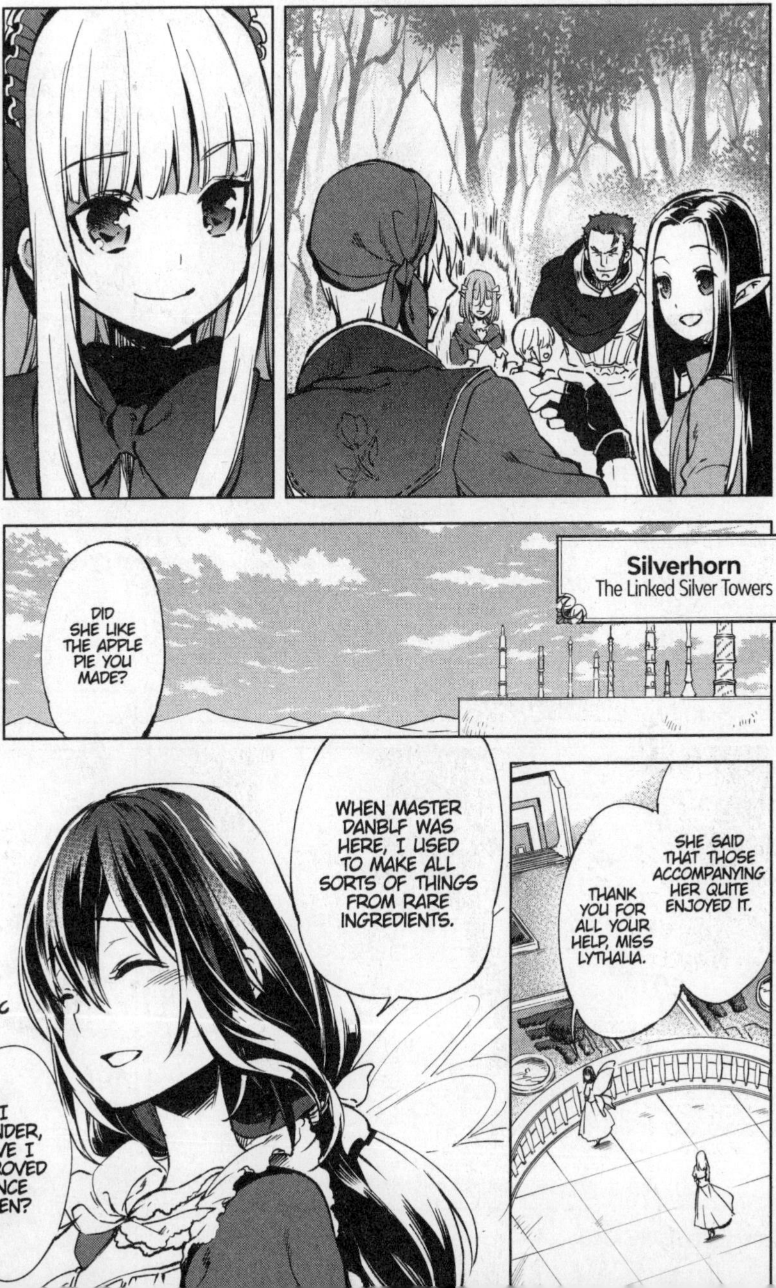
Silverhorn
The Linked Silver Towers
DID SHE LIKE THE APPLE PIE YOU MADE?
SHE SAID THAT THOSE ACCOMPANYING HER QUITE ENJOYED IT.
THANK YOU FOR ALL YOUR HELP, MISS LYTHALIA.
WHEN MASTER DANBLF WAS HERE, I USED TO MAKE ALL SORTS OF THINGS FROM RARE INGREDIENTS.
I WONDER, HAVE I IMPROVED SINCE THEN?

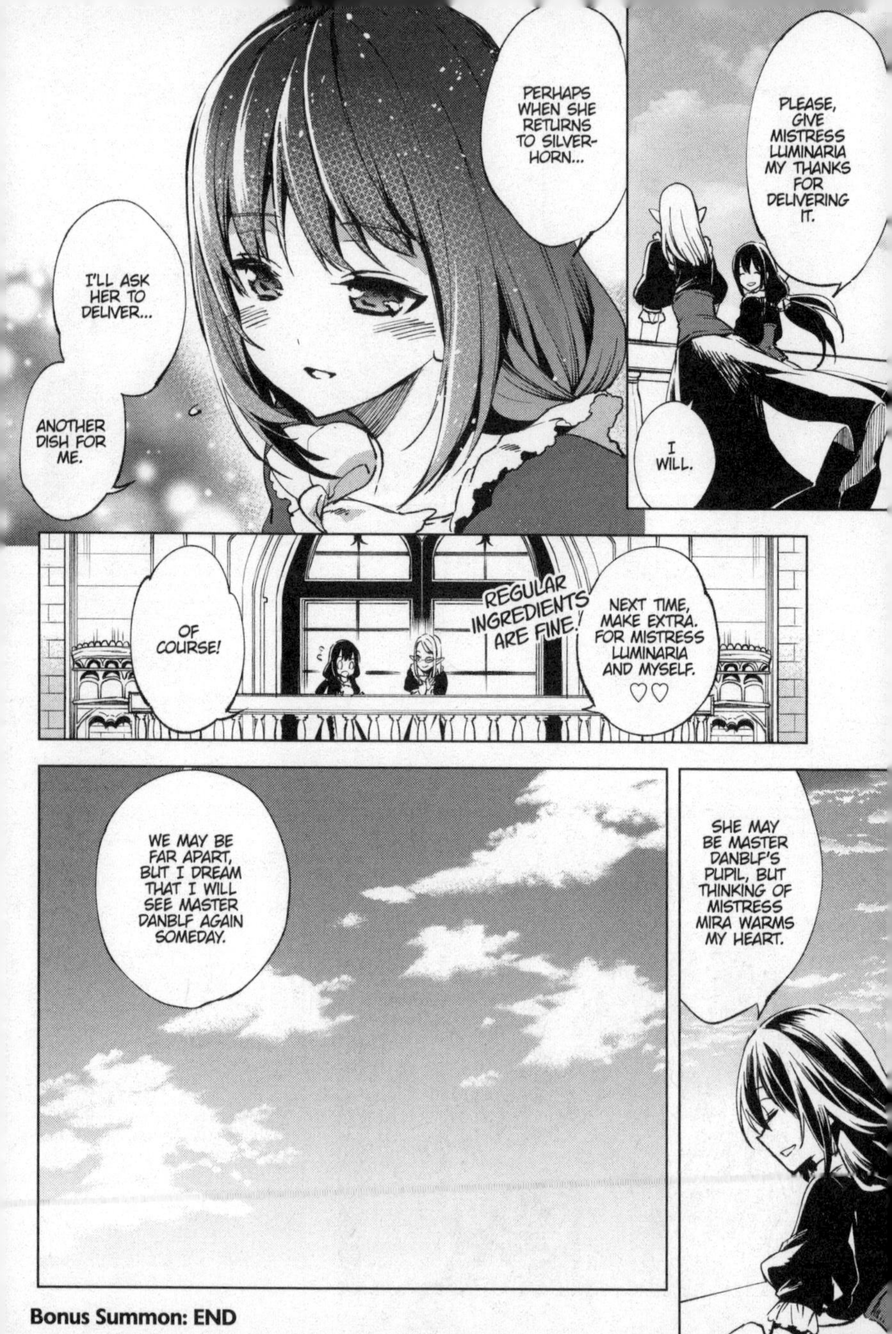
PLEASE, GIVE MISTRESS LUMINARIA MY THANKS FOR DELIVERING IT.
I WILL.
PERHAPS WHEN SHE RETURNS TO SILVER-HORN...
I'LL ASK HER TO DELIVER...
ANOTHER DISH FOR ME.
NEXT TIME, MAKE EXTRA. FOR MISTRESS LUMINARIA AND MYSELF. ♡♡
REGULAR INGREDIENTS ARE FINE!
OF COURSE!
SHE MAY BE MASTER DANBLF'S PUPIL, BUT THINKING OF MISTRESS MIRA WARMS MY HEART.
WE MAY BE FAR APART, BUT I DREAM THAT I WILL SEE MASTER DANBLF AGAIN SOMEDAY.

Bonus Summon: END

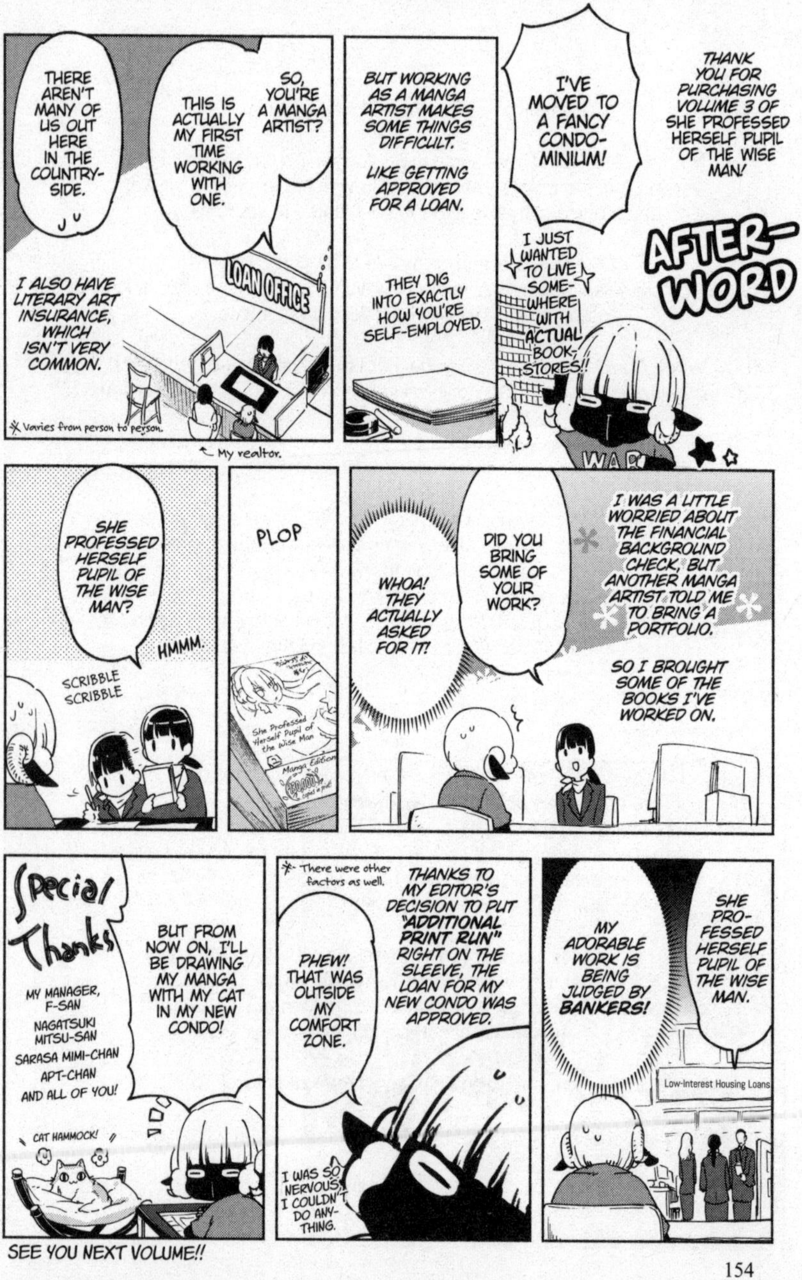
THANK YOU FOR PURCHASING VOLUME 3 OF SHE PROFESSED HERSELF PUPIL OF THE WISE MAN!
AFTER-WORD
I'VE MOVED TO A FANCY CONDO-MINIUM!
I JUST WANTED TO LIVE SOME-WHERE WITH ACTUAL BOOK-STORES!!
BUT WORKING AS A MANGA ARTIST MAKES SOME THINGS DIFFICULT.
LIKE GETTING APPROVED FOR A LOAN.
THEY DIG INTO EXACTLY HOW YOU'RE SELF-EMPLOYED.
SO, YOU'RE A MANGA ARTIST?
THIS IS ACTUALLY MY FIRST TIME WORKING WITH ONE.
THERE AREN'T MANY OF US OUT HERE IN THE COUNTRY-SIDE.
LOAN OFFICE
I ALSO HAVE LITERARY ART INSURANCE, WHICH ISN'T VERY COMMON.
※Varies from person to person.
← My realtor.
I WAS A LITTLE WORRIED ABOUT THE FINANCIAL BACKGROUND CHECK, BUT ANOTHER MANGA ARTIST TOLD ME TO BRING A PORTFOLIO.
DID YOU BRING SOME OF YOUR WORK?
WHOA! THEY ACTUALLY ASKED FOR IT!
SO I BROUGHT SOME OF THE BOOKS I'VE WORKED ON.
PLOP
She Professed Herself Pupil of the Wise Man
Manga Edition
SHE PROFESSED HERSELF PUPIL OF THE WISE MAN?
HMMM.
SCRIBBLE SCRIBBLE
SHE PRO-FESSED HERSELF PUPIL OF THE WISE MAN.
MY ADORABLE WORK IS BEING JUDGED BY BANKERS!
Low-Interest Housing Loans
※There were other factors as well.
THANKS TO MY EDITOR'S DECISION TO PUT "ADDITIONAL PRINT RUN" RIGHT ON THE SLEEVE, THE LOAN FOR MY NEW CONDO WAS APPROVED.
PHEW! THAT WAS OUTSIDE MY COMFORT ZONE.
I WAS SO NERVOUS I COULDN'T DO ANY-THING.
BUT FROM NOW ON, I'LL BE DRAWING MY MANGA WITH MY CAT IN MY NEW CONDO!
Special Thanks
MY MANAGER, F-SAN
NAGATSUKI MITSU-SAN
SARASA MIMI-CHAN
APT-CHAN
AND ALL OF YOU!
CAT HAMMOCK!
SEE YOU NEXT VOLUME!!

Thank you for purchasing this volume!

This is Ryusen Hirotsugu, the author of the original novel.
Volume 3 of the manga adaptation is now out in the wild. It's always
great to see something you've contributed to get released.

I'd like to express my gratitude to all of my readers,
dicca*suemitsu, and everyone else involved. Thank you so very much,
and congratulations on getting it out there!

When I read dicca*suemitsu's afterword to Volume 2 and discovered
that this was originally just a one-volume project, I was actually terrified.
But now we're up to Volume 3! Huzzah! And it really is thanks to
everyone who's purchased the books. Thank you over and
over again for all of your support!

I look forward to releasing as many volumes as we can, because
there's all sorts of sexy Mira scenes coming up, and if we keep
releasing the manga, they'll all be there! All you have to do is keep
buying the volumes as they come out. Of course, it helps if you can get
your friends and acquaintances to join in. It's the only way to guarantee
we'll be able to see Mira doing…this and that. Let's work
together to make those dreams come true!

Ahem.

Anyways, the seven Valkyrie sisters showed up in Volume 3.
In the novels, we only saw artwork for Alfina and Christina. But
here in the manga, we got to see the full crew! Aren't they lovely?
I'm amazed at how well they came out, given their rough descriptions.
It's a lot to take in! They'll show up again throughout the story,
so keep an eye out for them. I know I will!

Also, it makes it easier for me to visualize things in the future!
It's far better than when they're just some vague idea floating
about in my head. The day when each of them is summoned
individually might even be coming up.

Either way, the manga has given me lots of inspiration.

Oh, also, the novel version is available, too, so please check it out!

Ryusen Hirotsugu

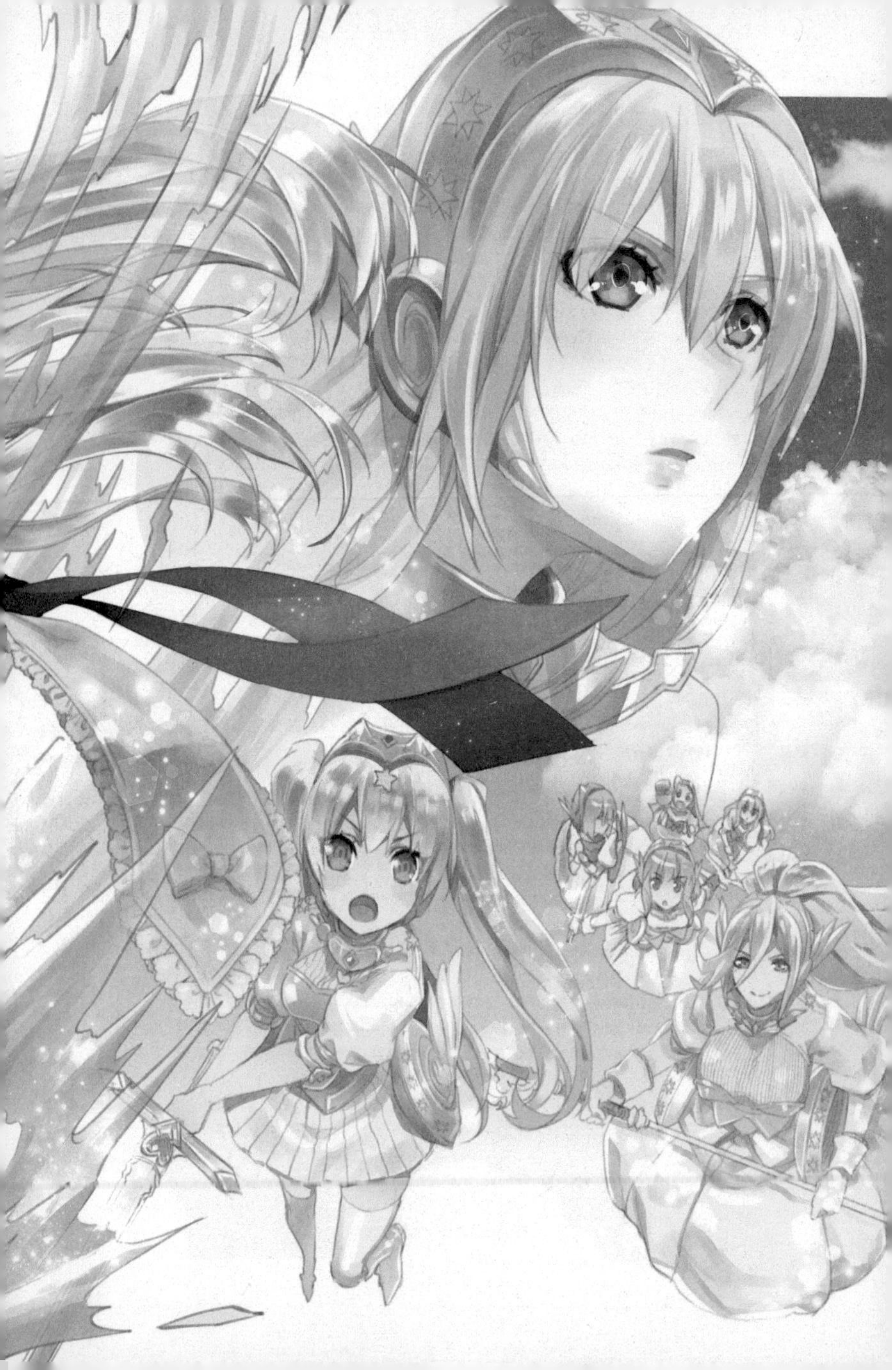

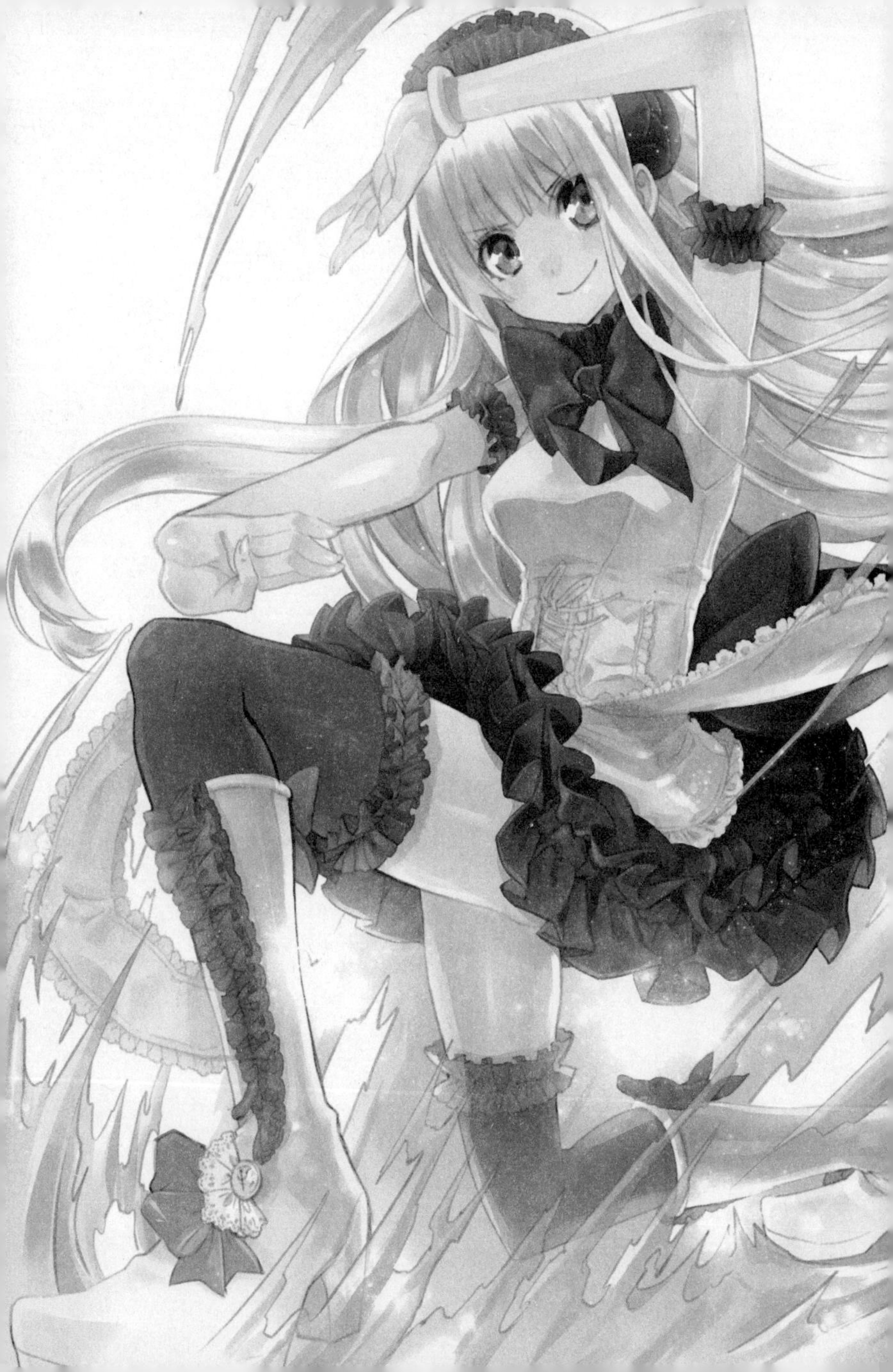

She
Professed
Herself
Pupil of the
Wise Man

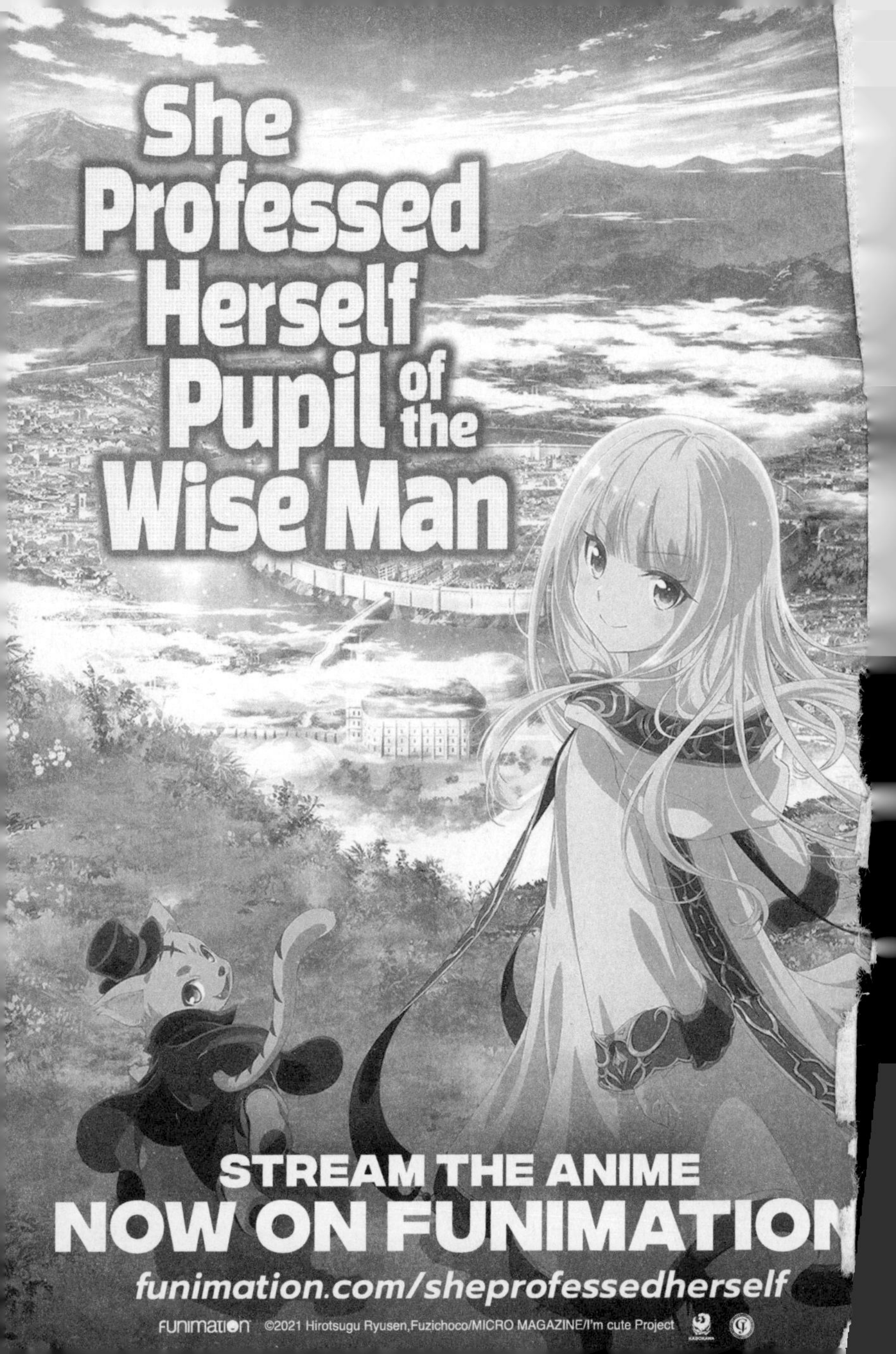
She Professed Herself Pupil of the Wise Man
STREAM THE ANIME
NOW ON FUNIMATION
funimation.com/sheprofessedherself
©2021 Hirotsugu Ryusen,Fuzichoco/MICRO MAGAZINE/I'm cute Project

SEVEN SEAS ENTERTAINMENT PRESENTS

She Professed Herself Pupil of the Wise Man

Vol. 3

ry by RYUSEN HIROTSUGU art by DICCA*SUEMITSU character design by FUZICHOCO

TRANSLATION
Wesley O'Donnell

ADAPTATION
C.A Hawksmoor

LETTERING
Carl Vanstiphout

COVER DESIGN
Nicky Lim

LOGO DESIGN
George Panella

PROOFREADER
Danielle King

EDITOR
Peter Adrian Behravesh

PRINT MANAGER
iannon Rasmussen-Silverstein

PRODUCTION ASSOCIATE
Christa Miesner

PRODUCTION MANAGER
Lissa Pattillo

MANAGING EDITOR
Julie Davis

ASSOCIATE PUBLISHER
Adam Arnold

PUBLISHER
Jason DeAngelis

Kenja no deshi wo nanoru kenja THE COMIC Vol. 3

This edition originally published in Japan in 2018 by
MICRO MAGAZINE, INC., Tokyo.
English translation rights arranged with MICRO MAGAZINE, INC., Tokyo.

Seven Seas press and purchase enquiries can be sent to Marketing Manager Lianne Sentar at press@gomanga.com. Information regarding the distribution and purchase of digital editions is available from Digital Manager CK Russell at digital@gomanga.com.

ISBN:978-1-64827-461-9
Printed in Canada
First Printing: December 2021
10 9 8 7 6 5 4 3 2 1

READING DIRECTIONS

This book reads from ***right to left***, Japanese style. If this is your first time reading manga, you start reading from the top right panel on each page and take it from there. If you get lost, just follow the numbered diagram here. It may seem backwards at first, but you'll get the hang of it! Have fun!!

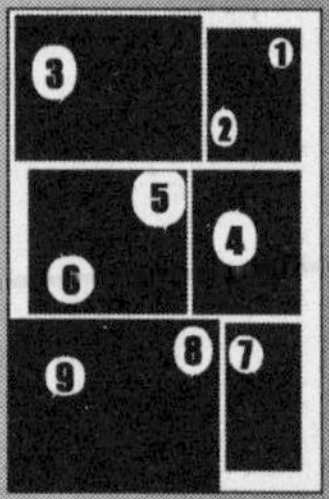
1
2
3
4
5
6
7
8
9

Follow us online: www.SevenSeasEntertainment.com